SECRET CODES for CONSOLES

D0288064

PLAYSTATION® 2

BASED ON A GAME RATED BY THE ESRB — EVERYONE E

AGASSI TENNIS GENERATION
ALIEN HOMINID
APE ESCAPE 3
ATV OFFROAD FURY 3
BRATZ: ROCK ANGELZ
CASPER SPIRIT DIMENSIONS
CASTLE SHIKIGAMI 2
CHICKEN LITTLE
CODENAME: KIDS NEXT DOOR: OPERATION V.I.D.E.O.G.A.M.E.
CRASH TAG TEAM RACING
DROME RACERS
DUEL MASTERS
EA SPORTS ARENA FOOTBALL
ESPN NBA 2K5
ESPN NFL 2K5
FIFA STREET 2
FROGGER: ANCIENT SHADOW
GRAFFITI KINGDOM
GRAN TURISMO 4
GRETZKY NHL 2005
HIGH ROLLERS CASINO
HOT SHOTS GOLF FORE!
ICE AGE 2: THE MELTDOWN
THE INCREDIBLES: RISE OF THE UNDERMINER
IN THE GROOVE
KARAOKE REVOLUTION VOLUME 2
KARAOKE REVOLUTION VOLUME 3
KATAMARI DAMACY
LEGO STAR WARS: THE VIDEO GAME
LOONEY TUNES SPACE RACE
MADDEN NFL 06

MAJOR LEAGUE BASEBALL 2K6
MEGA MAN 8
MEGA MAN X COLLECTION
MIDNIGHT CLUB 3: DUB EDITION REMIX
MIDWAY ARCADE TREASURES 3
MLB 06: THE SHOW
MLB 2005
MVP 06 NCAA BASEBALL
MVP BASEBALL 2005
MX UNLEASHED
MX VS. ATV UNLEASHED
NASCAR 06: TOTAL TEAM CONTROL
NBA 2K6
NBA BALLERS PHENOM
NBA LIVE 06
NBA LIVE 2005
NCAA FOOTBALL 06
NCAA MARCH MADNESS 06
NEED FOR SPEED UNDERGROUND 2
NFL STREET 2
NHL 2K6
OUTRUN 2006: COAST 2 COAST
PAC-MAN WORLD 3
R-TYPE FINAL
RAMPAGE: TOTAL DESTRUCTION
ROBOTS
SCALER
SHARK TALE
SHREK 2
SHREK SUPERSLAM
SLY 2: BAND OF THIEVES
SLY 3: HONOR AMONG THIEVES
SONIC MEGA COLLECTION PLUS
SPONGEBOB SQUAREPANTS: BATTLE FOR BIKINI BOTTOM

SPONGEBOB SQUAREPANTS: LIGHTS, CAMERA, PANTS!

SSX ON TOUR

STRIKE FORCE BOWLING

SUZUKI TT SUPERBIKES

TAK: THE GREAT JUJU CHALLENGE

TEENAGE MUTANT NINJA TURTLES 3: MUTANT NIGHTMARE

TIGER WOODS PGA TOUR 06

TIM BURTON'S THE NIGHTMARE BEFORE CHRISTMAS: OOGIE'S REVENGE

TY THE TASMANIAN TIGER 2: BUSH RESCUE

TY THE TASMANIAN TIGER 3: NIGHT OF THE QUINKAN

WHIPLASH

WORLD TOUR SOCCER 2005

YU-GI-OH! THE DUELIST OF THE ROSES

ZAPPER

BASED ON A GAME RATED BY THE ESRB **T** TEEN

AEON FLUX

AIRFORCE DELTA STRIKE

ALIAS

APE ESCAPE: PUMPED & PRIMED

THE BARD'S TALE

BATTLESTAR GALACTICA

CABELA'S DANGEROUS HUNTS 2

CABELA'S DEER HUNT 2005 SEASON

CAPCOM CLASSICS COLLECTION

CATWOMAN

CHAMPIONS OF NORRATH: REALMS OF EVERQUEST

THE CHRONICLES OF NARNIA: THE LION, THE WITCH AND THE WARDROBE

THE DA VINCI CODE

DESTROY ALL HUMANS!

DOG'S LIFE

DRAGON BALL Z: SAGAS

EPHEMERAL FANTASIA

FANTASTIC 4

FLATOUT

FUTURE TACTICS: THE UPRISING

GODZILLA: SAVE THE EARTH

GRADIUS V

GRAFFITI KINGDOM

GRAN TURISMO 4

GRETZKY NHL 2005

GROWLANSER GENERATIONS

GUITAR HERO

HEROES OF THE PACIFIC

THE INCREDIBLE HULK: ULTIMATE DESTRUCTION

JAK X: COMBAT RACING

JUICED

KYA: DARK LINEAGE

L.A. RUSH

MARVEL NEMESIS: RISE OF THE IMPERFECTS

MOTOCROSS MANIA 3

NEED FOR SPEED MOST WANTED

ONE PIECE: GRAND BATTLE

PETER JACKSON'S KING KONG: THE OFFICIAL GAME OF THE MOVIE

PRINCE OF PERSIA: THE SANDS OF TIME

PSYCHONAUTS

PUMP IT UP: EXCEED

RATCHET AND CLANK: UP YOUR ARSENAL

SAMURAI JACK: THE SHADOW OF AKU

SECRET WEAPONS OVER NORMANDY

SEEK AND DESTROY

SHAMAN KING: POWER OF SPIRIT

Games Listing

PLAYSTATION®2

5

AEON FLUX

BOMBER JACKET OUTFIT
Select Enter Cheat from the Extras menu and enter **JULIET ALPHA CHARLIE KILO ECHO TANGO**. Find the outfit under Outfits in the Extras menu.

FAME OUTFIT
Select Enter Cheat from the Extras menu and enter **GOLF ROMEO ALPHA YANKEE**. Find the outfit under Outfits in the Extras menu.

ALTERNATE OUTFITS
Select Enter Cheat from the Extras menu and enter **CHARLIE LIMA OSCAR TANGO HOTEL ECHO SIERRA**. Find the outfits under Outfits in the Extras menu. These outfits include the following: Freya, Monican Freya, Hostess Judy, Una, and Fashion Una.

MRS. GOODCHILD OUTFIT
Select Enter Cheat from the Extras menu and enter **WHISKEY HOTEL INDIA TANGO ECHO**. Find the outfit under Outfits in the Extras menu.

REVELATION OUTFIT
Select Enter Cheat from the Extras menu and enter **ALPHA ROMEO MIKE SIERRA**. Find the outfit under Outfits in the Extras menu.

SEEDS OUTFIT
Select Enter Cheat from the Extras menu and enter **MIKE OSCAR VICTOR INDIA ECHO**. Find the outfit under Outfits in the Extras menu.

WAR OUTFIT

Select Enter Cheat from the Extras menu and enter **BRAVO LIMA UNIFORM ROMEO**. Find the outfit under Outfits in the Extras menu.

ALL REPLAY EPISODES

Select Enter Cheat from the Extras menu and enter **BRAVO ALPHA YANKEE OSCAR UNIFORM**. Select Replay Episode from the Extras menu.

ALL SLIDESHOWS

Select Enter Cheat from the Extras menu and enter **PAPA INDIA XRAY ECHO SIERRA**. Select Slideshows from the Extras menu.

ACTION MOVIE CHEAT

Select Enter Cheat from the Extras menu and enter **BRAVO ALPHA GOLF MIKE ALPHA NOVEMBER** or **UNIFORM KILO GOLF ALPHA MIKE ECHO ROMEO**. Pause the game and select Cheats to access the code.

GOD MODE CHEAT

Select Enter Cheat from the Extras menu and enter **TANGO ROMEO INDIA ROMEO OSCAR XRAY**. Pause the game and select Cheats to access the code.

FREE FATALITIES CHEAT

Select Enter Cheat from the Extras menu and enter **CHARLIE UNIFORM TANGO INDIA OSCAR NOVEMBER ECHO**. Pause the game and select Cheats to access the code.

ONE-STRIKE KILLS CHEAT

Select Enter Cheat from the Extras menu and enter **BRAVO UNIFORM CHARLIE KILO FOXTROT SIERRA TANGO**. Pause the game and select Cheats to access the code.

RESTORE HEALTH CHEAT

Select Enter Cheat from the Extras menu and enter **HOTEL ECHO ALPHA LIMA MIKE ECHO**. Pause the game and select Cheats to access the code.

UNLIMITED AMMO CHEAT

Select Enter Cheat from the Extras menu and enter **FOXTROT UNIFORM GOLF**. Pause the game and select Cheats to access the code.

UNLIMITED HEALTH CHEAT

Select Enter Cheat from the Extras menu and enter **CHARLIE LIMA OSCAR NOVEMBER ECHO**. Pause the game and select Cheats to access the code.

UNLIMITED POWER STRIKES CHEAT

Select Enter Cheat from the Extras menu and enter **LIMA CHARLIE VICTOR GOLF**. Pause the game and select Cheats to access the code.

AGASSI TENNIS GENERATION

ALL PLAYERS
At the Main Menu, press **R2**, **L2**, **L3**, ◉, ✖, ◉.

AIRFORCE DELTA STRIKE

SELF DESTRUCT
Pause the game and press Up, Up, Down, Down, Left, Right, Left, Right, ✖, ◉.

REFILL HP AND MISSILES
Pause the game and press Up, Up, Down, Down, Left, Right, Left, Right, **L3**, **R3**.

ALIAS

LEVEL SELECT
Complete the game, then press **L1** + **R1** at the new game screen.

ALIEN HOMINID

ALL LEVELS, MINI-GAMES, & HATS
Select Player 1 Setup or Player 2 Setup and change the name to **ROYGBIV**.

HATS FOR 2-PLAYER GAME
Go to the Options and rename your alien one of the following:

abe	goodman
april	grrl
behemoth	princess
cletus	superfly
dandy	

APE ESCAPE 3

SECRET PASSWORDS
At the Title screen, press **L1** + **R1** + **L2** + **R2**. Now you can enter the following codes.

DARK MASTER ON THE LOOSE!

Enter **blackout** at the Secret Password screen.

MOVIE 28 AND 2 CINEMA FILES

Enter **2 snakes** at the Secret Password screen.

SHIMMY ON THE LOOSE!

Enter **2nd man** at the Secret Password screen.

MONKEY AS SPIKE

Enter **krops** at the Secret Password screen.

BLUE PIPOTRON

Enter **coolblue** at the Secret Password screen.

RED PIPOTRON

Enter **redmon** at the Secret Password screen.

YELLOW PIPOTRON

Enter **yellowy** at the Secret Password screen.

SAL-1000 MONKEY

Enter **grobyc** at the Secret Password screen.

SAL-3000 MONKEY

Enter **SAL3000** at the Secret Password screen.

APE ESCAPE: PUMPED & PRIMED

ALL GADGETS

Complete Story Mode. At the mode select, hold **R1 + L1 + R2 + L2** to access the password screen. Enter **Go Wild!**.

DISABLE ALL GADGETS CHEAT

Complete Story Mode. At the mode select, hold **R1 + L1 + R2 + L2** to access the password screen. Enter **Limited!**.

NORMAL DIFFICULTY

Complete Story Mode. At the mode select, hold **R1 + L1 + R2 + L2** to access the password screen. Enter **NORMAL!**.

HARD DIFFICULTY

Complete Story Mode. At the mode select, hold **R1 + L1 + R2 + L2** to access the password screen. Enter **HARD!**.

ATV OFFROAD FURY 3

UNLOCK EVERYTHING... OTHER THAN THE FURY BIKE

Select Player Profile from the options. Then, select Enter Cheat and enter **!SLACKER!**. This will not give the Fury.

ALL ATVS IN TRAINING

Select Player Profile from the options. Then, select Enter Cheat and enter **NOSKILLS**.

ALL RIDER GEAR

Select Player Profile from the options. Then, select Enter Cheat and enter **FITS**.

$1500

Select Player Profile from the options. Then, select Enter Cheat and enter **+foodstamps+**.

MUSIC VIDEOS

Select Player Profile from the options. Then, select Enter Cheat and enter **ROCKNROLL**.

THE BARD'S TALE

During a game, hold **L1** + **R1** and enter the following:

EVERYTHING ON (SILVER AND ADDERSTONES)
Press Up, Up, Down, Down, Left, Right, Left, Right.

FULL HEALTH AND MANA
Press Left, Left, Right, Right, Up, Down, Up, Down.

CAN'T BE HURT
Press Right, Left, Right, Left, Up, Down, Up, Down.

CAN'T BE STRUCK
Press Left, Right, Left, Right, Up, Down, Up, Down.

DAMAGE X100
Press Up, Down, Up, Down, Left, Right, Left, Right.

UNLOCK LEVELS
Press Right, Right, Left, Left, Up, Down, Up, Down.

DEBUG MENU
During a game, hold **L2** and press Right.

BATTLESTAR GALACTICA

MINI-SERIES MATERIALS
Select Extras and enter the following:

Left, Up, Left, Left, Down, Left, Up, Down.

Up, Up, Down, Down, Right, Up, Right, Down.

Right, Right, Down, Down, Left, Left, Up, Up.

Down(x4), Left(x4).

Up (x3), Down (x3), Left, Right.

Up, Left, Up, Right, Up, Left, Up, Right.

Right (x4), Down, Down, Left, Left.

Right, Right, Up, Up, Left, Left, Up, Up.

STARBUCK AND APOLLO AS WINGMEN
Select Extras and press Down, Down, Left, Down, Down, Up, Right, Right.

BRATZ: ROCK ANGELZ

CAMERON CHANGED
While in the Bratz Office, use the Cheat computer to enter **STYLIN**.

DYLAN CHANGED
While in the Bratz Office, use the Cheat computer to enter **MEYGEN**.

LONDON BOY CHANGED
While in the Bratz Office, use the Cheat computer to enter **BLINGZ**.

PARIS BOY CHANGED
While in the Bratz Office, use the Cheat computer to enter **ROCKIN**.

RECEIVE 1000 BLINGZ
While in the Bratz Office, use the Cheat computer to enter **YASMIN**.

RECEIVE 2000 BLINGZ
While in the Bratz Office, use the Cheat computer to enter **PHOEBE**.

RECEIVE 2100 BLINGZ
While in the Bratz Office, use the Cheat computer to enter **DANCIN**.

RECEIVE 3000 BLINGZ
While in the Bratz Office, use the Cheat computer to enter **WAYFAB**.

RECEIVE 6000 BLINGZ
While in the Bratz Office, use the Cheat computer to enter **HOTTIE**.

UNLOCKED RINGTONE 12
While in the Bratz Office, use the Cheat computer to enter **BLAZIN**.

UNLOCKED RINGTONE 15
While in the Bratz Office, use the Cheat computer to enter **FIANNA**.

UNLOCKED RINGTONE 16
While in the Bratz Office, use the Cheat computer to enter **ANGELZ**.

CABELA'S DANGEROUS HUNTS 2

DOUBLE HEALTH
Select Codes and enter Eye, Bolt, Skull, Hand, Boot.

HEALTH REGENERATES FASTER
Select Codes and enter Skull, Eye, Boot, Bolt, Hand.

DOUBLE DAMAGE
Select Codes and enter Hand, Boot, Skull, Eye, Bolt.

INFINITE AMMO
Select Codes and enter Bolt, Hand, Eye, Boot, Skull.

CABELA'S DEER HUNT 2005 SEASON

GPS
At the equipment menu, press ▲, ■, ●, R1, R2, ✕.

CAPCOM CLASSICS COLLECTION

ALL LOCKS OPENED
At the Title screen, press **L1**, **R1**, Up on Right Analog Stick, Down on Right Analog Stick, **L1**, **R1**, Up on Left Analog Stick, Down on Left Analog Stick, **L1**, **R1**, Up, Down.

CASPER SPIRIT DIMENSIONS

START GAME WITH GHOST POWER, FIRE ENHANCE, & ICE ENHANCE
At the Title screen, hold **L1** + **L2** + **R1** + **R2** until you hear a clucking sound.

CASTLE SHIKIGAMI 2

EXTRA CREDITS
Earn an extra credit for each hour of gameplay.

YOUNG FUMIKO
At the Character Select screen, highlight Fumiko and press Right, Right.

CATWOMAN

UNLOCK HIDDEN SURPRISES THROUGHOUT THE COMIC
Enter **1940** as a Vault code.

INCREASE HEALTH
Pause the game, hold **L1** + **L2** and press ■, ▲, Up, Down.

NEW COSTUME
Pause the game, hold **L1** + **L2** and press ▲, Up, ✕, ■, ▲, ●, Right.

CHAMPIONS OF NORRATH: REALMS OF EVERQUEST

LEVEL 20 CHARACTER
During a game, press and hold **L1** + **R2** + ▲ + **R3**. This makes your character level 20 with 75,000 coins and 999 skill points. This does *not* increase your character's main attributes.

CHICKEN LITTLE

INVINCIBILITY
Select Cheat Codes from the Extras menu and enter Baseball, Baseball, Baseball, Shirt.

BIG FEET
Select Cheat Codes from the Extras menu and enter Hat, Glove, Glove, Hat.

BIG HAIR

Select Cheat Codes from the Extras menu and enter Baseball, Bat, Bat, Baseball.

BIG HEAD

Select Cheat Codes from the Extras menu and enter Hat, Helmet, Helmet, Hat.

PAPER PANTS

Select Cheat Codes from the Extras menu and enter Bat, Bat, Hat, Hat.

SUNGLASSES

Select Cheat Codes from the Extras menu and enter Glove, Glove, Helmet, Helmet.

UNDERWEAR

Select Cheat Codes from the Extras menu and enter Hat, Hat, Shirt, Shirt.

THE CHRONICLES OF NARNIA: THE LION, THE WITCH AND THE WARDROBE

ENABLE CHEATS

At the Title screen, press ✖ and hold **L1** + **R1**, then press Down, Down, Right, Up. The text should turn green when entered correctly. Now you can enter the following codes.

LEVEL SELECT

At the wardrobe, hold **L1** and press Up, Up, Right, Right, Up, Right, Down.

ALL BONUS LEVELS

At the Bonus Drawer, hold **L1** and press Down, Down, Right, Right, Down, Right, Up.

LEVEL SKIP

During gameplay, hold **L1** and press Down, Left, Down, Left, Down, Right, Down, Right, Up.

INVINCIBILITY

During gameplay, hold **L1** and press Down, Up, Down, Right, Right.

RESTORE HEALTH

During gameplay, hold **L1** and press Down, Left, Left, Right.

10,000 COINS

During gameplay, hold **L1** and press Down, Left, Right, Down, Down.

ALL ABILITIES

During gameplay, hold **L1** and press Down, Left, Right, Left, Up.

FILL COMBO METER

During gameplay, hold **L1** and press Up, Up, Right, Up.

CODENAME: KIDS NEXT DOOR: OPERATION V.I.D.E.O.G.A.M.E.

INVINCIBILITY

Enter **432513** as a code.

CRASH TAG TEAM RACING

FASTER VEHICLES

At the Main menu, hold **L1** + **R1** and press ◉, ◉, ▲, ▲.

ONE-HIT KO

At the Main menu, hold **L1** + **R1** and press ✖, ◉, ◉, ✖.

DISABLE HUD
At the Main menu, hold **L1** + **R1** and press ✖, ■, ▲, ●.

CHICKEN HEADS
At the Main menu, hold **L1** + **R1** and press ✖, ●, ●, ■

JAPANESE CRASH
At the Main menu, hold **L1** + **R1** and press ■, ●, ■, ●.

DRIVE A BLOCK VEHICLE
At the Main menu, hold **L1** + **R1** and press ●, ●, ▲, ■.

THE DA VINCI CODE

GOD MODE
Select Codes from the Options screen
and enter **VITRUVIAN MAN**.

EXTRA HEALTH
Select Codes from the Options screen and enter **SACRED FEMININE**.

MISSION SELECT
Select Codes from the Options screen
and enter **CLOS LUCE 1519**.

ONE-HIT FIST KILL
Select Codes from the Options screen
and enter **PHILLIPS EXETER**.

ONE-HIT WEAPON KILL
Select Codes from the Options screen and enter **ROYAL HOLLOWAY**.

ALL VISUAL DATABASE
Select Codes from the Options screen
and enter **APOCRYPHA**.

**ALL VISUAL DATABASE AND
CONCEPT ART**
Select Codes from the Options screen
and enter **ET IN ARCADIA
EGO**.

DESTROY ALL HUMANS!

AMMO-A-PLENTY

Pause the game, hold **L2** and press Left, ●, **R2**, Right, **R1**, ●. This gives you unlimited ammo.

BULLETPROOF CRYPTO

Pause the game, hold **L2** and press ●, ●, Left, Left, ●, ●. This makes you invincible.

DEEP THINKER

Pause the game, hold **L2** and press **R1**, **R2**, ●, Right, **R2**, ●. This gives you unlimited Concentration.

AWARE LIKE A FOX

Pause the game, hold **L2** and press Right, ●, **R2**, **R1**, Right, **R2**. This maxes out the alert meter.

NOBODY LOVES YOU

Pause the game, hold **L2** and press **R2**, Right, **R2**, **R1**, ●, Right. This resets the alert meter.

FOUND KEY TO ORTHOPOX'S LAB

On the Mothership, hold **L2** and press ●, ●, Left, Left, ●, ●. This gives you access to the Upgrades at Pox's Lab.

MMMM BRAINS!

On the Mothership, hold **L2** and press **R1**, **R1**, **R2**, **R2**, Left, Right, Left, Right, **R2**, **R1**. This gives you extra DNA.

DOG'S LIFE

CHEAT MENU

During a game, press ● (Bark), ● (Bark), ● (Bark), hold ● (Growl), hold ● (Growl), hold ● (Growl), Left, Right, Down.

DRAGON BALL Z: SAGAS

PENDULUM ROOMS

Select Options from the Main menu and press Up, Down, Up, Down, Left, Right, Left, Right, Select, Start, Select, Start, ■, ●, ■, ●, ✕, ✕, Start. When entered correctly, the message "Pendulum Rooms Unlocked" will appear on-screen. This unlocks the Pendulum mode, all Extras, all Sagas, and all Upgrades.

INVINCIBILITY

Pause the game, select Controller and press Down, ✕, Select, Start, Right, ■, Left, ●, Up, ▲.

ALL UPGRADES

Pause the game, select Controller and press Up, Left, Down, Right, Select, Start, ■, ✕, ●, ▲.

DROME RACERS

INSTANT WIN

At the Main menu, press Left, Right, Left, Right, Up, Down, Up, Down, ■, ▲, ●. Press **L3** during a race to win.

ALL TRACKS

At the Main menu, press Left, Right, Left, Right, Up, Down, Up, Down, ▲, ▲, ✕.

PURPLE RAIN

At the Main menu, press Left, Right, Left, Right, Up, Down, Up, Down, Up, Down, ● (x3).

WIREFRAME MODE

At the Main menu, press Left, Right, Left, Right, Up, Down, Up, Down, ●, ●, ✕.

DUEL MASTERS

ALL LOCATIONS

At the map screen, hold **R3** and press ● (x3).

4 OF EVERY CARD AND UNLOCK CHUCK IN ARCADE MODE

At the deck building screen, hold **R3** and press **L1, L1, L1**.

PLAYER 1 LOSES SHIELD

During a duel, hold **R3** and press ▲, ■, ✕. Release **R3**.

PLAYER 2 LOSES SHIELD

During a duel, hold **R3** and press ▲, ●, ✕. Release **R3**.

PLAYER 1 GAINS SHIELD
During a duel, hold **R3** and press ✖, ■, ▲. Release **R3**.

PLAYER 2 GAINS SHIELD
During a duel, hold **R3** and press ✖, ●, ▲. Release **R3**.

PLAYER 1 WINS
During a duel, hold **R3** and press **L1**, **R1**, **L1**.

PLAYER 2 WINS
During a duel, hold **R3** and press **R1**, **L1**, **R1**.

TURN OFF DECK OUTS
During a duel, hold **R3** and press ■ (x3).

EA SPORTS ARENA FOOTBALL

BIG BALL
At the line of scrimmage, press **L1** + ▲, Up, Up.

SMALL BALL
At the line of scrimmage, press **L1** + ▲, Down, Down.

NORMAL SIZE BALL
At the line of scrimmage, press **L1** + ▲, Up, Down.

MAX STATS IN QUICK PLAY
Load a profile with the name **IronMen**. This will maximize all players' stats in Quick Play.

EPHEMERAL FANTASIA

ALL NOTES IN MIDDLE BAR
Select Pattimo from Items. Press **L2** (x3), **L1**, **L1**, Right (x3), ● before selecting your song.

NOTES MOVE FASTER AND FURTHER APART
Select Pattimo from Items. Press **L2**, **L1**, Right, ●, ● before selecting your song.

NOTES MOVE EVEN FASTER AND FURTHER APART
Select Pattimo from Items. Press **L2**, **L1**, Right, ●, ●, **L2**, **L1**, Right, ●, ● before selecting your song.

NOTES DISAPPEAR BEFORE HITTING TOP BAR
Select Pattimo from Items. Press **L2**, Right, **L1**, Right, **L2**, **L1** before selecting your song.

NOTES IN DIFFERENT PLACES
Select Pattimo from Items. Press Right, **L1**, **L1**, **L2**, **L1**, ● before selecting your song.

ESPN NBA 2K5

ALL 24/7 ITEMS
Create a player named **RAY GRAHAM**.

ESPN NFL 2K5

Enter these codes as your case-sensitive VIP name:

ALL CRIB ITEMS
Enter **CribMax**.

1,000,000 CRIB POINTS
Enter **PhatBank**.

ALL MILESTONE
Enter **MadSkilz**.

FANTASTIC 4

BARGE ARENA AND STAN LEE INTERVIEW #1
At the Main menu, press ■, ●, ■, Down, Down, ●, Up.

BONUS LEVEL
At the Main menu, press Right, Right, ■, ●, Left, Up, Down.

INFINITE COSMIC POWER
At the Main menu, press Up, ■, ●, ■, Left, Right, ●.

FIFA STREET 2

ALL VENUES
At the Main menu, hold **L1 + △** and press Left, Up, Up, Right, Down, Down, Right, Down.

FLATOUT

ALL CARS, CLASSES AND RACES
Create a new profile with the name **GIVEALL**.

$40,000

Create a new profile with the name **GIVECASH**.

EJECT YOURSELF FROM CAR

Create a new profile with the name **RAGDOLL**. Use the Gear Up button to throw yourself from the car without hitting anything.

FROGGER: ANCIENT SHADOW

LEVEL SELECT

For the following codes, choose Secret Code and enter the appropriate code to unlock the levels.

LEVEL	ENTER
Level 4-1	Berry, Lily, Lumpy, Lily.
Level 4-2	Finnius, Frogger, Frogger, Wani.
Level 5-1	Lily, Lily, Wani, Wani.
Level 5-2	Frogger, Berry, Finnius, Frogger.
Level 6-1	Lily, Wani, Lily, Wani.
Level 6-2	Frogger, Lily, Lily, Lily.
Level 6-3	Frogger, Frogger, Frogger, Berry.
Level 7-1	Lily, Lily, Wani, Lumpy.
Level 7-2	Lily, Frogger, Frogger, Lumpy.

UNLOCK LETTERS

To unlock the various letter, choose Secret Code and enter the following codes.

LETTER	ENTER
Hyacinth Letter	Lumpy, Frogger, Frogger, Berry
Cosmos Letter	Berry, Lumpy, Frogger, Lumpy
Rose Letter	Wani, Lily, Wani, Frogger
Pansy Letter	Lumpy, Berry, Lumpy, Finnius

UNLOCK WIGS

To unlock the various wigs, choose Secret Code and enter the following codes.

WIG	ENTER
Lobster Wig	Finnius, Wani, Lumpy, Frogger.
Bird Nest Wig	Lily, Lily, Lily, Lily.
Sail Boat Wig	Lumpy, Lumpy, Lumpy, Lumpy.
Skull Wig	Frogger, Lumpy, Lily, Frogger.

DEVELOPER PICTURE 1

Select Secret Code and enter Wani, Frogger, Wani, Frogger.

DEVELOPER PICTURE 2

Select Secret Code and enter Berry, Berry, Berry, Wani.

UNLOCK ARTWORK

To unlock the various artwork pieces, choose Secret Code and enter the following codes.

ART NAME	ENTER
Programmer Art 1	Wani, Wani, Wani, Wani.
Programmer Art 2	Lumpy, Frogger, Berry, Lily.
Programmer Art 3	Wani, Frogger, Lily, Finnius.
Additional Art 1	Frogger, Frogger, Frogger, Frogger.
Additional Art 2	Finnius, Finnius, Finnius, Finnius.
Additional Art 3	Berry, Berry, Berry, Berry.

FUTURE TACTICS: THE UPRISING

LEVEL SKIP

At the game select screen, press **L1**, ●, **R1**, **R1**, **R2**, ●, **L1**, **R1**, **R2**.

UNLIMITED TURNS AND MOVEMENT

During a game, press Up, Up, Down, Down, Left, Right, Left, Left, **R1**, **L1**.

BIG HEADS

During a game, press Up, Left, Down, Left, Down, Up, Up, Left.

DISCO MODE

During a game, press **L1**, Left, **L1**, Left, **R1**, Right, **R1**, Right.

LOW GRAVITY

During a game, press Up (x6), Down, Right, Up.

GODZILLA: SAVE THE EARTH

CHEAT MENU

At the Main menu, press and hold **L2**, ●, **R2** in order, then let go of ●, **R2**, **L2** in order. Now you can enter the following cheats.

ALL CITIES
Enter **659996**.

ALL MONSTERS
Enter **525955**.

UNLOCK CHALLENGES
Enter **975013**.

HEALTH REGENERATES
Enter **536117**.

ENERGY DOES NOT REGENERATE
Enter **122574**.

INDESTRUCTIBLE BUILDINGS
Enter **812304**.

100,000 POINTS
Enter **532459**.

150,000 POINTS
Enter **667596**.

200,000 POINTS
Enter **750330**.

PLAYER 1: 4X DAMAGE
Enter **259565**.

PLAYER 1: INFINITE ENERGY
Enter **819342**.

PLAYER 1: INVISIBLE
Enter **531470**.

PLAYER 1: INVULNERABLE
Enter **338592**.

PLAYER 2: 4X DAMAGE
Enter **927281**.

PLAYER 2: INFINITE ENERGY
Enter **324511**.

PLAYER 2: INVISIBLE
Enter **118699**.

PLAYER 2: INVULNERABLE
Enter **259333**.

PLAYER 3: 4X DAMAGE
Enter **500494**.

PLAYER 3: INFINITE ENERGY
Enter **651417**.

PLAYER 3: INVISIBLE
Enter **507215**.

PLAYER 3: INVULNERABLE
Enter **953598**.

PLAYER 4: 4X DAMAGE
Enter **988551**.

PLAYER 4: INFINITE ENERGY
Enter **456719**.

PLAYER 4: INVISIBLE
Enter **198690**.

PLAYER 4: INVULNERABLE
Enter **485542**.

GALLERY
Enter **294206**.

GODZILLA FINAL WARS
Enter **409014**.

GRADIUS V

You can use one of these for each level completed.

DOUBLE SHOT POWER
After the first boss, pause the game and press Up, Up, Down, Down, Left, Right, Left, Right, **L2**, **R2**.

LASER POWER
After the first boss, pause the game and press Up, Up, Down, Down, Left, Right, Left, Right, **L1**, **R1**.

GRAFFITI KINGDOM

PLAY AS FAKE PASTEL IN VS BOSSES
After completing the game, select VS Mode. Then hold **L2** + **R1** while selecting VS Bosses.

PLAY AS FAKE PIXEL IN VS BOSSES
After completing the game, select VS Mode. Then hold **L1** + **L2** while selecting VS Bosses.

PLAY AS PASTEL IN VS BOSSES
After completing the game, select VS Mode. Then hold **L1** + **R1** while selecting VS Bosses.

PLAY AS PIXEL IN VS BOSSES
After completing the game, select VS Mode. Then hold **L1** + **R2** while selecting VS Bosses.

FAKE PASTEL VS PASTEL IN 2 PLAYER TOURNAMENT
After completing the game, select VS Mode. Then hold **L1** + **L2** + **R1** while selecting 2 Player Tournament.

FAKE PASTEL VS PIXEL IN 2 PLAYER TOURNAMENT
After completing the game, select VS Mode. Then hold **L2** + **R1** while selecting 2 Player Tournament.

FAKE PIXEL VS FAKE PASTEL IN 2 PLAYER TOURNAMENT
After completing the game, select VS Mode. Then hold **L2** + **R2** while selecting 2 Player Tournament.

FAKE PIXEL VS PIXEL IN 2 PLAYER TOURNAMENT
After completing the game, select VS Mode. Then hold **L1** + **L2** while selecting 2 Player Tournament.

PASTEL VS FAKE PASTEL IN 2 PLAYER TOURNAMENT
After completing the game, select VS Mode. Then hold **L1** + **R1** while selecting 2 Player Tournament.

PASTEL VS FAKE PIXEL IN 2 PLAYER TOURNAMENT
After completing the game, select VS Mode. Then hold **R1** + **R2** while selecting 2 Player Tournament.

PIXEL VS FAKE PIXEL IN 2 PLAYER TOURNAMENT
After completing the game, select VS Mode. Then hold **L1** + **R2** while selecting 2 Player Tournament.

GRAN TURISMO 4

EXTRA TRACKS FOR ARCADE MODE
Play through the indicated amount of days to unlock the corresponding track in Arcade Mode.

DAYS	UNLOCK	DAYS	UNLOCK
15	Deep Forest Raceway	183	Cote d Azur
29	Opera Paris	197	Tahiti Maze
43	Fuji Speedway 80s	211	Twin Ring Motegi Road Course
57	Special Stage Route 5	225	George V Paris
71	Suzuka Circuit	239	Cathedral Rocks Trail I
85	Twin Ring Motegi Road Course East Short	253	Costa di Amalfi
99	Grand Valley Speedway	267	Circuit de la Sarthe 1
113	Hong Kong	281	Autumn Ring
127	Suzuka Circuit West Course	309	Chamonix
141	Fuji Speedway 2005 GT	309	Infineon Raceway Stock Car Course
155	Ice Arena	323	Fuji Speedway 2005 F
169	Apricot Hill Raceway	337	Tsukuba Circuit Wet
		351	Circuit de la Sarthe 2 (Not chicaned)

GRETZKY NHL 2005

EVERYTHING
At the Unlockables screen, press Start to bring up the code entry. Enter **shoenloc**.

GROWLANSER GENERATIONS

ALL ARMOR, GEMS AND MAX MONEY
At the world map, press Up, Right, **L2**, **L2**, Down, **R2**, **R2** Up, Down, **R2**, **L2**, Right, Left, ◉, ◉, ◉.

GUITAR HERO

UNLOCK ALL CHEATS
At the Main menu, press Yellow, Orange, Blue, Blue, Orange, Yellow, Yellow.

GUITAR HERO GUITAR CHEAT
At the Main menu, press Blue, Orange, Yellow, Blue, Blue.

CROWD METER CHEAT
At the Main menu, press Yellow, Blue, Orange, Orange, Blue, Blue, Yellow, Orange.

MONKEY HEAD CROWD CHEAT
At the Main menu, press Blue, Orange, Yellow, Yellow, Yellow, Blue, Orange.

SKULL HEAD CROWD CHEAT
At the Main menu, press Orange, Yellow, Blue, Blue, Orange, Yellow, Blue, Blue.

AIR GUITAR CHEAT
At the Main menu, press Orange, Orange, Blue, Yellow, Orange.

NO VENUE CHEAT
At the Main menu, press Blue, Yellow, Orange, Blue, Yellow, Orange.

HEROES OF THE PACIFIC

The following cheats will disable game saving.

CHEAT MENU
At the Main menu, press **L1**, **R2**, **L2**, **R3**, **R1**, **L3**.

PLANES AND MISSIONS
At the Main menu, press Up on Right Analog Stick , Down on Right Analog Stick , Left, **R2**, **L1**, Right on Right Analog Stick.

UPGRADE PLANES
At the Main menu, press **L1**, Left on Right Analog Stick, **R2**, Right on Right Analog Stick, Right, Down.

JAPANESE
At the Main menu, press ●, **R2**, **L1**, **L2**, Left, Up.

HIGH ROLLERS CASINO

CHEAT MODE
Enter your name as **SAM** and change the gender to female.

HOT SHOTS GOLF FORE!

Select Password from the Options menu and enter the following codes to enable these cheats:

ALL CHARACTERS AVAILABLE IN VS MODE
Enter **REZTWS**.

PRICE REDUCTION SALE IN SHOP
Enter **MKJEFQ**.

ALOHA BEACH RESORT COURSE IN SHOP
Enter **XSREHD**.

BAGPIPE CLASSIC COURSE IN SHOP
Enter **CRCNHZ**.

BLUE LAGOON C.C. COURSE IN SHOP
Enter **WVRJQS**.

DAY DREAM G.C. IN SHOP
Enter **OQUTNA**.

MINI-GOLF 2 G.C. IN SHOP
Enter **RVMIRU**.

SILKROAD CLASSIC COURSE IN SHOP
Enter **ZKOGJM**.

UNITED FOREST G.C. IN SHOP
Enter **UIWHLZ**.

WESTERN VALLEY COUNTRY CLUB COURSE AVAILABLE IN SHOP
Enter **LIBTFL** .

WILD GREEN C.C. COURSE IN SHOP
Enter **YZLOXE**.

CAPSULE 01 IN SHOP
Enter **WXAFSJ**.

CAPSULE 2 IN SHOP
Enter **OEINLK**.

CAPSULE 3 IN SHOP
Enter **WFKVTG**.

CAPSULE 4 IN SHOP
Enter **FCAVDO**.

CAPSULE 5 IN SHOP
Enter **YYPOKK**.

CAPSULE 6 IN SHOP
Enter **GDQDOF**.

CAPSULE 7 IN SHOP
Enter **HHXKPV**.

CAPSULE 8 IN SHOP
Enter **UOKXPS**.

CAPSULE 9 IN SHOP
Enter **LMIRYD**.

CAPSULE 10 IN SHOP
Enter **MJLJEQ**.

CAPSULE 11 IN SHOP
Enter **MHNCQI**

LOWER TOURNEY STAGE
Enter **XKWGFZ**.

CADDIE CLANK AVAILABLE
IN SHOP
Enter **XCQGWJ**.

CADDIE DAXTER AVAILABLE
IN SHOP
Enter **WSIKIN**.

CADDIE KAYLA AVAILABLE
IN SHOP
Enter **MZIMEL**.

CADDIE KAZ AVAILABLE IN
SHOP
Enter **LNNZJV**.

CADDIE MOCHI AVAILABLE
IN SHOP
Enter **MYPWPA**.

CADDIE SIMON AVAILABLE
IN SHOP
Enter **WRHZNB**.

CADDIE SOPHIE AVAILABLE
IN SHOP
Enter **UTWIVQ**.

BEGINNER'S BALL
AVAILABLE IN SHOP
Enter **YFQJJI**.

BIR AIR BALL AVAILABLE
IN SHOP
Enter **CRCGKR**.

INFINITY BALL AVAILABLE
IN SHOP
Enter **DJXBRG**.

PIN HOLE BALL AVAILABLE
IN SHOP
Enter **VZLSGP**.

SIDESPIN BALL AVAILABLE
IN SHOP
Enter **JAYQRK**.

TURBO SPIN BALL
AVAILABLE IN SHOP
Enter **XNETOK**.

100T HAMMER CLUB (B-
CLASS) AVAILABLE IN SHOP
Enter **NFSNHR**.

UPGRADE 100T HAMMER
CLUB (A-CLASS) AVAILABLE
IN SHOP
Enter **BVLHSI**.

UPGRADE 100T HAMMER
CLUB (S-CLASS) AVAILABLE
IN SHOP
Enter **MCSRUK**.

BIG AIR CLUB (B-CLASS)
AVAILABLE IN SHOP
Enter **DLJMFZ**.

UPGRADE BIG AIR CLUB (A-
CLASS) AVAILABLE IN SHOP
Enter **TOSXUJ**.

UPGRADE BIG AIR CLUB (S-
CLASS) AVAILABLE IN SHOP
Enter **JIDTQI**.

INFINITY CLUB AVAILABLE
IN SHOP
Enter **RZTQGV**.

UPGRADE INFINITY CLUB
(A-CLASS) AVAILABLE IN
SHOP
Enter **WTGFOR**.

UPGRADE INFINITY CLUB
(S-CLASS) AVAILABLE IN
SHOP
Enter **EIPCUL**.

PIN HOLE CLUB (B-CLASS) AVAILABLE IN SHOP
Enter **DGHFRP**.

UPGRADE PIN HOLE CLUB (A-CLASS) AVAILABLE IN SHOP
Enter **TTIMHT**.

UPGRADE PIN HOLE CLUB (S-CLASS) AVAILABLE IN SHOP
Enter **RBXVEL**.

UPGRADE TURBO SPIN CLUB (A-CLASS) AVAILABLE IN SHOP
Enter **NIWKWP**.

UPGRADE TURBO SPIN CLUB (S-CLASS) AVAILABLE IN SHOP
Enter **DTIZAB**.

EXTRA POSE CAM AVAILABLE IN SHOP
Enter **UEROOK**.

EXTRA SWING CAM AVAILABLE IN SHOP
Enter **RJIFQS**.

EXTRA VIDEO AVAILABLE IN SHOP
Enter **DPYHIU**.

HECKLETS AVAILABLE IN SHOP
Enter **DIXWFE**.

HSG CD/VOICE AVAILABLE IN SHOP
Enter **UITUGF**.

HSG CD/MUSIC AVAILABLE IN SHOP
Enter **PAJXLI**.

HSG RULES AVAILABLE IN SHOP
Enter **FKDHDS**.

LANDING GRID AVAILABLE IN SHOP
Enter **MQTIMV**.

REPLAY CAM A AVAILABLE IN SHOP
Enter **PVJEMF**.

REPLAY CAM B AVAILABLE IN SHOP
Enter **EKENCR**.

REPLAY CAM C AVAILABLE IN SHOP
Enter **ZUHHAC**.

MENU CHARACTER BRAD AVAILABLE IN SHOP
Enter **ZKJSIO**.

MENU CHARACTER PHOEBE AVAILABLE IN SHOP
Enter **LWVLCB**.

MENU CHARACTER RENEE AVAILABLE IN SHOP
Enter **AVIQXS**.

WALLPAPER SET 2 AVAILABLE IN SHOP
Enter **RODDHQ**.

MIKE'S COSTUME AVAILABLE IN SHOP
Enter **YKCFEZ**.

LIN'S COSTUME AVAILABLE IN SHOP
Enter **BBLSKQ**.

MEL'S COSTUME AVAILABLE IN SHOP
Enter **ARFLCR**.

PHOEBE'S COSTUME AVAILABLE IN SHOP
Enter **GJBCHY**.

ICE AGE 2: THE MELTDOWN

INFINITE PEBBLES
Pause the game and press Down, Down, Left, Up, Up, Right, Up, Down.

INFINITE ENERGY
Pause the game and press Down, Left, Right, Down, Down, Right, Left, Down.

INFINITE HEALTH
Pause the game and press Up, Right, Down, Up, Left, Down, Right, Left.

THE INCREDIBLE HULK: ULTIMATE DESTRUCTION

You must first collect a specific comic in the game to activate each code. Once you have collected the appropriate comic, you can enter the following. If you don't have the comic and enter the code, you get the following message: "That code cannot be activated...yet." Enable the cheats on the Code Input screen.

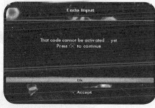 

UNLOCKED: CABS GALORE
Select Code Input from the Extras menu and enter **CABBIES**.

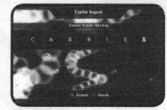

UNLOCKED: GORILLA INVASION
Select Code Input from the Extras menu and enter **kingkng**.

UNLOCKED: MASS TRANSIT
Select Code Input from the Extras menu and enter **TRANSIT**.

UNLOCKED: 5000 SMASH POINTS
Select Code Input from the Extras menu and enter **SMASH5**.

UNLOCKED: 10000 SMASH POINTS
Select Code Input from the Extras menu and enter **SMASH10**.

UNLOCKED: 15000 SMASH POINTS
Select Code Input from the Extras menu and enter **SMASH15**.

UNLOCKED: AMERICAN FLAG SHORTS
Select Code Input from the Extras menu and enter **AMERICA**.

UNLOCKED: CANADIAN FLAG SHORTS
Select Code Input from the Extras menu and enter **OCANADA**.

UNLOCKED: FRENCH FLAG SHORTS
Select Code Input from the Extras menu and enter **Drapeau**.

UNLOCKED: GERMAN FLAG SHORTS
Select Code Input from the Extras menu and enter **DEUTSCH**.

UNLOCKED: ITALIAN FLAG SHORTS
Select Code Input from the Extras menu and enter **MUTANDA**.

UNLOCKED: JAPANESE FLAG SHORTS
Select Code Input from the Extras menu and enter **FURAGGU**.

UNLOCKED: SPANISH FLAG SHORTS
Select Code Input from the Extras menu and enter **BANDERA**.

UNLOCKED: UK FLAG SHORTS
Select Code Input from the Extras menu and enter **FSHNCHP**.

UNLOCKED: COW MISSILES
Select Code Input from the Extras menu and enter **CHZGUN**.

UNLOCKED: DOUBLE HULK'S DAMAGE
Select Code Input from the Extras menu and enter **DESTROY**.

UNLOCKED: DOUBLE POWER COLLECTABLES
Select Code Input from the Extras menu and enter **BRINGIT**.

UNLOCKED: BLACK AND WHITE
Select Code Input from the Extras menu and enter **RETRO**.

UNLOCKED: SEPIA
Select Code Input from the Extras menu and enter **HISTORY**.

UNLOCKED: ABOMINATION
Select Code Input from the Extras menu and enter **VILLAIN**.

UNLOCKED: GRAY HULK
Select Code Input from the Extras menu and enter **CLASSIC**.

UNLOCKED: JOE FIXIT SKIN
Select Code Input from the Extras menu and enter **SUITFIT**.

UNLOCKED: WILD TRAFFIC
Select Code Input from the Extras menu and enter **FROGGIE**.

UNLOCKED: LOW GRAVITY
Select Code Input from the Extras menu and enter **PILLOWS**.

THE INCREDIBLES: RISE OF THE UNDERMINER

Pause the game, select Secrets, and enter the following.

EGOPROBLEM
Mr. Incredible and Frozone have huge funny heads!

MRIPROF
Mr. Incredible gains 1000 Experience Points.

FROZPROF
Frozone gains 1000 Experience Points.

MRIBOOM
Mr. Incredible gains a Super-Move.

FROZBOOM
Frozone gains a Super-Move.

ROLLCALL
Shows the game credits.

THISISTOOEASY
Cuts damage done to enemies in half, doubles damage done to the Supers, no health recovery, and Experience Points are halved!

THISISTOOHARD
Doubles damage done to enemies, halves damage done to the Supers, doubles amount of health recovery and Experience Points!

SHOWME
Unlocks every item in the Gallery!

MAXIMILLION
Doubles Experience Point rewards!

IN THE GROOVE

ALL SONGS
At the Main menu, press Up, Right, Up, Right, Left, Down, Left, Down, Up, Right, Down, Left, Up, Left, Down, Right.

JAK X: COMBAT RACING

DAXTER
Play for 5 hours to unlock Daxter in the Secrets Shop for 50,000 Orbs.

KIERA
Defeat the game.

KLEVER
Defeat Beachfront Drive Circuit Race

RAZER
Defeat Northern Tour Ciruit Race

SIG
Defeat Spargus City Death Race

UR-86
Defeat Kras City Qualifier

JAK
Make sure you have a Jak and Daxter save file on your memory card. Select Scan for Secret Characters from the Secrets Shop.

JAK II
Make sure you have a Jak II save file on your memory card. Select Scan for Secret Characters from the Secrets Shop.

JAK 3
Make sure you have a Jak 3 save file on your memory card. Select Scan for Secret Characters from the Secrets Shop.

RATCHET
Make sure you have a Ratchet: Deadlocked save file on your memory card. Select Scan for Secret Characters from the Secrets Shop.

HERO MODE
Complete the game with 100%. You can now purchase it for 50,000 Orbs at the Secret Shop.

JUICED

ARCADE/CUSTOM MODE UNLOCKED
Select Cheats from the Extras menu and enter **PINT**.

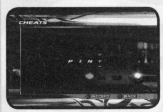

KARAOKE REVOLUTION VOLUME 2

At the Title screen, enter the following:

ALL SONGS
Press ●, ▲, Down, Left, Up, Right, **L2**, **R2**, Start.

ALL CHARACTERS
Press Up, ●, Right, ◉, ●, Left, ◉, Up, **L3**, **R3**.

ALL COSTUMES
Press Up, ◉, Left, ●, ●, Down, ◉, Right, **R3**, **L3**.

ALL VENUES
Press ●, ▲, Right, Up, Left, Down, **R2**, **L2**, Start.

GAME INFORMER T-SHIRT FOR ANGELA
Press Down, **L3** (x2), **R3** (x2), ◉, Right, ●, **L3**, **R3**.

GAMEPRO T-SHIRT
Press Down, **R3**, Up, **R3**, **L3**, Down, **L3**, Up, Down, ●.

GAME STAR T-SHIRT
Press Up, **R3**, Right, **R3** (x2), Left, **R3**, Down, ◉, ◉.

HARMONIX T-SHIRT FOR ISHANI

Press L3, ●, Up, ●, ■, L3, Down, Down, R3.

KONAMI T-SHIRT FOR DWAYNE

Press Right, R3, Right, R3, ●, Right, ●, ■, Down, Left.

PSM T-SHIRT FOR DEVRON

Press Left, Right, Left, L3, R3, Down, Up, Up, ●, ■.

Select Cheat Collection from Extras and enter the following or enter them during a game:

BANANA MICROPHONE

Press L1, L1, R2, R2, Right, Down, ●, Left, Up, ■.

DWAYNE DOLL MICROPHONE

Press ●, R2, ●, L1, R1, L2, ■, Up, ●, ■.

TOOTHBRUSH MICROPHONE

Press R1, L1, R2, L2, Right, Left, Down, Up, ●, ■.

BIG HEAD CHARACTER

Press Down (x3), Up, R1, L2, R2, L1, ●, ●.

SMALL HEAD CHARACTER

Press Right, Right, Up, Up, L2, L2, R2, R1, L1.

BIG EYE CHARACTER

Press ■ (x4), ●, Down, Down, R2, L2, R1.

GLASS CHARACTER

Press ■, ■, ●, R2, R2, L2, Down, Right, Right, Up.

OIL SLICK CHARACTER

Press L2, R2, L2, R2, ●, Down, ●, Up, Left, Right.

MERCURY CHARACTER

Press ●, L1, R2, Up, Up, Left, Left, ■, ■, R1.

WRAITH CHARACTER

Press R2, Left, R1, Right, Up, Up, ■, ●, Down, L2.

Select Cheat Collection from Extras and enter the following:

TOUGH CROWD

Press Right, Up, ● (x3), R2, R1, R1, L2, Down.

PIRATE CROWD

Press ■, ■, Left, Left, R2, L1, R2, R1, ●, L2.

ROBOT CROWD

Press ●, ●, Right, Right, R2, R1, R1, R2, ●, R2.

ZOMBIE CROWD

Press Left, L1, L2, ■, ■, L2, L2, L1, Left, Left.

KARAOKE REVOLUTION VOLUME 3

BANANA MICROPHONE

Score gold at each venue in Showtime mode. At the Extras menu, press Down, Up, Left, Right, ■, ●, ■, ● at Cheat Collection 1.

BIG EYED CHARACTER

Score gold at each venue in Showtime mode. At the Extras menu, press ●, ●, ■, ■, Down, Left, Left, Down at Cheat Collection 1.

DWAYNE DOLL MICROPHONE

Score gold at each venue in Showtime mode. At the Extras menu, press ■, ■, R3, ●, Up, Down, Right, Left at Cheat Collection 1.

TOOTHBRUSH MICROPHONE

Score gold at each venue in Showtime mode. At the Extras menu, press L2, L2, ■, ●, Down, Up, Left, L3 at Cheat Collection 1.

BIG HEAD CHARACTER

Score gold at each venue in Showtime mode. At the Extras menu, press ●, ■, ●, ■, Up, Right, Down, Left at Cheat Collection 2.

FISH MICROPHONE

Score gold at each venue in Showtime mode. At the Extras menu, press ■, Down, Up, Left, ■, ■, L2, L1 at Cheat Collection 2.

MERCURY CHARACTER

Score gold at each venue in Showtime mode. At the Extras menu, press Down, Down, Right, Left, Right, Left, ■, ● at Cheat Collection 2.

WRAITH CHARACTER

Score gold at each venue in Showtime mode. At the Extras menu, press L2, L2, Right, Right, ●, ■, R1, R1 at Cheat Collection 2.

GLASS CHARACTER

Score gold at each venue in Showtime mode. At the Extras menu, press Down, L2, R1, R2, L1, ●, ■, ● at Cheat Collection 3.

ICE CREAM MICROPHONE

Score gold at each venue in Showtime mode. At the Extras menu, press ■, ●, ■, ●, R2, L2, R1, L1 at Cheat Collection 3.

OIL SLICK CHARACTER

Score gold at each venue in Showtime mode. At the Extras menu, press L3, L3, R2, R1, L2, L1, Down, Up at Cheat Collection 3.

SMALL HEAD CHARACTER

Score gold at each venue in Showtime mode. At the Extras menu, press ●, R2, L2, R1, L1, Down, Down, Up at Cheat Collection 3.

ALIEN CROWD

Score gold at each venue in Showtime mode. At the Extras menu, press Up, Up, Down, ●, ●, L2, R2, ■ at Cheat Collection 4.

PIRATE CROWD

Score gold at each venue in Showtime mode. At the Extras menu, press Down, L2, L2, R2, R2, ■, ●, ■ at Cheat Collection 4.

ROBOT CROWD

Score gold at each venue in Showtime mode. At the Extras menu, press L3, Down, Down, R1, ●, ■, ●, ■ at Cheat Collection 4.

TOUGH AUDIO CROWD

Score gold at each venue in Showtime mode. At the Extras menu, press ●, L1, L2, R1, R2, Right, Right, Down at Cheat Collection 4.

ZOMBIE CROWD

Score gold at each venue in Showtime mode. At the Extras menu, press ■, ■, ●, ●, Up, Right, Right, Up at Cheat Collection 4.

KATAMARI DAMACY

COMETS

Finish a "Make a Star" level under a certain time to earn a comet. Use the following table to find the times you must beat to earn a comet.

LEVEL	FINISH WITHIN
Make a Star 1	1 minute
Make a Star 2	3 minutes
Make a Star 3	4 minutes
Make a Star 4	6 minutes
Make a Star 5	8 minutes

LEVEL	FINISH WITHIN
Make a Star 6	8 minutes
Make a Star 7	8 minutes
Make a Star 8	12 minutes
Make a Star 9	15 minutes
Make the Moon	20 minutes

KYA: DARK LINEAGE

BONUS GALLERY
At the Main menu, press ▲, Up, ●, Right, Down, Down, ■, Left.

RESTORE LIFE
Pause the game and press **L1**, **R2**, **L2**, **R1**, Up, Up, Left, ■, Right, ●, Start.

SHRINK JAMGUT
Pause the game and press **R2**, **R2**, ●, **R2**, **L2**, **L2**, Left, **L2**, ▲.

L.A. RUSH

$5,000
During a game, press Up, Down, Left, Right, ●, Left, **R2**, Up.

DISABLE POLICE
During a game, press Up, Down, Left, Right, **R2**, ■, Right, **R1**, Left.

UNLIMITED N20
During a game, press Up, Down, Left, Right, ■, Up, Down, ●, Up.

ALL CARS IN GARAGE PIMPED
During a game, press Up, Down, Left, Right, ●, ■, **R2**, **R1**, Up, Down, Left, Right.

FAST TRAFFIC
During a game, press Up, Down, Left, Right, ■, Right, ●, Left.

NO CATCH UP
Use **C-VHARD** as a profile name.

LEGO STAR WARS: THE VIDEO GAME

Extras

Pause the game and select Extras to toggle these cheats on and off.

INVINCIBILITY

At Dexter's Diner, select Enter Code and enter **4PR28U**.

BIG BLASTERS

At Dexter's Diner, select Enter Code and enter **IG72X4**.

CLASSIC BLASTERS

At Dexter's Diner, select Enter Code and enter **L449HD**.

SILLY BLASTERS

At Dexter's Diner, select Enter Code and enter **NR37W1**.

BRUSHES

At Dexter's Diner, select Enter Code and enter **SHRUB1**.

TEA CUPS

At Dexter's Diner, select Enter Code and enter **PUCEAT**.

MINIKIT DETECTOR

At Dexter's Diner, select Enter Code and enter **LD116B**.

MOUSTACHES

At Dexter's Diner, select Enter Code and enter **RP924W**.

PURPLE

At Dexter's Diner, select Enter Code and enter **YD77GC**.

SILHOUETTES

At Dexter's Diner, select Enter Code and enter **MS999Q**.

These codes make each character available for purchase from Dexter's Diner.

BATTLE DROID

At Dexter's Diner, select Enter Code and enter **987UYR**.

BATTLE DROID (COMMANDER)

At Dexter's Diner, select Enter Code and enter **EN11K5**.

BATTLE DROID (GEONOSIS)

At Dexter's Diner, select Enter Code and enter **LK42U6**.

BATTLE DROID (SECURITY)

At Dexter's Diner, select Enter Code and enter **KF999A**.

BOBA FETT

At Dexter's Diner, select Enter Code and enter **LA811Y**.

CLONE

At Dexter's Diner, select Enter Code and enter **F8B4L6**.

CLONE (EPISODE III)

At Dexter's Diner, select Enter Code and enter **ER33JN**.

CLONE (EPISODE III, PILOT)

At Dexter's Diner, select Enter Code and enter **BHU72T**.

CLONE (EPISODE III, SWAMP)

At Dexter's Diner, select Enter Code and enter **N3T6P8**.

CLONE (EPISODE III, WALKER)

At Dexter's Diner, select Enter Code and enter **RS6E25**.

COUNT DOOKU

At Dexter's Diner, select Enter Code and enter **14PGMN**.

DARTH MAUL

At Dexter's Diner, select Enter Code and enter **H35TUX**.

DARTH SIDIOUS

At Dexter's Diner, select Enter Code and enter **A32CAM**.

DISGUISED CLONE

At Dexter's Diner, select Enter Code and enter **VR832U**.

DROIDEKA
At Dexter's Diner, select Enter Code and enter **DH382U**.

GENERAL GRIEVOUS
At Dexter's Diner, select Enter Code and enter **SF321Y**.

GEONOSIAN
At Dexter's Diner, select Enter Code and enter **19D7NB**.

GRIEVOUS' BODYGUARD
At Dexter's Diner, select Enter Code and enter **ZTY392**.

GONK DROID
At Dexter's Diner, select Enter Code and enter **U63B2A**.

JANGO FETT
At Dexter's Diner, select Enter Code and enter **PL47NH**.

KI-ADI MUNDI
At Dexter's Diner, select Enter Code and enter **DP55MV**.

KIT FISTO
At Dexter's Diner, select Enter Code and enter **CBR954**.

LUMINARA
At Dexter's Diner, select Enter Code and enter **A725X4**.

MACE WINDU (EPISODE III)
At Dexter's Diner, select Enter Code and enter **MS952L**.

PADMÉ
At Dexter's Diner, select Enter Code and enter **92UJ7D**.

PK DROID
At Dexter's Diner, select Enter Code and enter **R840JU**.

PRINCESS LEIA
At Dexter's Diner, select Enter Code and enter **BEQ82H**.

REBEL TROOPER
At Dexter's Diner, select Enter Code and enter **L54YUK**.

ROYAL GUARD
At Dexter's Diner, select Enter Code and enter **PP43JX**.

SHAAK TI
At Dexter's Diner, select Enter Code and enter **EUW862**.

SUPER BATTLE DROID
At Dexter's Diner, select Enter Code and enter **XZNR21**.

LOONEY TUNES SPACE RACE

ALL BONUSES
Select Cheats from the Options screen and enter **MADAESAN**.

NO GAG CRATES
Select Cheats from the Options screen and enter **ENGARDE**.

INFINITE TURBO
Select Cheats from the Options screen and enter **KABOOM**.

ALL TOURNAMENTS & ACME EVENTS
Select Cheats from the Options screen and enter **TRUTHOR**.

ALL GALLERIA ITEMS
Select Cheats from the Options screen and enter **ALLMINE**.

MIRROR MODE
Select Cheats from the Options screen and enter **ITIS2LAFF**.

MARVIN THE MARTIAN
Select Cheats from the Options screen and enter **Q32**.

PORKY PIG
Select Cheats from the Options screen and enter **20LBHAM**.

THE KING
Select Cheats from the Options screen and enter **KOTIM**.

ASTEROID BELT TRACK
Select Cheats from the Options screen and enter **WHATISUI**.

NEBULA TRACK
Select Cheats from the Options screen and enter **CLOSEIT**.

PLANET ACME 2 TRACK
Select Cheats from the Options screen and enter **HLORALPH**.

PYRAMIDS OF MARS 2 TRACK
Select Cheats from the Options screen and enter **TORGO**.

WILD WEST QUADRANT 2 TRACK
Select Cheats from the Options screen and enter **GULLIBLE**.

GALACTORAMA PARK 2 STAGE
Select Cheats from the Options screen and enter **124ADIME**.

NORTH POLE STAR 2 STAGE
Select Cheats from the Options screen and enter **PLANETX**.

MADDEN NFL 06

Select Madden Cards from My Madden. Then select Madden Codes and enter the following:

PASSWORD	CARD
8Q2J2X	#55 Donovan McNabb Gold
2W4P9T	#188 First and Fifteen Bronze
2Y7L8B	#189 First and Five Bronze
2Z2F4H	#190 Unforced Errors Bronze
3D3Q3P	#191 Extra Credit Bronze
3D8X6T	#192 Tight Fit Bronze
3E9R4V	#193 5th Down Bronze
3F9G4J	#194 3rd Down Bronze
3H3U7F	#195 Human Plow Bronze
3H8M5U	#196 Super Dive Bronze
3J3S9Y	#197 Da Boot Bronze

MAJOR LEAGUE BASEBALL 2K6

UNLOCK EVERYTHING
Select Enter Cheat Code from the
My 2K6 menu and enter **Derek
Jeter**.

TOPPS 2K STARS
Select Enter Cheat Code from the My 2K6 menu and enter **Dream Team**.

SUPER WALL CLIMB
Select Enter Cheat Code from the
My 2K6 menu and enter **Last
Chance**. Enable the cheats by
selecting My Cheats or selecting
Cheat Codes from the Options screen
in-game.

SUPER PITCHES
Select Enter Cheat Code from the My 2K6 menu and enter **Unhittable**.
Enable the cheats by selecting My Cheats or selecting Cheat Codes from the
Options screen in-game.

ROCKET ARMS
Select Enter Cheat Code from the My 2K6 menu and enter **Gotcha**.
Enable the cheats by selecting My Cheats or selecting Cheat Codes from the
Options screen in-game.

BOUNCY BALL
Select Enter Cheat Code from the My 2K6 menu and enter **Crazy Hops**.
Enable the cheats by selecting My Cheats or selecting Cheat Codes from the
Options screen in-game.

MARVEL NEMESIS: RISE OF THE IMPERFECTS

UNLOCKS ALL FANTASTIC FOUR COMICS
Select Cheats from the Options and enter **SAVAGELAND**.

UNLOCKS ALL TOMORROW PEOPLE COMICS
Select Cheats from the Options and enter **NZONE**.

ELEKTRA BONUS CARD
Select Cheats from the Options and enter **THEHAND**.

SOLARA BONUS CARD
Select Cheats from the Options and enter **REIKO**.

STORM BONUS CARD
Select Cheats from the Options and enter **MONROE**.

MEGA MAN X8

PLAY AS ALIA
At the Title screen, press Down, **R1**, Up, **L1**, ⬛, ✖, 🔺, ⬤.

PLAY AS LAYER
At the Title screen, press ⬛, ⬛, Right, ✖, **R1**.

BATTLE CUTMAN
At the Title screen, press Left, ⬤, Up, 🔺, Down, ✖, Right, ⬛, **L1**, **R1**, **L2**, **R2**.

SIGMA BLADE
At the Title screen, press **L3**, **L3**, **R3**, **L3**, **L3**, **R3**, **L3**, **L3**, **R3**, **L3**, **L3**, **R3**.

BLACK ZERO
At the Title screen, press **L1**, **L1**, **R1**, **R1**, **L1**, **L1**, **L1**, **L1**.

PALLETE
At the Title screen, press **R1**, ✖, Left, ⬛, ⬛.

ULTIMATE ARMOR X
At the Title screen, press Left, Left, Left, Right, Right, Right, Left, Left, Left, Left, Right, Right, Right, Right.

WHITE AXL
At the Title screen, press **L2**, **L2**, **L2**, **R2**, **R2**, **R2**, **L2**, **L2**, **L2**, **R2**.

MEGA MAN X COLLECTION

Mega Man X4

BLACK ZERO
At the Character Select screen, highlight Zero, hold **R1** and press Right (x6). Then release **R1**, hold ◉ and press Start. Continue holding ◉ until the game starts.

ULTIMATE ARMOR FOR MEGA MAN X
At the Character Select screen, highlight Mega Man X, press ◉, ◉, Left (x6), hold **L1** + **R2** and press Start. Continue holding **L1** + **R2** until the game starts. Complete the level, then find the Leg power-up in the Jungle.

Mega Man X5

BLACK ZERO
At the Character Select screen, highlight Zero and press Down, Down, Up (x9).

ULTIMATE ARMOR FOR MEGA MAN X
At the Character Select screen, highlight Mega Man X and press Up, Up, Down (x9).

Mega Man X6

BLACK ZERO
At the Main menu, highlight Game Start and press **L1**, **L1**, **L1**, **R2**.

ULTIMATE ARMOR FOR MEGA MAN X
At the Main menu, highlight Game Start and press Left, Left, Left, Right.

MIDNIGHT CLUB 3: DUB EDITION REMIX

ALL CITIES AND RACES IN ARCADE MODE
Select Cheat Codes from the Options screen and enter **urbansprawl**, **roadtrip** or **crosscountry**.

NO DAMAGE
Select Cheat Codes from the Options screen and enter **ontheroad**.

ARGO SPECIAL MOVE
Select Cheat Codes from the Options screen and enter **dfens**.

ROAR SPECIAL MOVE
Select Cheat Codes from the Options screen and enter **Rjnr**.

ZONE SPECIAL MOVE
Select Cheat Codes from the Options screen and enter **allin**.

ADD $1 TO CAREER MONEY
Select Cheat Codes from the Options screen and enter **kubmir**.

SUBTRACT $1 OF CAREER MONEY
Select Cheat Codes from the Options screen and enter **rimbuk**.

BUNNY HEAD
Select Cheat Codes from the Options screen and enter **getheadl**.

CHROME HEAD
Select Cheat Codes from the Options screen and enter **haveyouseenthisboy**.

FLAMING HEAD
Select Cheat Codes from the Options screen and enter **trythisathome**.

SNOWMAN HEAD
Select Cheat Codes from the Options screen and enter **getheadm**.

PUMPKIN HEAD
Select Cheat Codes from the Options screen and enter **getheadk**.

YELLOW SMILE HEAD
Select Cheat Codes from the Options screen and enter **getheadj**.

MIDWAY ARCADE TREASURES 3

RUSH 2049

ACTIVATE CHEAT MENU
At the Main menu, highlight Options and press **L1** + **R1** + ■ + ●. Now you can enter the following cheats.

ALL CARS
At the Cheat menu, press ✖, ✖, ●, ●, **L1**, **L1**, hold **R1** and press ■, release **R1**, hold **L1** and press ✖.

ALL TRACKS
At the Cheat menu, hold ✖ + ■ and press **R1**, release the buttons, hold ■ + ● and press **L1**, release the buttons, ✖, ✖, ●, ●, hold **L1** + **R1** and press ■.

ALL PARTS
At the Cheat menu, hold ■ and press ●, ✖, **L1**, **R1**, release ■, hold ● and press ✖, release ●, ■, ■.

RESURRECT IN PLACE
At the Cheat menu, press **R1**, **R1**, **L1**, **L1**, ✖, ■, ●.

FRAME SCALE
At the Cheat menu, hold **L1** and press ✖, ✖, ●, release **L1**, hold **R1** and press ✖, ✖, ●.

TIRE SCALING
At the Cheat menu, press ■, ●, ✖, ■, ●, ✖, hold **R1** and press ✖.

FOG COLOR
At the Cheat menu, hold **L1** and press ■, release **L1**, hold ✖ and press ■, release ✖, hold ● and press ■, release ●, hold **R1** and press ■.

CAR COLLISIONS
At the Cheat menu, hold **L1** + **R1** and press ■, ●, ✖, release the buttons, ■, ●, ✖.

CONE MINES
At the Cheat menu, hold ● and press **R1**, **L1**, release ●, ■, hold ✖ and press ■, release ✖, ■.

CAR MINES
At the Cheat menu, Hold **L1** + **R1** + ■ and press ✖, ●, release the buttons, ✖, ●.

TRACK ORIENTATION
At the Cheat menu, hold **L1**+**R1** and press ■, release the buttons, ✖, ■, ●, hold **L1**+**R1** and press ■.

AUTO ABORT
At the Cheat menu, press ✖, **L1**, ■, **R1**, ●, hold **L1**+**R1** and press ✖, ■.

SUPER SPEED
At the Cheat menu, hold ● + **R1** and press **L1**, release the buttons, hold ✖ and press ■, release ✖, ✖, ✖, ✖.

INVINCIBLE
At the Cheat menu, hold **L1** + ■ and press ●, ✖, release the buttons, hold **R1** and press ✖, ■, ●.

INVISIBLE CAR
At the Cheat menu, hold **L1** and press ■, release **L1**, hold **R1** and press ●, release **R1**, ✖, hold **L1** + **R1** and press ■, release the buttons, ●, ●, ●.

INVISIBLE TRACK
At the Cheat menu, press R1, L1, ●, ■, ✖, ✖, ■, ●, hold L1 + R1 and press ✖.

BRAKES
At the Cheat menu, press ●, ●, ●, hold L1 + ■ + ✖ and press R1.

SUPER TIRES
At the Cheat menu, hold R1 and press ■, ■, ■, release R1, hold L1 and press ✖, ✖, ●.

MASS
At the Cheat menu, hold ✖ and press ●, ■, ●, release ✖, L1, R1.

BATTLE PAINT SHOP
At the Cheat menu, hold ✖ and press L1, R1, L1, R1, release ✖, ■, ●, ■.

DEMOLITION BATTLE
At the Cheat menu, hold L1 + ✖ and press ●, ■, release the buttons, hold R1 + ✖ and press ●, ■.

RANDOM WEAPONS
At the Cheat menu, hold L1 + ✖ and press ■, ●, release the buttons, hold R1 + ✖ and press ■, ●.

HYDRO THUNDER

ALL TRACKS AND BOATS
Get a high score and enter ?PB as your initials.

MLB 2005

ALL PLAYERS
At the Main menu, press Left, Up, Left, Right, Down, Right, Left, Up.

ALL TEAMS
At the Main menu, press Left, Right, Right, Down, Down, Left, Up, Up.

ALL UNIFORMS
At the Main menu, press Up, Down, Right, Left, Down, Right, Down, Up.

ALL STADIUMS
At the Main menu, press Down, Up, Left, Right, Up, Right, Up, Down.

BEANS
At the Main menu, press Right(x6), Left, Down.

BIG BALL
At the Main menu, press Up, Up, Right, Left, Up, Up, Right, Left.

BIG HEAD
At the Main menu, press Left, Right, Left, Right, Up, Down, Up, Down.

SMALL HEAD
At the Main menu, press Up, Down, Up, Up, Right (x3), Left.

BLACK AND WHITE
At the Main menu, press Up, Up, Down, Down, Left, Right, Left, Right.

FASTER RUNNERS
At the Main menu, press Left, Right, Left, Right, Left, Right, Up, Up.

SLOWER RUNNERS
At the Main menu, press Right, Left, Right, Left, Right, Left, Down, Down.

SUPER PITCH BREAK
At the Main menu, press Right, Left, Right, Left, Right, Left, Up, Up.

SUPER PITCH SPEED
At the Main menu, press Up (x3), Left (x3), Left, Right.

SUPER SIX PITCHES
At the Main menu, press Down, Up, Down, Right (x4), Left.

MLB '06: THE SHOW

ALL TEAMS
At the Main menu, press Left, Right, Right, Down, Down, Left, Up, Up.

ALL PLAYERS
At the Main menu, press Left, Up, Left, Right, Down, Right, Left, Up.

ALL UNIFORMS
At the Main menu, press Up, Down, Right, Left, Down, Right, Down, Up.

ALL STADIUMS
At the Main menu, press Down, Up, Left, Right, Up, Right, Up, Down.

BIG BALL
Pause the game and press Up, Right, Down, Left, Right, Down, Left, Up.

MAX PITCH
Pause the game and press Right, Right, Up, Up, Down, Down, Left, Left Break.

MAX PITCH SPEED
Pause the game and press Up, Up, Left, Right, Left, Right, Up, Up.

RUN FASTER
Pause the game and press Left, Left, Left, Up, Right, Right, Right, Down.

RUN SLOWER
Pause the game and press Right, Right, Right, Up, Left, Left, Left, Down.

MOTOCROSS MANIA 3

ALL TRACKS
At the Main menu, press Up, Left, Down, Right, Up, Left, Down, Left, Left, ■.

ALL RIDERS & BIKES
At the Main menu, press Up, Left, Down, Right, Up, Left, Down, Up, ■.

ALL BIKE UPGRADES
At the Main menu, press Up, Left, Down, Right, Up, Down, Down, Left, Down, ■.

ALL WEAPONS & ARMOR
At the Main menu, press Up, Left, Down, Right, Up, Left, Down, Left, Down, ■.

FREESTYLE

At the Main menu, press Up, Left, Down, Right, Up, Left, Down, Left, Left, ●. Go into another menu and back out to access Freestyle.

MVP 06 NCAA BASEBALL

ALL CHALLENGE ITEMS
In Dynasty Mode, create a player with the name **Dee Jay Randall**.

LEVEL 1 CHALLENGE ITEMS
In Dynasty Mode, create a player with the name **Peter Termouth**.

ALL LEVEL 2 CHALLENGE ITEMS
In Dynasty Mode, create a player with the name **Trey Smith**.

MVP BASEBALL 2005

ALL STADIUMS, PLAYERS, UNIFORMS AND REWARDS
Create a player named **Katie Roy**.

RED SOX ST. PATRICK'S DAY UNIFORM
Create a player named **Neverlose Sight**.

BAD HITTER WITH THIN BAT
Create a player named **Erik Kiss**.

GOOD HITTER WITH BIG BAT
Create a player named **Isaiah Paterson**, **Jacob Paterson** or **Keegan Paterson**.

BIGGER BODY
Create a player named **Kenny Lee**.

MX UNLEASHED

Select Cheat Codes from the Options menu, then highlight the desired cheat and press ● to access a keyboard. Enter the following codes.

SUPERCROSS TRACKS
Enter **STUPERCROSS**.

NATIONAL TRACKS
Enter **ECONATION**.

FREESTYLE TRACKS
Enter **BUSTBIG**.

PRO PHYSICS
Enter **SWAPPIN**.

EXPERT AI
Enter **OBTGOFAST**.

MACHINES
Enter **MINIGAMES**.

50CC BIKES
Enter **SQUIRRELDOG**.

500CC BIKES
Enter **BIGDOGS**.

CAREER COMPLETION
Enter **CLAPPEDOUT**.

AI BOWLING
Enter **WRECKINGBALL**.

MX VS. ATV UNLEASHED

UNLOCK EVERYTHING
Select Cheat Codes from the Options and enter **TOOLAZY**.

1,000,000 POINTS
Select Cheat Codes from the Options and enter **BROKEASAJOKE**. After entering the code, press Done multiple times for more points.

ALL PRO RIDERS
Select Cheat Codes from the Options and enter **WANNABE**.

ALL GEAR
Select Cheat Codes from the Options and enter **WARDROBE**.

50CC BIKE CLASS
Select Cheat Codes from the Options and enter **MINIMOTO**.

ALL MACHINES
Select Cheat Codes from the Options and enter **LEADFOOT**.

ALL FREESTYLE TRACKS
Select Cheat Codes from the Options and enter **HUCKIT**.

NASCAR 06: TOTAL TEAM CONTROL

UNLOCK EVERYTHING
In Fight to the Top mode, select Edit Driver. Enter **Gimme Gimme** as the first and last names.

$10,000,000
In Fight to the Top mode, select Edit Driver. Enter **Walmart Money** as the first and last names.

WALMART DRIVER AND TRACK
In Fight to the Top mode, select Edit Driver. Enter **Walmart Exclusive** as the first and last names.

MAX FAN LEVEL
In Fight to the Top mode, select Edit Driver. Enter **Super Star** as the first and last names.

MAX PRESTIGE
In Fight to the Top mode, select Edit Driver. Enter **MeMyself AndI** as the first and last names.

MAX TEAM PRESTIGE
In Fight to the Top mode, select Edit Driver. Enter **All ForOne** as the first and last names.

NBA 2K6

CELEBRITY STREET OPTION
Select Codes from the Features menu and enter **ballers**.

2KSPORTS TEAM
Select Codes from the Features menu and enter **2ksports**.

2K6 TEAM
Select Codes from the Features menu and enter **nba2k6**.

VC TEAM
Select Codes from the Features menu and enter **vcteam**.

NIKE SHOX MTX SHOES
Select Codes from the Features menu and enter **crazylift**.

NIKE ZOOM 20-5-5 SHOES
Select Codes from the Features menu and enter **lebronsummerkicks**.

NIKE ZOOM KOBE 1 SHOES
Select Codes from the Features menu and enter **kobe**.

NIKE ZOOM LEBRON III ALL-STAR COLORWAY SHOES
Select Codes from the Features menu and enter **lb allstar**.

NIKE ZOOM LEBRON III BLACK/CRIMSON SHOES
Select Codes from the Features menu and enter **lb crimsonblack**.

NIKE ZOOM LEBRON III SPECIAL BIRTHDAY EDITION SHOES
Select Codes from the Features menu and enter **lb bday**.

NIKE ZOOM LEBRON III WHITE/GOLD SHOES
Select Codes from the Features menu and enter **lb whitegold**.

NIKE UP TEMPO PRO SHOES
Select Codes from the Features menu and enter **anklebreakers**.

ALTERNATE UNIFORMS
For the following codes, choose Codes from the Features menu and enter the appropriate code.

UNIFORM	ENTER
2006 All-Star	fanfavorites
St. Patrick's Day	gogreen
Bulls Retro	chi retro
Cavaliers Alternate	cle 2nd
Celtics Alternate	bos 2nd
Clippers Retro	lac retro
Grizzlies Retro	mem retro
Heat Retro	mia retro
Hornets Retro	no retro
Kings Alternate	sac 2nd
Knicks Retro	ny retro
Magic Retro	orl retro
Nets Retro	nj retro
Nuggets Alternate	den 2nd

UNIFORM	ENTER
2005-06 Pacers Uniform	31andonly

Pistons Alternate	det 2nd
Rockets Retro	hou retro
Sonics Retro	sea retro
Suns Retro	phx retro
Wizards Retro	was retro

+10 BONUS FOR DEFENSIVE AWARENESS
Find the PowerBar vending machine in The Crib. Choose Enter Code and enter **lockdown**.

+10 BONUS FOR OFFENSIVE AWARENESS
Find the PowerBar vending machine in The Crib. Choose Enter Code and enter **getaclue**.

MAX DURABILITY
Find the PowerBar vending machine in The Crib. Choose Enter Code and enter **noinjury**.

UNLIMITED STAMINA
Find the PowerBar vending machine in The Crib. Choose Enter Code and enter **nrgmax**.

POWERBAR TATTOO
Find the PowerBar vending machine in The Crib. Choose Enter Code and enter **pbink**. You can now use it in the game's Create Player feature.

ALL ITEMS IN THE CRIB
Find the PowerBar vending machine in The Crib. Choose Enter Code and enter **criball**.

NBA BALLERS: PHENOM

VERSUS SCREEN CHEATS

You can enter the following codes at the Vs screen. The ● button corresponds to the first number in the code, the ▲ is the second number, and the ⦿ button corresponds to the last number. Press the D-pad in any direction to enter the code.

EFFECT	CODE
Tournament Mode	0 1 1

Big Head	1 3 4

Kid Ballers	4 3 3

EFFECT	CODE
Speedy Players	2 1 3
Alternate Gear	1 2 3

NBA LIVE 2005

50,000 DYNASTY POINTS
Enter **YISS55CZ0E** as an NBA Live Code.

ALL CLASSICS HARDWOOD JERSEYS
Enter **PRYI234N0B** as an NBA Live Code.

ALL TEAM GEAR
Enter **1NVDR89ER2** as an NBA Live Code.

ALL SHOES
Enter **FHM389HU80** as an NBA Live Code.

AIR UNLIMITED SHOES
Enter **XVLJD9895V** as an NBA Live Code.

HUARACHE 2K4 SHOES
Enter **VNBA60230T** as an NBA Live Code.

NIKE BG ROLLOUT SHOES
Enter **0984ADF90P** as an NBA Live Code.

NIKE SHOX ELITE SHOES
Enter **2388HDFCBJ** as an NBA Live Code.

ZOOM GENERATION LOW SHOES
Enter **234SDJF9W4** as an NBA Live Code.

ZOOM LEBRON JAMES II SHOES
Enter **1KENZO23XZ** as an NBA Live Code.

ATLANTA HAWKS ALTERNATE UNIFORM
Enter **HDI834NN9N** as an NBA Live Code.

BOSTON CELTICS ALTERNATE UNIFORM
Enter **XCV43MGMDS** as an NBA Live Code.

DALLAS MAVERICKS ALTERNATE UNIFORM
Enter **AAPSEUD09U** as an NBA Live Code.

NEW ORLEANS HORNETS ALTERNATE UNIFORM
Enter **JRE7H4D90F** as a NBA Live Code.

NEW ORLEANS HORNETS ALTERNATE UNIFORM 2
Enter **JRE7H4D9WH** as a NBA Live Code.

SEATTLE SONICS ALTERNATE UNIFORM
Enter **BHD87YY27Q** as a NBA Live Code.

GOLDEN STATE WARRIORS ALTERNATE UNIFORM
Enter **NAVNY29548** as an NBA Live Code.

NBA LIVE 06

EASTERN ALL-STARS 2005-06 AWAY JERSEYS
Select NBA Codes from My NBA Live and enter **XCVB5387EQ**.

EASTERN ALL-STARS 2005-06 HOME JERSEY
Select NBA Codes from My NBA Live and enter **234SDFGHMO**.

WESTERN ALL-STARS 2005-06 AWAY JERSEY
Select NBA Codes from My NBA Live and enter **39N56B679J**.

WESTERN ALL-STARS 2005-06 HOME JERSEY
Select NBA Codes from My NBA Live and enter **2J9UWABNP1**.

BOSTON CELTICS 2005-06 ALTERNATE JERSEY
Select NBA Codes from My NBA Live and enter **193KSHU88J**.

CLEVELAND CAVALIERS 2005-06 ALTERNATE JERSEY
Select NBA Codes from My NBA Live and enter **9922NVDKVT**.

DENVER NUGGETS 2005-06 ALTERNATE JERSEYS
Select NBA Codes from My NBA Live and enter **XWETJK72FC**.

DETROIT PISTONS 2005-06 ALTERNATE JERSEY
Select NBA Codes from My NBA Live and enter **JANTWIKBS6**.

INDIANA PACERS 2005-06 ALTERNATE AWAY JERSEY
Select NBA Codes from My NBA Live and enter **PSDF90PPJN**.

INDIANA PACERS 2005-06 ALTERNATE HOME JERSEY
Select NBA Codes from My NBA Live and enter **SDF786WSHW**.

SACRAMENTO KINGS 2005-06 ALTERNATE JERSEY
Select NBA Codes from My NBA Live and enter **654NNBFDWA**.

A3 GARNETT 3
Select NBA Codes from My NBA Live and enter **DRI239CZ49**.

JORDAN MELO V.5 WHITE & BLUE
Select NBA Codes from My NBA Live and enter **5223WERPII**.

JORDAN MELO V.5 WHITE & YELLOW
Select NBA Codes from My NBA Live and enter **ZXDR7362Q1**.

JORDAN XIV BLACK & RED
Select NBA Codes from My NBA Live and enter **144FVNHM35**.

JORDAN XIV WHITE & GREEN
Select NBA Codes from My NBA Live and enter **67YFH9839F**.

JORDAN XIV WHITE & RED
Select NBA Codes from My NBA Live and enter **743HFDRAU8**.

S. CARTER III LE
Select NBA Codes from My NBA Live and enter **JZ3SCARTVY**.

T-MAC 5 BLACK
Select NBA Codes from My NBA Live and enter **258SHQW95B**.

T-MAC 5 WHITE
Select NBA Codes from My NBA Live and enter **HGS83KP234P**.

ANSWER DMX 10
Select NBA Codes from My NBA Live and enter **RBKAIUSAB7**.

ANSWER IX AND THE RBK ANSWER IX VIDEO
Select NBA Codes from My NBA Live and enter **AI9BUBBA7T**.

THE QUESTION AND THE MESSAGE FROM ALLEN IVERSON VIDEO
Select NBA Codes from My NBA Live and enter **HOYAS3AI6L**.

NCAA FOOTBALL 06

IMPACT PLAYERS IN THE ZONE IN PRACTICE
Create a Profile with the name **ZoneOut**.

PENNANT CODES
Select Pennant Collection from My NCAA. Press Select and enter the following codes:

Code	Pennant	Code	Pennant
Sic Em	#16 Baylor	Geaux Tigers	#285 All-LSU
Oskee Wow	#63 Illinois	Raising Cane	#286 All-Miami
Fight	#160 Texas Tech	Go Blue	#287 All-Michigan
Thanks	#200 First and Fifteen	Hail State	#288 All-Mississippi State
For	#201 Blink	Go Big Red	#289 All-Nebraska
Registering	#202 Boing	Rah Rah	#290 All-North Carolina
With EA	#204 Butter Fingers	Golden Domer	#291 All-Notre Dame
Tiburon	#205 Crossed The Line	Killer Nuts	#292 All-Ohio State
EA Sports	#206 Cuffed	Boomer	#293 All-Oklahoma
Touchdown	#207 Extra Credit	Go Pokes	#294 All-Oklahoma State
In The Zone	#208 Helium	Quack Attack	#295 All-Oregoon
Turnover	#209 Hurricane	We Are	#296 All-Penn State
Impact	#210 Instant Freplay	Lets Go Pitt	#297 All-Pittsburgh
Heisman	#211 Jumbalaya	Boiler Up	#298 All-Purdue
Game Time	#212 Molasses	Orange Crush	#299 All-Syracuse
Break Free	#213 Nike Free	Big Orange	#300 All-Tennessee
Hand Picked	#214 Nike Magnigrip	Hook Em	#301 All-Texas
No Sweat	#215 Nike Pro	Gig Em	#302 All-Texas A&M
Light Speed	#216 Nike Speed TD	Mighty	#303 All-UCLA
Elite 11	#219 QB Dud	Fight On	#304 All-USC
NCAA	#222 Stiffed	Wahoos	#305 All-Virginia
Football	#224 Take Your Time	Tech Triumph	#306 All-Virginia Tech
06	#225 Thread & Needle	Bow Down	#307 All-Washington
Offense	#226 Tough As Nails	U Rah Rah	#308 All-Wisconsin
Defense	#227 Trip	Bear Down	#311 Ark Mascot
Blitz	#228 What a Hit!	Red And Gold	#333 ISU Mascot
Sideline	#229 Kicker Hex	Rock Chalk	#335 KU Mascot
Fumble	#273 2004 All-Americans	Go Green	#346 Michigan State Mascot
Roll Tide	#274 All-Alabama	Rah Rah Rah	#341 Minn Mascot
Woopigsooie	#276 All-Arkansas	Hotty Totty	#342 Miss Mascot
War Eagle	#277 All-Auburn	Mizzou Rah	#344 Mizzou Mascot
Death Valley	#278 All-Clemson	Go Pack	#349 NCSU Mascot
Glory	#279 All-Colorado	Go Cats	#352 NU Mascot
Great To Be	#280 All-Florida	On On UK	#371 UK Mascot
Uprising	#281 All-FSU	Go Deacs Go	#382 Wake Mascot
Hunker Down	#282 All-Georgia	All Hail	#385 WSU Mascot
On Iowa	#283 All-Iowa	Hail WV	#386 WVU Mascot
Victory	#284 All-Kansas State		

NCAA MARCH MADNESS 06

ALL TEAMS
Select My NCAA, then Cheat Codes from the lounge. Enter **PSDF9078VT**.

AIR JORDAN III SHOES
Select My NCAA, then Cheat Codes from the lounge. Enter **39N56BXC4S**.

FIRST AIR JORDANS
Select My NCAA, then Cheat Codes from the lounge. Enter **2J9UWAS44L**.

NEED FOR SPEED MOST WANTED

BURGER KING CHALLENGE
At the Title screen, press Up, Down, Up, Down, Left, Right, Left, Right.

CASTROL SYNTEC VERSION OF THE FORD GT
At the Title screen, press Left, Right, Left, Right, Up, Down, Up, Down.

MARKER IN BACKROOM OF THE ONE-STOP SHOP
At the Title screen, press Up, Up, Down, Down, Left, Right, Up, Down.

NEED FOR SPEED UNDERGROUND 2

ALL CIRCUIT TRACKS
At the Title screen, press Down, **R1**, **R1**, **R1**, **R2**, **R2**, **R2**, ●.

$200 IN CAREER MODE
At the Title screen, press Up, Up, Up, Left, **R1**, **R1**, **R1**, Down.

$1000 IN CAREER MODE
At the Title screen, press Left, Left, Right, ●, ●, Right, **L1**, **R1**. This code also unlocks the RX-8 and Skyline in Quick Race.

HUMMER H2 CAPONE
At the Title screen, press Up, Left, Up, Up, Down, Left, Down, Left.

NISSAN SKYLINE
At the Title screen, press Down, Down, **L1**, **L2**, **L1**, **L2**, **L1**, Down.

SHINESTREET LEXUS IS300
At the Title screen, press Up, Down, Left, Up, Left, Up, Right, Left.

BEST BUY VINYL
At the Title screen, press Up, Down, Up, Down, Down, Up, Right, Left.

BURGER KING VINYL
At the Title screen, press Up, Up, Up, Up, Down, Up, Up, Left.

UNIQUE VINYL
At the Title screen, press Down, Up, Down, Left, **L1**, **L1**, **L1**, Down.

PERFORMANCE LEVEL 1
At the Title screen, press **L1**, **R1**, **L1**, **R1**, Left, Left, Right, Up.

PERFORMANCE LEVEL 2
At the Title screen, press **R1**, **R1**, **L1**, **R1**, Left, Right, Up, Down.

VISUAL LEVEL 1
At the Title screen, press **R1**, **R1**, Up, Down, **L1**, **L1**, Up, Down.

VISUAL LEVEL 2
At the Title screen, press **L1**, **R1**, Up, Down, **L1**, Up, Up, Down.

NFL STREET 2

FUMBLE MODE
Enter **GreasedPig** as a code.

MAX CATCH
Enter **MagnetHands** as a code.

NO CHAINS MODE
Enter **NoChains** as a code.

NO FUMBLE MODE
Enter **GlueHands** as a code.

UNLIMITED TURBO
Enter **NozBoost** as a code.

EA FIELD
Enter **EAField** as a code.

AFC EAST ALL STARS
Enter **EAASFSCT** as a code.

AFC NORTH ALL STARS
Enter **NAOFRCTH** as a code.

AFC SOUTH ALL STARS
Enter **SAOFUCTH** as a code.

AFC WEST ALL STARS
Enter **WAEFSCT** as a code.

NFC EAST ALL STARS
Enter **NNOFRCTH** as a code.

NFC NORTH ALL STARS
Enter **NNAS66784** as a code.

NFC SOUTH ALL STARS
Enter **SNOFUCTH** as a code.

NFC WEST ALL STARS
Enter **ENASFSCT** as a code.

TEAM REEBOK
Enter **Reebok** as a code.

TEAM XZIBIT
Enter **TeamXzibit** as a code.

NHL 2K6

UNLOCK EVERYTHING
Select Manage Profiles from the Options screen. Create a New Profile with the name **Turco813**.

ONE PIECE: GRAND BATTLE

CHOPPER'S 3RD COSTUME
At the Title screen, hold **L1** or **L2** and press Left, Right ✖, ■, ✖, ▲.

LUFFY'S 3RD COSTUME
At the Title screen, hold **L1** or **L2** and press Up, Up, ✖, ■, ✖, ✖.

ROBIN'S 3RD COSTUME
At the Title screen, hold **L1** or **L2** and press Down, Right, ✖, ■, ✖, ✖.

SANJI'S 3RD COSTUME
At the Title screen, hold **L1** or **L2** and press Up, Down, ✖, ■, ✖, ●.

NAMI'S 3RD COSTUME
At the Title screen, hold **L1** or **L2** and press Left, Left, ✖, ■, ✖.

USOPP'S 3RD COSTUME
At the Title screen, hold **L1** or **L2** and press Right, Right, ✖, ■, ✖, ▲.

ZORO'S 3RD COSTUME
At the Title screen, hold **L1** or **L2** and press Down, Down, ✖, ■, ✖, ▲.

OUTRUN 2006: COAST 2 COAST

100% COMPLETE/UNLOCK EVERYTHING

Edit your license and change the name to **ENTIRETY**. Select Done, then back out of all menus.

1,000,000 OUTRUN MILES

Edit your license and change the name to **MILESANDMILES**. Select Done, then back out of all menus.

PAC-MAN WORLD 3

ALL LEVELS AND MAZES

At the Main menu, highlight Level Select and press Left, Right, Left, Right, ●, Up.

PETER JACKSON'S KING KONG: THE OFFICIAL GAME OF THE MOVIE

At the Main menu, hold **L1** + **R1** and press Down, ●, Up, ●, Down, Down, Up, Up. Release **L1** + **R1** to get the Cheat option on the menu. The Cheat option will also be available from the pause menu.

GOD MODE
Select Cheat and enter **8wonder**.

ALL CHAPTERS
Select Cheat and enter **KKst0ry**.

AMMO 999
Select Cheat and enter **KK 999 mun.**

MACHINE GUN
Select Cheat and enter **KKcapone**.

REVOLVER
Select Cheat and enter **KKtigun**.

SNIPER RIFLE
Select Cheat and enter **KKsn1per**.

INFINITE SPEARS
Select Cheat and enter **lance 1nf**.

ONE-HIT KILLS
Select Cheat and enter **GrosBras**.

EXTRAS
Select Cheat and enter
KKmuseum.

PRINCE OF PERSIA: THE SANDS OF TIME

CLASSIC PRINCE OF PERSIA
Start a new game and while on the balcony, hold **L3** and enter ❌, ◼, ▲,
⬤, ▲, ❌, ◼, ⬤.

CLASSIC PASSWORDS

LEVEL	PASSWORD	LEVEL	PASSWORD
2	KIEJSC	8	SVZMSC
3	VNNNPC	9	DBJRPC
4	IYVPTC	10	MZFYSC
5	RWSWWC	11	BRAYQC
6	GONWUC	12	UUGTPC
7	DEFNUC	Jafar	LRARUC

PSYCHONAUTS

ALL POWERS
Hold **L1** and **R1** and press ⬤, ⬤,
▲, **R2**, **L3**, ▲.

9999 LIVES
Hold **L1** and **R1** and press **L3**, **R2**,
R2, ⬤, ❌, **R3**.

9999 AMMO
Hold **L1** and **R1** and press **R3**, ❌,
L3, **L3**, ▲, ⬤.

GLOBAL ITEMS
Hold **L1** and **R1** and press **R3**, ⬤,
R2, **R2**, **L3**, ▲.

ALL POWERS UPGRADED
Hold **L1** and **R1** and press **L3**, **R3**,
L3, **R2**, ⬤, **R2**.

10K ARROWHEADS
Hold **L1** and **R1** and press ❌, **R3**,
R3, **R2**, ▲, ◼.

PUMP IT UP: EXCEED

ARROWS DISAPPEAR
At the song select, press Up/Left,
Up/Right, Down/Left, Down/Right,
Center.

ARROW SPEED CHANGES THROUGHOUT SONG
At the song select, press Up/Left,
Up/Right, Up/Left, Up/Right, Up/
Left, Up/Right, Up/Left, Up/Right,
Center.

DOUBLE SPEED
At the song select, press Up/Left, Up/
Right Up/Left Up/Right center 2X
speed. Enter this code again to get
3x speed; a third time for 4x speed;
a fourth time to get 8x speed.

DEACTIVATES THESE MODIFIERS
At the song select, press Down/Left,
Down/Right, Down/Left, Down/
Right, Down/Left, Down/Right.

R-TYPE FINAL

INVINCIBILITY
Pause the game, press and hold **L2**, then press Right, Right, Left, Right, Left, Left, Right, Left, **L1**, Up, Up, Down, Down, Up, Down, Up, Down, **L1**. Re-enter the code to disable it.

99.9% CHARGE DOSE
Pause the game, press and hold **L2**, then press **R2**, **R2**, Left, Right, Up, Down, Right, Left, Up, Down, ▲.

FULL BLUE POWER, MISSILES, AND BITS
Pause the game, press and hold **L2**, then press **R2**, **R2**, Left, Right, Up, Down, Right, Left, Up, Down, ●.

FULL RED POWER, MISSILES, AND BITS
Pause the game, press and hold **L2**, then press **R2**, **R2**, Left, Right, Up, Down, Right, Left, Up, Down, ■.

FULL YELLOW POWER, MISSILES, AND BITS
Pause the game, press and hold **L2**, then press **R2**, **R2**, Left, Right, Up, Down, Right, Left, Up, Down, ✖.

LADY LOVE SHIP (#3)
At the R Museum, enter **5270 0725** as a password.

STRIDER SHIP (#24)
At the R Museum, enter **2078 0278** as a password.

MR. HELI SHIP (#59)
At the R Museum, enter **1026 2001** as a password.

CURTAIN CALL SHIP (#100)
At the R Museum, enter **1009 9201** as a password.

RAMPAGE: TOTAL DESTRUCTION

ALL MONSTERS
At the Main menu, press **R2** + **L2** to access the Cheat menu and enter **141421**.

INVULNERABLE TO ATTACKS
At the Main menu, press **R2** + **L2** to access the Cheat menu and enter **986960**.

ALL SPECIAL ABILITIES
At the Main menu, press **R2** + **L2** to access the Cheat menu and enter **011235**.

ALL LEVELS
At the Main menu, press **R2** + **L2** to access the Cheat menu and enter **271828**.

CPU VS CPU DEMO
At the Main menu, press **R2** + **L2** to access the cheat menu and enter **082864**.

FAST CPU VS CPU DEMO
At the Main menu, press **R2** + **L2** to access the Cheat menu and nter **874098**.

ONE-HIT DESTROYS BUILDINGS
At the Main menu, press **R2** + **L2** to access the Cheat menu and enter **071767**.

OPENING MOVIE
At the Main menu, press **R2** + **L2** to access the Cheat menu and enter **667300**.

ENDING MOVIE
At the Main menu, press **R2** + **L2** to access the Cheat menu and enter **667301**.

CREDITS
At the Main menu, press **R2** + **L2** to access the Cheat menu and enter **667302**.

VERSION INFORMATION
At the Main menu, press **R2** + **L2** to access the Cheat menu and enter **314159**.

CLEAR CHEATS
At the Main menu, press **R2** + **L2** to access the Cheat menu and enter **000000**.

RATCHET AND CLANK: UP YOUR ARSENAL

DUEL BLADE LASER SWORD
Pause the game and press ●, ■, ●, ■, Up, Down, Left, Left.

QWARK'S ALTERNATE COSTUME
Start a game of Qwark Vid-Comic and press Up, Up, Down, Down, Left, Right, ●, ●, ■.

PIRATE VS NINJA MINI-GAME
At the Qwark Comics Issue select, press ● to bring up a password screen. Enter _**MEGHAN**_ as a password.

4-PLAYER BOMB MINI-GAME
At the Qwark Comics Issue select, press ● to bring up a password screen. Enter **YING_TZU** as a password. Press Start, Select to return to Starship Phoenix.

SLY 2: BAND OF THIEVES DEMO
At the Title screen, hold **L1** + **L2** + **R1** + **R2**.

ROBOTS

BIG HEAD
Pause the game and press Up, Down, Down, Up, Right, Right, Left, Right.

UNLIMITED HEALTH
Pause the game and press Up, Right, Down, Up, Left, Down, Right, Left.

UNLIMITED SCRAP
Pause the game and press Down, Down, Left, Up, Up, Right, Up, Down.

SAMURAI JACK: THE SHADOW OF AKU

MAXIMUM HEALTH
During a game, hold Left on the Left Analog Stick + Right on the Right Analog Stick, and press ✖, ◉, ⬓, ⬛.

MAXIMUM ZEN
During a game, hold Left on the Left Analog Stick + Right on the Right Analog Stick, and press ◉, ✖, ⬛, ⬓.

CRYSTAL SWORD
During a game, press Left on the Left Analog Stick, Down + Up on the Right Analog Stick, then press ✖, ◉, ⬛, ⬓.

FIRE SWORD
During a game, press Down on the Left Analog Stick + Up on the Right Analog Stick, then press ⬛, ✖, ◉, ⬓.

LIGHTNING SWORD
During a game, press Down on the Left Analog Stick + Up on the Right Analog Stick, then press ◉, ✖, ⬓, ⬛.

SCALER

FULL HEALTH
Pause the game, select audio from the options and press **R1**, **L1**, **R1**, **L1**, ◉, ◉, ⬛, ⬛, **R1**, ⬛.

200,000 KLOKKIES
Pause the game, select audio from the options and press **L1**, **L1**, **R1**, **R1**, ◉, ⬛, ◉.

INFINITE ELECTRIC BOMBS
Pause the game, select audio from the options and press **R1**, **R1**, **L1**, **L1**, ◉, ◉, ⬛.

SECRET WEAPONS OVER NORMANDY

ALL PLANES, ENVIRONMENTS, AND MISSIONS
At the Main menu, press ⬛(x3), ◉(x3), ⬓, ⬛, then enter **R2**, **R2**, **L2**, **L2**.

ALL ENVIRONMENTS IN INSTANT ACTION
At the Main menu, press Up, Down, Left, Right, **L1**, **R1**, **L1**, **R1**.

INVINCIBILITY
At the Main menu, press Up, Down, Left, Right, Left, Left, Right, Right, **L1**, **L1**, **R1**, **R1**, **L2**, **R2**.

UNLIMITED AMMUNITION
At the Main menu, press Up, Right, Down, Left, Up, Right, Down, Left, **L1**, **R1**.

BIG HEADS
At the Main menu, press Right, Up, Left, Down, Right, Up, Left, Down, Right, **L1**, **R1**, **L1**, **R1**.

SEEK AND DESTROY

Enter the following passwords at the pink tank in the first town to get different bonuses:

1000 GOLD
At the pink tank, enter **KWNOHIRO**.

AIR GATLING GUN
At the pink tank, enter **GSASINRI**.

BOUND BOMB
At the pink tank, enter **KKHWEEEE**.

GRAND FLAG
At the pink tank, enter **ODGRITRO**.

SHAMAN KING: POWER OF SPIRIT

VERSUS MODE
Complete all 20 episodes in story mode.

MASKED MERIL IN VERSUS MODE
Press select on Meril.

MATILDA IN VERSUS MODE
Press select on Kanna.

MARION FAUNA IN VERSUS MODE
Press select on Matilda.

ZEKE ASAKURA IN VERSUS MODE
Press select on Yoh Asakura.

SHARK TALE

REPLACE PEARLS WITH FISH KING COINS
During a level with Pearls, press Select, then hold **L1** and press ◉, ✕, ◉ (x3), ✕, ◉, ◉. Release **L1** to enable the cheat.

ATTACK
During a game, press Select, then hold **L1** and press ◉ (x4), ✕, ◉ x4). Release **L1** to enable the cheat.

CLAMS AND FAME
During a game, press Select, then hold **L1** and press ◉, ◉, ✕, ✕, ◉, ✕, ◉, ◉. Release **L1** to enable the cheat.

SHREK 2

BONUS GAMES
Pause the game and select Scrapbook. Press Left, Up, ✕, ◉, Left, Up, ✕, ◉, Left, Up, ✕, ◉, ■, ◉, ■, ◉, ■, ◉. Exit the level and select Bonus to access the games.

CHAPTER SELECT
Pause the game and select Scrapbook. Press Left, Up, ✕, ◉, Left, Up, ✕, ◉, Left, Up, ✕, ◉, Up, Up, Up, Up, Up. Exit the level and select Chapter Select to change chapters.

FULL HEALTH
Pause the game and select Scrapbook. Press Left, Up, ✕, ○, Left, Up, ✕, ○, Left, Up, ✕, ○, Up, Right, Down, Left, Up.

1,000 COINS
Pause the game and select Scrapbook. Press Left, Up, ✕, ○, Left, Up, ✕, ○, Left, Up, ✕, ○ (x6).

SHREK SUPERSLAM

ALL CHARACTERS AND LEVELS
At the Title screen, press **L1**, **R1**, ■, ○.

ALL CHALLENGES
At the Title screen, press ▲, ▲, ▲, ○, ○, ○, ▲, ■, ○, ■, ■, ■, Up, Down, Left, Right, **L1**, **R1**.

ALL STORY MODE CHAPTERS
At the Title screen, press ▲, ■, **R1**, ○.

ALL MEDALS & TROPHIES
At the Title screen, press **R1**, **L1**, ▲, ■.

SUPER SPEED MODIFIER
At the Title screen, press **L1**, **L1**, **R1**, **R1**, **L1**, **R1**, **L1**, **R1**, ■, ○, ▲, ▲.

PIZZA ONE
At the Title screen, press Up, Up, ▲, ▲, Right, Right, ○, ○, Down, Down, **L1**, **R1**, Left, Left, ■, ■, **L1**, **R1**.

PIZZA TWO
At the Title screen, press ○, ○, ■, ■, Right, Right, Left, Left, **L1**, **L1**.

PIZZA THREE
At the Title screen, press Down, Down, Right, ○, Up, ▲, Left, ■, **L1**, **L1**.

SLAMMAGEDDON
At the Title screen, press Up, Up, Down, Down, Left, Right, Left, Right, ▲, ■, ■, **L1**, **R1**.

THE SIMS BUSTIN' OUT

Pause the game, then enter the following codes. You must enter the Enable Cheats code first. After entering another code, select the gnome to access it.

ENABLE CHEATS
Press **R2**, **L1**, **R1**, **L2**, Left, ○. A gnome appears in your yard when the code is entered correctly.

FILL ALL MOTIVES
Press **L2**, **R1**, Left, ○, Up.

GIVE MONEY
Press **L1**, **R2**, Right, ■, **L3**. Select the gnome to give money.

UNLOCK ALL LOCATIONS
Press **R2**, **R3**, **L3**, **L2**, **R1**, **L1**.

UNLOCK ALL OBJECTS
Press **L2**, **R2**, Up, ▲, **L3**.

UNLOCK ALL SKINS
Press **L1**, **R2**, ✕, ○, Up, Down.

UNLOCK ALL SOCIAL OPTIONS
Press **L1**, **R1**, Down, ✕, **L3**, **R3**.

SLY 2: BAND OF THIEVES

RESTART EPISODE
Pause the game and press Left, **R1**, Up, Down, Up, Left.

SKIP TO TUTORIAL
Pause the game and press Right, Left, Up, Up, Up, **R1**, Start.

SKIP TO EPISODE 1: THE BLACK CHATEAU
Pause the game and press Down, **R1**, Left, Right, **R1**, Down, Start.

SKIP TO EPISODE 2: A STARRY EYED ENCOUNTER
Pause the game and press **R1**, Left, Right, **R1**, Left, Down, Start.

SKIP TO EPISODE 3: THE PREDATOR AWAKES
Pause the game and press Up, Left, Right, Left, Down, Up, Start.

SKIP TO EPISODE 4: JAILBREAK
Pause the game and press Up, Right, Right, Up, Left, Left, Start.

SKIP TO EPISODE 5: A TANGLED WEB
Pause the game and press Left, **R1**, Down, Down, Up, Right, Start.

SKIP TO EPISODE 6: HE WHO TAMES THE IRON HORSE
Pause the game and press Down, Up, **R1**, **R1**, Left, Down, Start.

SKIP TO EPISODE 7: MENACE IN THE NORTH, EH?
Pause the game and press Left, Left, Left, Down, Down, **R1**, Start.

SKIP TO EPISODE 8: ANATOMY FOR DISASTER
Pause the game and press Down, Up, Left, Left, **R1**, Right, Start.

TOM GADGET
Pause the game and press Left, Left, Down, Right, Left, Right.

TIME RUSH GADGET
Pause the game and press Down, Down, Up, Down, Right, Left.

EPISODE EASTER EGGS
After each boss fight, leave the game on the Episode Menu of the level with the boss you just fought. If you don't touch a button or move to another menu for approximately 8-10 seconds, Carmelita's Badge will appear in the bottom-left corner of the screen and start flashing for just a few seconds. As soon as you see it, press ● to access a secret movie. There are a total of five secret clips, one for each level with a boss fight.

1: Episode 1: The Black Chateau—Sly 2: Band of Thieves promo trailer.

2: Episode 3: The Predator Awakes—MTV Lala promo.

3: Episode 5: A Tangled Web—Sly 2: Band of Thieves 15-second television commercial.

4: Episode 7: Menace in the North, Eh?—Sly Cooper "Making of" video.

5: Episode 8: Anatomy for Disaster—Credits Roll and "Where are they now" clips.

SLY 3: HONOR AMONG THIEVES

TOONAMI PLANE
While flying the regular plane, pause the game and press **R1**, **R1**, Right, Down, Down, Right.

Comix Zone

INVINCIBILITY

Select the jukebox from the options and play the following tracks in order:
3, 12, 17, 2, 2, 10, 2, 7, 7, 11.

STAGE SELECT

Select the jukebox from the options and play the following tracks in order:
14, 15, 18, 5, 13, 1, 3, 18, 15, 6.

Dr. Robotnik's Mean Bean Machine

EASY PASSWORDS

Continue a game with the following passwords:

LEVEL	PASSWORD
2	Red Bean, Red Bean, Red Bean, Has Bean
3	Clear Bean, Purple Bean, Clear Bean, Green Bean
4	Red Bean, Clear Bean, Has Bean, Yellow Bean
5	Clear Bean, Blue Bean, Blue Bean, Purple Bean
6	Clear Bean, Red Bean, Clear Bean, Purple Bean
7	Purple Bean, Yellow Bean, Red Bean, Blue bean
8	Yellow Bean, Green Bean, Purple Bean, Has Bean
9	Yellow Bean, Purple Bean, Has Bean, Blue Bean
10	Red Bean, Yellow Bean, Clear Bean, Has Bean
11	Green Bean, Purple Bean, Blue Bean, Clear Bean
12	Red Bean, Has Bean, Has Bean, Yellow Bean
13	Yellow Bean, Has Bean, Blue Bean, Blue Bean

NORMAL PASSWORDS

LEVEL	PASSWORD
2	Has Bean, Clear Bean, Yellow Bean, Yellow Bean
3	Blue Bean, Clear Bean, Red Bean, Yellow Bean
4	Yellow Bean, Blue Bean, Clear Bean, Purple Bean
5	Has Bean, Green Bean, Blue Bean, Yellow Bean
6	Green Bean, Purple Bean, Purple Bean, Yellow Bean
7	Purple Bean, Blue Bean, Green Bean, Has Bean
8	Green Bean, Has Bean, Clear Bean, Yellow Bean
9	Blue Bean, Purple Bean, Has Bean, Has Bean
10	Has Bean, Red Bean, Yellow Bean, Clear Bean
11	Clear Bean, Red Bean, Red Bean, Blue Bean
12	Green Bean, Green Bean, Clear Bean, Yellow Bean
13	Purple Bean, Yellow Bean, Has Bean, Clear Bean

HARD PASSWORDS

LEVEL	PASSWORD
2	Green Bean, Clear Bean, Yellow Bean, Yellow Bean
3	Yellow Bean, Clear Bean, Purple Bean, Clear Bean
4	Blue Bean, Green Bean, Clear Bean, Blue Bean
5	Red Bean, Purple Bean, Green Bean, Green Bean
6	Yellow Bean, Yellow Bean, Clear Bean, Green Bean
7	Purple Bean, Clear Bean, Blue Bean, Blue Bean
8	Clear Bean, Yellow Bean, Has Bean, Yellow Bean
9	Purple Bean, Blue Bean, Blue Bean, Green Bean
10	Clear Bean, Green Bean, Red Bean, Yellow Bean
11	Blue Bean, Yellow Bean, Yellow Bean, Has Bean
12	Green Bean, Clear Bean, Clear Bean, Blue bean
13	Has Bean, Clear Bean, Purple Bean, Has Bean

HARDEST PASSWORDS

LEVEL	PASSWORD
2	Blue Bean, Blue Bean, Green Bean, Yellow Bean
3	Green Bean, Yellow Bean, Green Bean, Clear Bean
4	Purple Bean, Purple Bean, Red Bean, Has Bean
5	Green Bean, Red Bean, Purple Bean, Blue Bean
6	Blue Bean, Purple Bean, Green Bean, Yellow Bean
7	Blue Bean, Purple Bean, Green Bean, Has Bean
8	Clear Bean, Purple Bean, Has Bean, Yellow Bean
9	Purple Bean, Green Bean, Has Bean, Clear Bean
10	Green Bean, Blue Bean, Yellow Bean, Has Bean
11	Green Bean, Purple Bean, Has Bean, Red Bean
12	Red Bean, Green Bean, Has Bean, Blue Bean
13	Red Bean, Red Bean, Clear Bean, Yellow Bean

RISTAR

LEVEL SELECT
Enter **ILOVEU** as a password.

FIGHT ONLY BOSSES
Enter **MUSEUM** as a password.

TIME ATTACK
Enter **DOFEEL** as a password.

TONE DEAF SOUNDS
Enter **MAGURO** as a password.

TRUE SIGHT
Enter **MIEMIE** as a password.

SUPER HARD
Enter **SUPER** as a password.

VERY HARD
Enter **SUPERB** as a password.

CANCEL CODES
Enter **XXXXXX** as a password.

Sonic the Hedgehog

LEVEL SELECT
At the title screen press Up, Down, Right, Left. Hold ● and press Start.

Sonic the Hedgehog 2

LEVEL SELECT

Select Sound Test from the Options. Play the following in this order: 19, 65, 09, 17. Exit the Options and immediately hold ⬤ and press Start.

Sonic the Hedgehog 3

LEVEL SELECT

While the game is loading, press Up, Up, Down, Down, Up, Up, Up, Up. Scroll down past Competition.

Sonic Spinball

ROUND SELECT

At the Options, press ⬤, Down, ✖, Down, ⬤, Down, ⬤, ✖, Up, ⬤, ⬤, Up, ✖, ⬤, Up. Then, at the title screen, hold ⬤ and press Start for Round 2. Hold ✖ and press Start for Round 3. Hold ⬤ and press Start for Round 4.

SPIDER-MAN 2

TREYARCH PASSWORD

Start a New Game and enter **HCRAYERT** as your name. You will start at 44% complete, 201,000 Hero Points, some upgrades, and more.

SPONGEBOB SQUAREPANTS: BATTLE FOR BIKINI BOTTOM

You must quickly enter the following codes.

RESTORE HEALTH

Pause the game, hold **L1** + **L2** + **R1** + **R2** and press ⬤, ⬤, ⬤, ⬤, ⬤, ⬤, ⬤, ⬤, ⬤, ⬤, ⬤, ⬤.

EXPERT MODE

Pause the game, hold **L1** + **L2** + **R1** + **R2** and press ⬤, ⬤, ⬤, ⬤, ⬤, ⬤, ⬤, ⬤, ⬤, ⬤, ⬤, ⬤, ⬤, ⬤, ⬤, ⬤.

EARN 1,000 SHINY OBJECTS

Pause the game, hold **L1** + **L2** + **R1** + **R2** and press ⬤, ⬤, ⬤, ⬤, ⬤, ⬤, ⬤, ⬤.

EARN 10 GOLD SPATULAS

Pause the game, hold **L1** + **L2** + **R1** + **R2** and press ⬤, ⬤, ⬤, ⬤, ⬤, ⬤, ⬤, ⬤.

BUBBLE BOWL POWER-UP

Pause the game, hold **L1** + **L2** + **R1** + **R2** and press ⬤, ⬤, ⬤, ⬤, ⬤, ⬤, ⬤, ⬤. Press ⬤ to use the power-up.

CRUISE BUBBLE POWER-UP
Pause the game, hold **L1** + **L2** + **R1** + **R2** and press ■, ●, ■, ●, ■, ■, ●, ●. Press **L1** to use the power-up.

INCREASE VALUE OF SHINY OBJECTS
Pause the game, hold **L1** + **L2** + **R1** + **R2** and press ■, ●, ■, ●, ●, ■, ●, ●, ●, ■, ■, ■, ●, ●, ■.

MODIFIED CRUISE BUBBLE CONTROLS
Pause the game, hold **L1** + **L2** + **R1** + **R2** and press ●, ●, ●, ●, ■, ■, ●, ●, ■, ●, ■, ■.

VILLAGERS GIVE SHINY OBJECTS WHEN HIT
Pause the game, hold **L1** + **L2** + **R1** + **R2** and press ■, ■, ■, ■, ■, ●, ●, ●, ●, ■, ●, ■.

VILLAGERS RESTORE HEALTH WHEN NEAR
Pause the game, hold **L1** + **L2** + **R1** + **R2** and press ■, ■, ■, ■, ■, ●, ■, ●, ●, ●, ■, ■.

NO PANTS
Pause the game, hold **L1** + **L2** + **R1** + **R2** and press ●, ●, ●, ●, ■, ●, ●, ■, ●, ■, ■, ●.

BIG PLANKTON
Pause the game, hold **L1** + **L2** + **R1** + **R2** and press ■, ■, ■, ■, ●, ■, ●, ■, ●, ●, ●, ●.

SMALL CHARACTERS
Pause the game, hold **L1** + **L2** + **R1** + **R2** and press ■, ■, ■, ■, ●, ■, ●, ■, ■, ■, ■, ■.

SMALL VILLAGERS
Pause the game, hold **L1** + **L2** + **R1** + **R2** and press ■, ■, ■, ■, ■, ●, ■, ●, ■, ●, ■, ■.

SPONGEBOB BREAKS APART WHEN DEFEATED
Pause the game, hold **L1** + **L2** + **R1** + **R2** and press ●, ●, ●, ●, ■, ■, ●, ■, ●, ●, ●, ■.

SPONGEBOB SQUAREPANTS: LIGHTS, CAMERA, PANTS!

SILVER STORY MODE
Select Rewards from the Bonuses menu. Then select Codes and enter **486739**.

ALL ACTION FIGURES
Select Rewards from the Bonuses menu. Then select Codes and enter **977548**.

HOOK, LINE & CHEDDAR GAME
Select Rewards from the Bonuses menu. Then select Codes and enter **893634**.

SSX ON TOUR

NEW THREADS
Select Cheats from the Extras menu and enter **FLYTHREADS**.

THE WORLD IS YOURS
Select Cheats from the Extras menu and enter **BACKSTAGEPASS**.

SHOW TIME (ALL MOVIES)
Select Cheats from the Extras menu and enter **THEBIGPICTURE**.

BLING BLING (INFINITE CASH)
Select Cheats from the Extras menu and enter **LOOTSNOOT**.

FULL BOOST, FULL TIME
Select Cheats from the Extras menu and enter **ZOOMJUICE**.

MONSTERS ARE LOOSE (MONSTER TRICKS)
Select Cheats from the Extras menu and enter **JACKALOPESTYLE**

SNOWBALL FIGHT
Select Cheats from the Extras menu and enter **LETSPARTY**.

FEEL THE POWER (STAT BOOST)
Select Cheats from the Extras menu and enter **POWERPLAY**.

CHARACTERS ARE LOOSE
Select Cheats from the Extras menu and enter **ROADIEROUNDUp**.

UNLOCK CONRAD
Select Cheats from the Extras menu and enter **BIGPARTYTIME**.

UNLOCK MITCH KOOBSKI
Select Cheats from the Extras menu and enter **MOREFUNTHANONE**.

UNLOCK NIGEL
Select Cheats from the Extras menu and enter **THREEISACROWD**.

UNLOCK SKI PATROL
Select Cheats from the Extras menu and enter **FOURSOME**.

S

STAR WARS: BATTLEFRONT II

INFINITE AMMO
Pause the game, hold **L2** + **R2** and press Up, Down, Left, Down, Down, Left, Down, Down, Left, Down, Down, Down, Left, Right.

INVINCIBILITY
Pause the game, hold **L2** + **R2** and press Up, Up, Up, Left, Down, Down, Down, Left, Up, Up, Up, Left, Right.

NO HUD
Pause the game, hold **L2** + **R2** and press Up, Up, Up, Up, Left, Up, Up, Down, Left, Down, Up, Up, Left, Right. Re-enter the code to enable HUD again.

ALTERNATE SOLDIERS
Pause the game, hold **L2** + **R2** and press Down, Down, Down, Up, Up, Left, Down, Down, Down, Down, Down, Left, Up, Up, Up, Left.

ALTERNATE SOUNDS
Pause the game, hold **L2** + **R2** and press Up, Up, Up, Left, Up, Down, Up, Up, Left, Down, Down, Down, Left, Up, Down, Down, Left, Right.

FUNNY MESSAGES WHEN REBELS DEFEATED
Pause the game, hold **L2** + **R2** and press Up, Down, Left, Down, Left, Right.

STRIKE FORCE BOWLING

ALL NIGHT ENVIRONMENTS AND MARS
Name your bowler **!LEVELS!**.

THREE HIDDEN CHARACTERS
Name your bowler **!BOWLER!**.

SUZUKI TT SUPERBIKES

CHEAT SCREEN
At the Main menu, press **R1**, **R2**, **L1**, **L2**, **R1**, **R2**, **L1**, **L2**. Now you can enter the following:

ALL EVENTS
Enter **BORN FREE**.

RED BULL MAD SUNDAY EVENTS
Enter **SUNDAYSUNDAY**.

ALL HELMETS
Enter **SKID LIDS**.

ALL LEATHERS
Enter **COLORED HIDE**.

ALL BIKES
Enter **ROCKETS**.

ALL WHEELS
Enter **TIRE CITY**.

ALL COLLECTION BOOK
Enter **COUCH POTATO**.

TAITO LEGENDS

EXTRA GAMES
At the Title screen, press **L1**, **R1**, **R2**, **L2**, Select, Start.

TAK: THE GREAT JUJU CHALLENGE

BONUS SOUND EFFECTS
In Juju's Potions, select Universal Card and enter 20, 17, 5 for Bugs, Crystals and Fruits respectively.

BONUS SOUND EFFECTS 2
In Juju's Potions, select Universal Card and enter 50, 84, 92 for Bugs, Crystals and Fruits respectively.

BONUS MUSIC TRACK 1
In Juju's Potions, select Universal Card and enter 67, 8, 20 for Bugs, Crystals and Fruits respectively.

BONUS MUSIC TRACK 2
In Juju's Potions, select Universal Card and enter 6, 18, 3 for Bugs, Crystals and Fruits respectively.

MAGIC PARTICLES
In Juju's Potions, select Universal Card and enter 24, 40, 11 for Bugs, Crystals and Fruits respectively.

MORE MAGIC PARTICLES
In Juju's Potions, select Universal Card and enter 48, 57, 57 for Bugs, Crystals and Fruits respectively.

VIEW JUJU CONCEPT ART
In Juju's Potions, select Universal Card and enter Art 33, 22, 28 for Bugs, Crystals and Fruits respectively.

VIEW VEHICLE ART
In Juju's Potions, select Universal Card and enter 11, 55, 44 for Bugs, Crystals and Fruits respectively.

VIEW WORLD ART
In Juju's Potions, select Universal Card and enter 83, 49, 34 for Bugs, Crystals and Fruits respectively.

TEENAGE MUTANT NINJA TURTLES 3: MUTANT NIGHTMARE

INVINCIBILITY
Select Passwords from the Options screen and enter **MDLDSSLR**.

HEALTH POWER-UPS BECOME SUSHI
Select Passwords from the Options screen and enter **SLLMRSLD**.

NO HEALTH POWER-UPS
Select Passwords from the Options screen and enter **DMLDMRLD**.

ONE-HIT DEFEATS TURTLE
Select Passwords from the Options screen and enter **LDMSLRDD**.

MAX OUGI
Select Passwords from the Options screen and enter **RRDMLSDL**.

UNLIMITED SHURIKEN
Select Passwords from the Options screen and enter **LMDRRMSR**.

NO SHURIKEN
Select Passwords from the Options screen and enter **LLMSRDMS**.

DOUBLE ENEMY ATTACK
Select Passwords from the Options screen and enter **MSRLSMML**.

DOUBLE ENEMY DEFENSE
Select Passwords from the Options screen and enter **SLRMLSSM**.

TIGER WOODS PGA TOUR 06

T

ALL GOLFERS
Select Password from the Options and enter **WOOGLIN**.

ALL CLUBS
Select Password from the Options and enter **CLUB11**.

LEVEL 2 NIKE ITEMS
Select Password from the Options and enter **JUSTDOIT**.

ALL COURSES
Select Password from the Options and enter **ITSINTHEHOLE**.

TIGER WOODS IN HAT AND TIE
Select Password from the Options and enter **GOLDENAGE**.

TIGER WOODS IN STRIPED PANTS
Select Password from the Options and enter **TECHNICOLOR**.

TIGER WOODS IN OLD GOLF OUTFIT
Select Password from the Options and enter **OLDSKOOL**.

TIGER WOODS IN A DIFFERENT OLD GOLF OUTFIT
Select Password from the Options and enter **THROWBACK**.

ARNOLD PALMER
Select Password from the Options and enter **ARNIESARMY**.

BEN HOGAN
Select Password from the Options and enter **THEHAWK**.

JACK NICKLAUS
Select Password from the Options and enter **GOLDENBEAR**.

OLD TOM MORRIS
Select Password from the Options and enter **FEATHERIE**.

TOMMY BLACK
Select Password from the Options and enter **IDONTHAVEAPROBLEM**.

WESLEY ROUNDER
Select Password from the Options and enter **POCKETPAIR**.

PLAYSTATION® 2

TIM BURTON'S THE NIGHTMARE BEFORE CHRISTMAS: OOGIE'S REVENGE

PUMPKIN JACK AND SANTA JACK COSTUMES
During gameplay, press Down, Up, Right, Left, **L3**, **R3**.

TONY HAWK'S AMERICAN WASTELAND

ALWAYS SPECIAL
Select Cheat Codes from the Options screen and enter **uronfire**. Pause the game and select Cheats from the Game Options to enable the cheat.

PERFECT RAIL
Select Cheat Codes from the Options screen and enter **grindxpert**. Pause the game and select Cheats from the Game Options to enable the cheat.

PERFECT SKITCH
Select Cheat Codes from the Options screen and enter **h!tchar!de**. Pause the game and select Cheats from the Game Options to enable the cheat.

PERFECT MANUAL
Select Cheat Codes from the Options screen and enter **2wheels!**. Pause the game and select Cheats from the Game Options to enable the cheat.

MOON GRAVITY
Select Cheat Codes from the Options screen and enter **2them00n**. Pause the game and select Cheats from the Game Options to enable the cheat.

MAT HOFFMAN
Select Cheat Codes from the Options screen and enter **the_condor**.

JASON ELLIS
Select Cheat Codes from the Options screen and enter **sirius-dj**.

T

TONY HAWK'S UNDERGROUND 2

Select Cheat Codes from the Game Options and enter the following. For the cheats, pause the game and select Cheats to turn them on.

ALL LEVELS
Enter **d3struct**.

ALL SKATERS EXCEPT FOR SECRET SKATERS
Enter **costars!**.

THPS1 TONY HAWK AND ALL THUG2 MOVIES
Enter **boxoffice**.

NATAS KAUPAS
Enter **oldskool**.

NIGEL BEAVERHAUSEN
Enter **sellout**.

PHIL MARGERA
Enter **aprilsman**.

INFINITE RAIL CHEAT
Enter **straightedge**.

ALWAYS SPECIAL
Enter **likepaulie**.

TY THE TASMANIAN TIGER 2: BUSH RESCUE

ALL BUNYIP KEYS
During a game, press Start, ▲, Start, Start, ▲, ■, ●, ■, ✕.

ALL FIRST-LEVEL RANGS
During a game, press Start, ▲, Start, Start, ▲, ●, ■, ●, ■.

ALL SECOND-LEVEL RANGS
During a game, press Start, ▲, Start, Start, ▲, ■, ●, ■, ▲.

GET 100,000 OPALS
During a game, press Start, ▲, Start, Start, ▲, ●, ✕, ●, ✕.

HIGHLIGHT ALL COLLECTIBLES
During a game, press Start, ▲, Start, Start, ▲, Up, Down, Left, Right.

TY THE TASMANIAN TIGER 3: NIGHT OF THE QUINKAN

100,000 OPALS
During a game, press Start, Start, ▲, Start, Start, ▲, ●, ✕, ●, ✕.

ALL 'RANG CHASSIS
During a game, press Start, Start, ▲, Start, Start, ▲, ●, ■, ●, ■.

THE URBZ: SIMS IN THE CITY

CHEAT GNOME
During a game, press ◉, L1, L2, R2, R1.

JUMP AHEAD SIX HOURS
Enter the Cheat Gnome code and then press R2, R3, L3, L2, R1, L2.

ACQUIRE SKILL OBJECT
Enter the Cheat Gnome code and then press L1, R2, Right, ◉, L3

MAX ARTISTIC SKILL
Enter the Cheat Gnome code and then press L3, R3, R1, R2, ◉

MAX MENTAL SKILL
Enter the Cheat Gnome code and then press L1, R2, ✕, ◉, Up

MAX PHYSICAL SKILL
Enter the Cheat Gnome code and then press L1, R1, Down, ✕, L3

ALL SOCIALS
Enter the Cheat Gnome code and then press L2, R2, Up, ▲, L3, ✕.

POWER SOCIALS
Enter the Cheat Gnome code and then press ▲, R2, L1, ✕, ◉.

RAISE MOTIVES
Enter the Cheat Gnome code and then press R2, L1, R1, L2, Left, ◉.

DEVELOPMENT TEAM
Enter the Cheat Gnome code and then press Up, Down, ◉, Up, Down.

ULTIMATE SPIDER-MAN

ALL CHARACTERS
Pause the game and select Controller Setup from the Options. Press Right, Down, Right, Down, Left, Up, Left, Right.

ALL CONCEPT ART
Pause the game and select Controller Setup from the Options. Press Down, Down, Down, Up, Down, Up, Left, Left.

ALL COVERS
Pause the game and select Controller Setup from the Options. Press Left, Left, Right, Left, Up, Left, Left, Down.

ALL LANDMARKS
Pause the game and select Controller Setup from the Options. Press Up, Right, Down, Left, Down, Up, Right, Left.

WHIPLASH

INVINCIBILITY

Pause the game, select Abilities and Power-ups and press ● to access the Restricted screen. Press ●, ▲, Up, Down, ◉, Up, ▲.

ALL ABILITIES

Pause the game, select Abilities and Power-ups and press ●. Press ●, Left, ◉, ◉, ▲, Left, Up, ✖, ◉, Right.

HYPER BUNNY

Pause the game, select Abilities and Power-ups and press ● to access the Restricted screen. Press ●, Down, Right, Down, Up, Down.

WORLD TOUR SOCCER 2005

ALL TEAMS AND STADIUMS

At the Main menu, press **L1**, **R1**, **R2**, **L2**, Up, Down, Left, Right.

QA LIVERPOOL, TIF OLDBOYS, TIF NEWBIES, AND TOUCHLINE TEAMS

At the Main menu, press Down, Right, **L2**, **R1**, Left, **R1**.

TIMEWARP TEAMS

At the Main menu, press **R2**, **L2**, **R2**, **L2**, Up, **L1**.

ALL BONUSES

At the Main menu, press **L2**, **L2**, **L1**, **R1**, Left, Up, Left, Down.

UNLIMITED MONEY

At the Main menu, press Right, Right, Left, Up (x3).

MORE TRANSFER MONEY

At the Main menu, press **L1**, **L1**, **R1**, Down, Left, Right.

UNLIMITED SKILL FOR CUSTOM TEAMS

At the Main menu, press Up, Up, **R1**, **L2**, Up, **L1**.

UNLIMITED TIF TOKENS

At the Main menu, press Up, Down, Up, Down, **R1**, **R1**, **R2**, **R2**, Up, Down, Up, Down.

ALL MOVIES

At the Main menu, press **L2**, **L1** (x3), **L2**, **L2**.

FASTER ANNOUNCERS

At the Main menu, press **L2**, **R2**, **R1**, **R2**, **L2**, **R2**.

CLOWN SOUNDS

At the Main menu, press **L1**, **L1**, **L2**, **R2**, **R2**, **R1**.

FARM SOUNDS

At the Main menu, press **L1**, **L1**, **R2**, Up, Down, Right.

CREDITS

At the Main menu, press **L2**, **L1**, **L1**, **L2** (x3).

WORMS 3D

2 BLIMPS

Generate a new landscape with the code **igotworms**.

3 SUBMARINES

Generate a new landscape with the code **CANDY**.

TINY ISLAND

Generate a new landscape with the code **Smashsumfruit**..

X-MEN LEGENDS II: RISE OF APOCALYPSE

ALL CHARACTERS

At the Team Management screen, press Right, Left, Left, Right, Up, Up, Up, Start.

ALL SKINS

At the Team Management screen, press Down, Up, Left, Right, Up, Up, Start

ALL SKILLS

At the Team Management screen, press Left, Right, Left, Right, Down, Up, Start.

LEVEL 99

At the Team Management screen, press Up, Down, Up, Down, Left, Up, Left, Right, Start.

GOD MODE

Pause the game and press Down, Up, Down, Up, Right, Down, Right, Left, Start.

MOVE FASTER

Pause the game and press Up, Up, Up, Down, Up, Down, Start.

UNLIMITED XTREME TOKENS

Pause the game and press Left, Down, Right, Down, Up, Up, Down, Up, Start.

TOUCH OF DEATH

During a game, press Left, Left, Right, Left, Right, Up, Start.

100,000 TECH-BITS

At Forge or Beast's store, press Up, Up, Up, Down, Right, Right, Start.

ALL DANGER ROOM COURSES

At the Danger Room Course menu, press Right, Right, Left, Left, Up, Down, Up, Down, Start.

ALL COMICS

Select Review from the Main menu and press Right, Left, Left, Right, Up, Up, Right, Start.

ALL CINEMATICS
Select Review from the Main menu and press Left, Right, Right, Left, Down, Down, Left, Start.

ALL CONCEPTS
Select Review from the Main menu and press Left, Right, Left, Right, Up, Up, Down, Start.

ALL SCREENS
Select Review from the Main menu and press Right, Left, Right, Left, Up, Up, Down, Start.

X-MEN: THE OFFICIAL GAME

DANGER ROOM ICEMAN
At the Cerebro Files menu, press Right, Right, Left, Left, Down, Up, Down, Up, Start.

DANGER ROOM NIGHTCRAWLER
At the Cerebro Files menu, press Up, Up, Down, Down, Left, Right, Left, Right, Start.

DANGER ROOM WOLVERINE
At the Cerebro Files menu, press Down, Down, Up, Up, Right, Left, Right, Left, Start.

XGRA: EXTREME-G RACING ASSOCIATION

ALL LEVELS OF RACING
Enter **FREEPLAY** at the Cheat Menu.

ALL TRACKS
Enter **WIBBLE** at the Cheat Menu.

O2 LIVERIED
Enter **UCANDO** at the Cheat Menu.

MESSAGE IN CREDITS
Enter **MUNCHKIN**, **EDDROOLZ** or **EDDIEPOO** at the Cheat Menu.

YS: THE ARK OF NAPISHTIM

HOW TO ENTER CHEAT CODES
1. Select **New Game**.
2. Select **Cheat** to enter the Cheat Room.
3. To activate Cheat Mode, strike the colored crystals in this sequence: Red, Blue, Yellow, Red, Blue, Yellow. The sequence appears at the top left as you strike each crystal.

4. Perform a Downward Thrust strike on the center pedestal to complete the code and activate Cheat Mode.

5. You can now use the same method to enter one of the cheat codes listed below, then exit the Cheat Room.

6. The game selection buttons are now red. Games saved with the Cheat Mode enabled will appear in red.

CLEARFLAG

Hit the crystals in the following order: Red, Red, Red, Red, Blue, Blue, Blue, Blue, Yellow, Yellow, Yellow, Yellow, Blue, Blue, Yellow, Yellow, Red, Red. This turns on all special features normally available only after you've completed the game once—Nightmare Mode, Time Attack, and Red Spirit Monuments. **Note:** When enabled, Red Spirit Monuments appear after you reach Port Rimorge. They allow you to warp between the Rehdan Village and Port Rimorge monuments to save travel time.

OPENING MOVIE WITH ENGLISH VOICE/ENGLISH TEXT

Hit the crystals in the following order: Blue, Blue, Yellow, Red.

OPENING MOVIE WITH ENGLISH VOICE/JAPANESE TEXT

Hit the crystals in the following order: Blue, Blue, Blue, Yellow, Red.

OPENING MOVIE WITH JAPANESE VOICE/ENGLISH TEXT

Hit the crystals in the following order: Blue, Blue, Blue, Blue, Yellow, Red.

OPENING MOVIE WITH JAPANESE VOICE/NO TEXT

Hit the crystals in the following order: Blue, Yellow, Red.

ALTERNATE OPENING MOVIE

Hit the crystals in the following order: Red, Blue, Red.

BEACH MOVIE WITH ENGLISH VOICE/ENGLISH TEXT

Hit the crystals in the following order: Blue, Blue, Red, Yellow

BEACH MOVIE WITH ENGLISH VOICE/JAPANESE TEXT

Hit the crystals in the following order: Blue, Blue, Blue, Red, Yellow.

BEACH MOVIE WITH JAPANESE VOICE/ENGLISH TEXT

Hit the crystals in the following order: Blue, Red, Red, Yellow.

BEACH MOVIE WITH JAPANESE VOICE/JAPANESE TEXT

Hit the crystals in the following order: Blue, Red, Yellow.

ROMUN FLEET ENTRANCE ANIME MOVIE

Hit the crystals in the following order: Blue, Red, Yellow, Red, Red, Yellow, Blue, Blue, Blue.

ROMUN FLEET ENTRANCE CG MOVIE

Hit the crystals in the following order: Blue, Red, Yellow, Red, Red, Yellow, Blue.

ROMUN FLEET DESTROYED ANIME MOVIE

Hit the crystals in the following order: Blue, Red, Yellow, Red, Red, Yellow, Red, Red, Red.

ROMUN FLEET DESTROYED CG MOVIE

Hit the crystals in the following order: Blue, Red, Yellow, Red, Red, Yellow, Red.

NAPISHTIM DESTROYED MOVIE WITH ENGLISH VOICE/ENGLISH TEXT

Hit the crystals in the following order: Blue, Red, Yellow, Red, Red, Blue, Yellow, Yellow.

NAPISHTIM DESTROYED MOVIE WITH ENGLISH VOICE/JAPANESE TEXT

Hit the crystals in the following order: Blue, Red, Yellow, Red, Red, Blue, Yellow, Yellow, Yellow.

NAPISHTIM DESTROYED MOVIE WITH JAPANESE VOICE/ENGLISH TEXT

Hit the crystals in the following order: Blue, Red, Yellow, Red, Red, Blue, Yellow, Yellow, Yellow, Yellow.

NAPISHTIM DESTROYED MOVIE WITH JAPANESE VOICE/JAPANESE TEXT

Hit the crystals in the following order: Blue, Red, Yellow, Red, Red, Blue, Yellow.

OLHA DEMO AFTER CLEARING TIME ATTACK ON HARD (JAPANESE)

Hit the crystals in the following order: Red, Red, Red, Red, Red, Blue, Blue, Blue, Yellow, Red, Blue, Blue, Yellow, Yellow, Yellow.

GAME IN JAPANESE

Hit the crystals in the following order: Yellow, Yellow, Red, Blue.

LEVEL 10

Hit the crystals in the following order: Red, Blue, Blue, Red, Red, Blue.

LEVEL 20

Hit the crystals in the following order: Red, Blue, Blue, Red, Red, Blue, Blue.

LEVEL 30

Hit the crystals in the following order: Red, Red, Blue, Blue, Red, Red, Blue, Blue.

LEVEL 40

Hit the crystals in the following order: Red, Red, Blue, Red, Red, Blue, Blue, Yellow.

LEVEL 60

Hit the crystals in the following order: Red, Red, Blue, Blue, Yellow, Yellow, Red, Red, Blue, Blue, Yellow, Yellow.

HALF PRICE ITEMS

Hit the crystals in the following order: Yellow, Yellow, Blue, Blue, Red, Red, Red, Yellow, Yellow, Yellow, Red, Red, Blue, Blue.

20 ITEM TOOL MAX INCREASE

Hit the crystals in the following order: Yellow, Yellow, Red, Red, Blue, Blue, Yellow, R.

MAXED OUT BLIRANTE SWORD

Hit the crystals in the following order: Blue, Blue, Yellow, Yellow, Yellow, Red, Blue, Red, Red, Red, Yellow, Yellow.

MAXED OUT LIVART SWORD

Hit the crystals in the following order: Blue, Blue, Blue, Yellow, Yellow, Red, Blue, Red, Red, Yellow, Yellow, Yellow.

MAXED OUT ERICCIL SWORD

Hit the crystals in the following order: Blue, Yellow, Yellow, Red, Red, Red, Blue, Blue, Blue, Red, Red, Yellow.

MAXED OUT ALL 3 SWORDS

Hit the crystals in the following order: Blue, Yellow, Red, Blue, Blue, Blue, Red, Red, Red, Yellow, Yellow, Yellow, Blue, Yellow, Red.

ALTERNATE ENDING MOVIES

In the Rehdan Village (Festival at Night): Toksa and Nahrya look toward Adol as he walks by.

At the Entrance of the Village: Isha runs toward the back, then returns.

On the Tres Mares: The cat is on the front of the ship.

ENDING CHANGE CRITERIA

Direction Calman is facing: Faces Adol if he has gotten the Gold Locket.

Number of Pikkards: Found all four pikkards and returned them to Emilio.

YU-GI-OH! THE DUELIST OF THE ROSES

PASSWORDS

At the Build Deck screen, press **R3** and enter the following passwords:

NUMBER	CARD	PASSWORD
#001	Seiyaryu	2H4D85J7
#019	Meteor Dragon	86985631
#042	Fairy's Gift	NVE7A3EZ
#043	Magician of Faith	GME1S3UM
#057	Left Arm of the Forbidden One	A5CF6HSH
#058	Exodia the Forbidden One	37689434
#146	Swordstalker	AHOPSHEB
#149	Greenkappa	YBJMCD6Z
#152	Tactical Warrior	054TC727
#191	Swordsman from a Foreign Land	CZ81UVGR
#478	Aqua Dragon	JXCB6FU7
#655	Ancient Tree of Enlightenment	EKJHQ109
#502	Barrel Dragon	GTJXSBJ7
#567	Beustking of the Swamps	QXNTQPAX
#291	Birdface	N54T4TY5
#348	Dragon Seeker	81EZCH8B
#372	Mystical Capture Chains	N1NDJMQ3
#458	Serpentine Princess	UMQ3WZUZ
#506	Blast Sphere	CZN5GD2X
#510	Robotic Knight	S5S7NKNH
#670	Fairy King Truesdale	YF07QVEZ
#674	Slate Warrior	73153736
#687	Mimicat	69YDQM85
#699	Dark Hole	UMJ1OMQB
#702	Harpy's Feather Duster	8HJHQPNP
#732	Change of Heart	SBYDQM8B
#750	Earthshaker	Y34PN1SV
#758	Flf's Light	E5G3NRAD
#765	Horn of the Unicorn	S14FGKQ1
#794	Crush Card	SRA7L5YR
#806	Gravity Bind	OIINFG9WX
#814	Goblin Fan	92886423
#825	Royal Decree	8TETQHE1
#829	Mirror Wall	53297534

ZAPPER

INFINITE LIVES

Pause the game, hold **L1** and press Up, Up, Up, Left, Left, Right, Left, Right.

INFINITE SHIELDS

Pause the game, hold **L1** and press Up, Down, Up, Left, Right, Down, Up.

XBOX®

AMPED 2
APEX
CHICKEN LITTLE
CRASH TAG TEAM RACING
DANCE DANCE REVOLUTION ULTRAMIX 2
DANCE DANCE REVOLUTION ULTRAMIX 3
EA SPORTS ARENA FOOTBALL
FIFA STREET
FORZA MOTORSPORT
FROGGER: ANCIENT SHADOW
ICE AGE 2: THE MELTDOWN
THE INCREDIBLES
THE INCREDIBLES: RISE OF THE UNDERMINER
LEGO STAR WARS: THE VIDEO GAME
LMA MANAGER 2005
MADDEN NFL 2005
MADDEN NFL 06
MAJOR LEAGUE BASEBALL 2K5
MAJOR LEAGUE BASEBALL: WORLD SERIES EDITION
MAJOR LEAGUE BASEBALL 2K6
MVP BASEBALL 2005
MVP 06 NCAA BASEBALL
MX vs. ATV UNLEASHED
NASCAR 06: TOTAL TEAM CONTROL
NASCAR 2005: CHASE FOR THE CUP
NBA 2K6
NBA BALLERS
NBA BALLERS: PHENOM
NBA LIVE 2004
NBA LIVE 06

NBA STREET 2
NCAA FOOTBALL 2005
NCAA FOOTBALL 06
NCAA MARCH MADNESS 06
NEED FOR SPEED MOST WANTED
NEED FOR SPEED UNDERGROUND 2
NFL STREET 2
NHL 2K6
OUTRUN 2
OUTRUN 2006: COAST 2 COAST
PINBALL HALL OF FAME: THE GOTTLIEB COLLECTION
RALLISPORT CHALLENGE 2
ROBOTS
RUGBY LEAGUE 2
SCALER
SHREK 2
SHREK SUPERSLAM
SONIC HEROES
SONIC MEGA COLLECTION PLUS
SPONGEBOB SQUAREPANTS: BATTLE FOR BIKINI BOTTOM
SPONGEBOB SQUAREPANTS: LIGHTS, CAMERA, PANTS!
SPONGEBOB SQUAREPANTS: THE MOVIE
SSX 3
SSX ON TOUR
STRIKE FORCE BOWLING
TAK 2: THE STAFF OF DREAMS
TAK: THE GREAT JUJU CHALLENGE
TAZ WANTED
TEENAGE MUTANT NINJA TURTLES 3: MUTANT NIGHTMARE
TIGER WOODS PGA TOUR 2005
TIGER WOODS PGA TOUR 06

TIM BURTON'S THE NIGHTMARE BEFORE CHRISTMAS: OOGIE'S REVENGE

TY THE TASMANIAN TIGER 2: BUSH RESCUE

TY THE TASMANIAN TIGER 3: NIGHT OF THE QUINKAN

WORLD CHAMPIONSHIP POOL 2004

WORLD RACING

YU-GI-OH! THE DAWN OF DESTINY

ZAPPER

ADVENT RISING

AEON FLUX

ALIEN HOMINID

THE BARD'S TALE

BLAZING ANGELS: SQUADRONS OF WWII

CABELA'S BIG GAME HUNTER 2005 ADVENTURES

CABELA'S DANGEROUS HUNTS 2

CAPCOM CLASSICS COLLECTION

THE CHRONICLES OF NARNIA: THE LION, THE WITCH AND THE WARDROBE

COLD WAR

CRIMSON SKIES: HIGH ROAD TO REVENGE

THE DA VINCI CODE

DESTROY ALL HUMANS!

DIGIMON RUMBLE ARENA 2

DRAGON BALL Z: SAGAS

DUNGEONS & DRAGONS HEROES

FANTASTIC 4

FUTURE TACTICS: THE UPRISING

GOBLIN COMMANDER: UNLEASH THE HORDE

GODZILLA: SAVE THE EARTH

GREG HASTINGS' TOURNAMENT PAINTBALL

GUN METAL

HEROES OF THE PACIFIC

THE INCREDIBLE HULK: ULTIMATE DESTRUCTION

L.A. RUSH

MAGIC: THE GATHERING— BATTLEGROUNDS

MARVEL NEMESIS: RISE OF THE IMPERFECTS

MIDNIGHT CLUB II

MIDNIGHT CLUB 3: DUB EDITION

MLB SLUGFEST: LOADED

MOTOCROSS MANIA 3

NIGHTCASTER

ODDWORLD: STRANGER'S WRATH

PANZER DRAGOON ORTA

CRIMSON SKIES: HIGH ROAD TO REVENGE

THE DA VINCI CODE

DESTROY ALL HUMANS!

DIGIMON RUMBLE ARENA 2

DRAGON BALL Z: SAGAS

DUNGEONS & DRAGONS HEROES

FANTASTIC 4

FUTURE TACTICS: THE UPRISING

GOBLIN COMMANDER: UNLEASH THE HORDE

GODZILLA: SAVE THE EARTH

GREG HASTINGS' TOURNAMENT PAINTBALL

GUN METAL

HEROES OF THE PACIFIC

THE INCREDIBLE HULK: ULTIMATE DESTRUCTION

L.A. RUSH

MAGIC: THE GATHERING—
BATTLEGROUNDS

MARVEL NEMESIS: RISE OF THE
IMPERFECTS

MIDNIGHT CLUB II

MIDNIGHT CLUB 3: DUB EDITION

MLB SLUGFEST: LOADED

MOTOCROSS MANIA 3

NIGHTCASTER

ODDWORLD: STRANGER'S WRATH

PANZER DRAGOON ORTA

PETER JACKSON'S KING KONG: THE
OFFICIAL GAME OF THE MOVIE

PRINCE OF PERSIA: THE SANDS
OF TIME

PSYCHONAUTS

ROBOTECH: INVASION

SECRET WEAPONS OVER NORMANDY

SHATTERED UNION

SID MEIER'S PIRATES!

THE SIMS 2

THE SIMS BUSTIN' OUT

SPIDER-MAN 2

SPIKEOUT: BATTLE STREET

SPY VS. SPY

STAR WARS: BATTLEFRONT

STAR WARS EPISODE III:
REVENGE OF THE SITH

STAR WARS KNIGHTS OF THE OLD
REPUBLIC II: THE SITH LORDS

STAR WARS: OBI-WAN

STAR WARS REPUBLIC COMMANDO

STARSKY AND HUTCH

STOLEN

TEENAGE MUTANT NINJA TURTLES 2:
BATTLE NEXUS

TOM & JERRY: WAR OF THE WHISKERS

TOMB RAIDER: LEGEND

TONY HAWK'S UNDERGROUND

TONY HAWK'S UNDERGROUND 2

TONY HAWK'S AMERICAN
WASTELAND

ULTIMATE SPIDER-MAN

WRATH UNLEASHED

WWE WRESTLEMANIA 21

XGRA: EXTREME-G RACING
ASSOCIATION

X-MEN LEGENDS II: RISE OF
APOCALYPSE

X-MEN: THE OFFICIAL GAME

YAGER

Games Listing

XBOX®

ADVENT RISING

CHEAT MENU

Pause the game and press Up, Up, Down, Down, Left, Right, Left, Right, White, Black, **X**.

AEON FLUX

BOMBER JACKET OUTFIT

Select Enter Cheat from the Extras menu and enter **JULIET ALPHA CHARLIE KILO ECHO TANGO**. Look for the outfit under Outfits in the Extras menu.

FAME OUTFIT

Select Enter Cheat from the Extras menu and enter **GOLF ROMEO ALPHA YANKEE**. Look for the outfit under Outfits in the Extras menu.

MULTIPLE OUTFITS

Select Enter Cheat from the Extras menu and enter **CHARLIE LIMA OSCAR TANGO HOTEL ECHO SIERRA**. Look for the outfits under Outfits in the Extras menu. The outfits include the following: Freya, Monican Freya, Hostess Judy, Una, and Fashion Una.

MRS. GOODCHILD OUTFIT

Select Enter Cheat from the Extras menu and enter **WHISKEY HOTEL INDIA TANGO ECHO**. Look for the outfit under Outfits in the Extras menu.

REVELATION OUTFIT

Select Enter Cheat from the Extras menu and enter **ALPHA ROMEO MIKE SIERRA**. Look for the outfit under Outfits in the Extras menu.

SEEDS OUTFIT

Select Enter Cheat from the Extras menu and enter **MIKE OSCAR VICTOR INDIA ECHO**. Look for the outfit under Outfits in the Extras menu.

WAR OUTFIT

Select Enter Cheat from the Extras menu and enter **BRAVO LIMA UNIFORM ROMEO**. Look for the outfit under Outfits in the Extras menu.

ALL REPLAY EPISODES

Select Enter Cheat from the Extras menu and enter **BRAVO ALPHA YANKEE OSCAR UNIFORM**. Then select Replay Episode from the Extras menu to view the episodes.

ALL SLIDESHOWS

Select Enter Cheat from the Extras menu and enter **PAPA INDIA XRAY ECHO SIERRA**. Then select Slideshows from the Extras menu to view the slideshows.

ACTION MOVIE CHEAT

Select Enter Cheat from the Extras menu and enter **BRAVO ALPHA GOLF MIKE ALPHA NOVEMBER**. Or, enter **UNIFORM KILO GOLF ALPHA MIKE ECHO ROMEO**. Pause the game and select Cheats to access the code.

GOD MODE

Select Enter Cheat from the Extras menu and enter **TANGO ROMEO INDIA ROMEO OSCAR XRAY**. Pause the game and select Cheats to access God Mode.

FREE FATALITIES CHEAT

Select Enter Cheat from the Extras menu and enter **CHARLIE UNIFORM TANGO INDIA OSCAR NOVEMBER ECHO**. Pause the game and select Cheats to access the code.

ONE-STRIKE KILLS

Select Enter Cheat from the Extras menu and enter **BRAVO UNIFORM CHARLIE KILO FOXTROT SIERRA TANGO**. Pause the game and select Cheats to access the code.

RESTORE HEALTH

Select Enter Cheat from the Extras menu and enter **HOTEL ECHO ALPHA LIMA MIKE ECHO**. Pause the game and select Cheats to access the code.

UNLIMITED AMMO

Select Enter Cheat from the Extras menu and enter **FOXTROT UNIFORM GOLF**. Pause the game and select Cheats to access the code.

UNLIMITED HEALTH

Select Enter Cheat from the Extras menu and enter **CHARLIE LIMA OSCAR NOVEMBER ECHO**. Pause the game and select Cheats to access the code.

UNLIMITED POWER STRIKES

Select Enter Cheat from the Extras menu and enter **LIMA CHARLIE VICTOR GOLF**. Pause the game and select Cheats to access the code.

ALIEN HOMINID

ALL LEVELS, MINI-GAMES, AND HATS

Select Player 1 Setup or Player 2 Setup and change the name to **ROYGBIV**.

HATS FOR 2-PLAYER GAME

Go to the Options menu and rename your alien one of the following:

ABE	Top Hat	#11
APRIL	Blond Wig	#4
BEHEMOTH	Red Cap	#24
CLETUS	Hunting Hat	#3
DANDY	Flower Petal Hat	#13
GOODMAN	Black Curly Hair	#7
GRRL	Flowers	#10
PRINCESS	Tiara	#12
SUPERFLY	Afro	#6
TOMFULP	Brown Messy Hair	#2

AMPED 2

Enter the following as a code. Note that the cheats will disable the saving feature.

LEVEL SELECT
Enter **AllLevels**.

ALL CHARACTERS
Enter **AllMyPeeps**.

PLAY AS BIGFOOT
Enter **BrotherOfYeti**.

PLAY AS BONES
Enter **FunnyBone**.

PLAY AS BUNNY
Enter **Bunny**.

PLAY AS FROSTY JACK
Enter **FrostByte**.

PLAY AS HERMIT JOE
Enter **GetOffMyLand**.

PLAY AS MOCAP MAN
Enter **MoCapMan**.

PLAY AS RADICAL
Enter **Radical**.

PLAY AS SHINY GAL
Enter **MetalMaam**.

PLAY AS STEEZY
Enter **ChillinWSteezy**.

PLAY AS YETI
Enter **GoTeamYeti**.

MAXIMUM STATS
Enter **MaxSkills**.

FAST BOARDER
Enter **FastMove**.

FAST SPINS
Enter **SuperSpin**.

ALL GRABS
Enter **TrickedOut**.

LOW GRAVITY
Enter **LowGravity**.

NO CRASHING
Enter **DontCrash**.

NO COLLISIONS
Enter **NoCollisions**.

ICY COURSES
Enter **AllIce**.

ALL MOVIES
Enter **ShowRewards**.

DISABLE CODES
Enter **noCheats**.

APEX

ALL TRACKS AND CIRCUITS
Start a new game in Dream mode and enter **WORLD** as a brand name.

ALL CONCEPT CARS
Start a new game in Dream mode and enter **DREAMY** as a brand name.

ALL PRODUCTION CARS
Start a new game in Dream mode and enter **REALITY** as a brand name.

THE BARD'S TALE

During a game, hold Left Trigger + Right Trigger and enter the following:

EVERYTHING ON (SILVER AND ADDERSTONES)
Press Up, Up, Down, Down, Left, Right, Left, Right

FULL HEALTH AND MANA
Press Left, Left, Right, Right, Up, Down, Up, Down

CAN'T BE HURT
Press Right, Left, Right, Left, Up, Down, Up, Down

CAN'T BE HIT
Press Left, Right, Left, Right, Up, Down, Up, Down

DAMAGE X100
Press Up, Down, Up, Down, Left, Right, Left, Right

BLAZING ANGELS: SQUADRONS OF WWII

ALL MISSIONS, MEDALS, & PLANES
At the Main menu, hold Left Trigger + Right Trigger and press X, White, Black, Y, Y, Black, White, X.

GOD MODE
Pause the game, hold Left Trigger and press X, Y, Y, X. Release Left Trigger, hold Right Trigger and press Y, X, X, Y. Re-enter the code to disable it.

DAMAGE INCREASED
Pause the game, hold Left Trigger and press White, White, Black. Release Left Trigger, hold Right Trigger and press Black, Black, White. Re-enter the code to disable it.

CABELA'S BIG GAME HUNTER 2005 ADVENTURES

UNLIMITED ENERGY
During a game, press Black, Black, Left Trigger, Black, X, Y, B, A.

CABELA'S DANGEROUS HUNTS 2

DOUBLE HEALTH
Select Codes and enter Eye, Bolt, Skull, Hand, Boot.

HEALTH REGENERATES FASTER
Select Codes and enter Skull, Eye, Boot, Bolt, Hand.

DOUBLE DAMAGE
Select Codes and enter Hand, Boot, Skull, Eye, Bolt.

INFINITE AMMO
Select Codes and enter Bolt, Hand, Eye, Boot, Skull.

CAPCOM CLASSICS COLLECTION

ALL LOCKS OPENED
At the Title screen, press Left Trigger, Right Trigger, Up on Right Analog Stick, Down on Right Analog Stick, Left Trigger, Right Trigger, Up on Left Analog Stick, Down on Left Analog Stick, Left Trigger, Right Trigger, Up, Down.

CHICKEN LITTLE

INVINCIBILITY
Select Cheat Codes from the Extras menu and enter Baseball, Baseball, Baseball, Shirt.

BIG FEET
Select Cheat Codes from the Extras menu and enter Hat, Glove, Glove, Hat.

BIG HAIR
Select Cheat Codes from the Extras menu and enter Baseball, Bat, Bat, Baseball.

BIG HEAD
Select Cheat Codes from the Extras menu and enter Hat, Helmet, Helmet, Hat.

PAPER PANTS
Select Cheat Codes from the Extras menu and enter Bat, Bat, Hat, Hat.

SUNGLASSES
Select Cheat Codes from the Extras menu and enter Glove, Glove, Helmet, Helmet.

UNDERWEAR
Select Cheat Codes from the Extras menu and enter Hat, Hat, Shirt, Shirt.

THE CHRONICLES OF NARNIA: THE LION, THE WITCH AND THE WARDROBE

ENABLE CHEATS
At the Title screen, press **A** and hold Left Trigger + Right Trigger and press Down, Down, Right, Up. The text should turn green when entered correctly. When this occurs, you can enter the following codes.

LEVEL SELECT
At the wardrobe, hold Left Trigger and press Up, Up, Right, Right, Up, Right, Down.

ALL BONUS LEVELS
At the Bonus Drawer, hold Left Trigger and press Down, Down, Right, Right, Down, Right, Up.

LEVEL SKIP
During gameplay, hold Left Trigger and press Down, Left, Down, Left, Down, Right, Down, Right, Up.

INVINCIBILITY
During gameplay, hold Left Trigger and press Down, Up, Down, Right, Right.

RESTORE HEALTH
During gameplay, hold Left Trigger and press Down, Left, Left, Right.

ALL ABILITIES
During gameplay, hold Left Trigger and press Down, Left, Right, Left, Up.

10,000 COINS
During gameplay, hold Left Trigger and press Down, Left, Right, Down, Down.

FILL COMBO METER
During gameplay, hold Left Trigger and press Up, Up, Right, Up.

COLD WAR

INVULNERABILITY
Pause the game and press **X**, White, **Y**, Black, Left.

WIN CURRENT LEVEL
Pause the game and press **X**, White, **Y**, Black, **X**.

ALL ITEMS, GADGETS, & TECH POINTS
Pause the game and press **X**, White, **Y**, Black, **Y**.

CRASH TAG TEAM RACING

FASTER VEHICLES
At the Main menu, hold Left Trigger + Right Trigger and press **B, B, Y, Y**.

JAPANESE CRASH
At the Main menu, hold Left Trigger + Right Trigger and press **X, B, X, B**.

ONE-HIT KO
At the Main menu, hold Left Trigger + Right Trigger and press **A, B, B, A**.

DRIVE A BLOCK VEHICLE
At the Main menu, hold Left Trigger + Right Trigger and press **B, B, Y, X**.

DISABLE HUD
At the Main menu, hold Left Trigger + Right Trigger and press **A, X, Y, B**.

CHICKEN HEADS
At the Main menu, hold Left Trigger + Right Trigger and press **A, B, B, X**.

CRIMSON SKIES: HIGH ROAD TO REVENGE

GOD MODE
During a game, press **Y, A, X, B**, Black.

ALL PLANES
During a game, press **Y, X, B, Y**, Black.

$5,000
During a game, press **A, Y, A, Y**, Black.

SUPER PRIMARY WEAPON
During a game, press **B, X, A, B**, Black.

10 TOKENS
During a game, press **X, B, X, B**, Black.

ULTRA HARD DIFFICULTY
During a game, press **X, B, A, X**, Black.

DANCE DANCE REVOLUTION ULTRAMIX 2

ALL SONGS
With a controller in port four, select Credits from the Options screen. Then press Up, Up, Down, Down, Left, Right, Left, Right, **B**, **A**, Up, Up, Down, Down, Left, Right, Left, Right, **A**, **B**.

KONSENTO:03 AND MAID-ZUKIN CHARACTERS
With a controller in port four, select Dancers from the Options screen. Then press and hold **X** + **Y** for five seconds.

DANCE DANCE REVOLUTION ULTRAMIX 3

ALL SONGS
Select Credits from the Options screen and play the Credits mini-game, then press the opposite of what the game indicates. (For example, press Up when it says Down and so on. Or, if it says Left + Right, press Up + Down.) You'll hear applause when the code is entered correctly.

THE DA VINCI CODE

GOD MODE
Select Codes from the Options screen and enter **VITRUVIAN MAN**.

EXTRA HEALTH
Select Codes from the Options screen and enter **SACRED FEMININE**.

MISSION SELECT
Select Codes from the Options screen and enter **CLOS LUCE 1519**.

ONE-HIT FIST KILL
Select Codes from the Options screen and enter **PHILLIPS EXETER**.

ONE-HIT WEAPON KILL
Select Codes from the Options screen and enter **ROYAL HOLLOWAY**.

ALL VISUAL DATABASE
Select Codes from the Options screen and enter **APOCRYPHA**.

ALL VISUAL DATABASE AND CONCEPT ART
Select Codes from the Options screen and enter **ET IN ARCADIA EGO**.

DESTROY ALL HUMANS!

AMMO-A-PLENTY
Pause the game, hold Left Trigger and press Left, **Y**, White, Right, Black, **X**. This gives you unlimited ammo.

BULLETPROOF CRYPTO
Pause the game, hold Left Trigger and press **X**, **Y**, Left, Left, **Y**, **X**. This makes you invincible.

D

DEEP THINKER
Pause the game, hold Left Trigger and press Black, White, **Y**, Right, White, **Y**. This gives you unlimited concentration.

AWARE LIKE A FOX
Pause the game, hold Left Trigger and press Right, Right, **X**, White, Black, Right, White. This maxes out the alert meter.

NOBODY LOVES YOU
Pause the game, hold Left Trigger and press White, Right, White, Black, **X**, Right. This resets the alert meter.

FIND KEY TO ORTHOPOX'S LAB
On the Mothership, hold Left Trigger and press **X**, **Y**, Left, Left, **Y**, **X**. This gives you access to the Upgrades at Pox's Lab.

MMMM BRAINS!
On the Mothership, hold Left Trigger and press Black, Black, White, White, Left, Right, Left, Right, White, Black. This gives you extra DNA.

DIGIMON RUMBLE ARENA 2

ONE-HIT KILLS
At the Title screen, press Right, Up, Left, Down, **A**, Left Trigger + Right Trigger.

EVOLVE ENERGY ITEM
At the Title screen, press **Y**, Right, Down, **B**, Left Trigger, **A**, Right Trigger, **A**, **Y**.

EVOLVE METER ALWAYS FULL
At the Title screen, press **X**, Right, **A**, **Y**, Left, **B**, Left Trigger + Right Trigger.

DRAGON BALL Z: SAGAS

ALL UPGRADES
Pause the game, select Controller and press Up, Left, Down, Right, Back, Start, **Y**, **X**, **A**, **B**.

INVINCIBILITY
Pause the game, select Controller and press Down, **A**, Up, **Y**, Back, Start, Right, **X**, Left, **B**.

DUNGEONS AND DRAGONS HEROES

During a game, hold Left Trigger and press **A** + **Y**. Now you can enter the following:

INVINCIBILITY
Enter **PELOR**.

NIGHTMARE DIFFICULTY SETTING
Enter **MPS LABS**.

UNLIMITED MYSTICAL WILL
Enter **OBADHAI**.

10,000 EXPERIENCE POINTS
Enter **DSP633**.

500,000 GOLD
Enter **KNE637**.

DEXTERITY UP 10
Enter **YAN** or **ZXE053**.

CONSTITUTION UP 10
Enter **N STINE**.

10 ANTI-VENOM
Enter **SPINRAD**.

10 BERSERK BREW
Enter **THOMAS**.

10 FASH FREEZE
Enter **ESKO**.

10 FIRE BOMB
Enter **WEBER**.

10 FIRE FLASK
Enter **BROPHY**.

10 FIREY OIL
Enter **EHOFF**.

10 GLOBE POTION
Enter **WRight**.

10 INSECT PLAGUE
Enter **DERISO**.

10 KEYS
Enter **KEIDEL**.

10 KEYS
Enter **SNODGRASS**.

10 LARGE HEALING POTIONS
Enter **THOMPSON**.

10 LARGE WILL POTIONS
Enter **GEE**.

10 MEDIUM POTIONS OF WILL
Enter **LU**.

10 POTIONS OF HASTE
Enter **UHL**.

10 PYROKINS
Enter **SMITH**.

10 ROD OF DESTRUCTION
Enter **AUSTIN**.

10 ROD OF FIRE
Enter **DELUCIA**.

10 ROD OF MIRACLES
Enter **JARMAN**.

10 ROD OF MISSILES
Enter **MILLER**.

10 ROD OF REFLECTION
Enter **WHITTAKE**.

10 ROD OF SHADOWS
Enter **DINOLT**.

10 THROWN AXE OF RUIN
Enter **RAMERO**.

10 THROWN DAGGERS OF STUNNING
Enter **BELL**.

10 THROWN DAGGERS
Enter **MOREL**.

10 THROWN HALCYON HAMMER
Enter **PRASAD**.

10 THROWN HAMMER
Enter **BRATHWAI**.

10 THROWN VIPER AXE
Enter **FRAZIER**.

10 THROWN VIPER AXE
Enter **HOWARD**.

10 THUDERSTONE
Enter **ELSON**.

10 TOMES OF LESSONS
Enter **PAQUIN**.

10 TOMES OF THE APPRENTICE
Enter **BILGER**.

10 TOMES OF THE TEACHER
Enter **MEFFORD**.

10 TOMES OF THE MASTER
Enter **SPANBURG**.

10 WARP STONES
Enter **HOPPENST**.

10 HOLY WATER
Enter **CRAWLEY**.

VIEW CONCEPT ART
Enter **CONCEPTS**.

VIEW CREDITS
Enter **CREDITS**.

DISABLE CHEATS
Enter **UNBUFF**.

EA SPORTS ARENA FOOTBALL

BIG BALL
While at the line of scrimmage, press
Left Trigger + **Y**, Up, Up.

SMALL BALL
While at the line of scrimmage, press Left Trigger + **Y**, Down, Down.

NORMAL SIZE BALL
While at the line of scrimmage, press Left Trigger + **Y**, Up, Down.

MAX STATS IN QUICK PLAY
Load a profile with the name **IronMen**. This will maximize all players' stats in Quick Play.

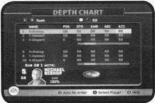

FANTASTIC 4

BARGE ARENA AND STAN LEE INTERVIEW #1
At the Main menu, press **X**, **B**, **X**, Down, Down, **B**, Up.

INFINITE COSMIC POWER
At the Main menu, press Up, **X**, **X**, **X**, Left, Right, **B**.

BONUS LEVEL
At the Main menu, press Right, Right, **X**, **B**, Left, Up, Down.

FIFA STREET

ALL CLOTHES
At the Main menu, hold Left Trigger + **Y** and press Right, Right, Left, Up (x3), Down, Left.

SMALL PLAYERS
Pause the game, hold Left Trigger + **Y** and press Up, Left, Down, Down, Right, Down, Up, Left.

NORMAL SIZE PLAYERS
Pause the game, hold Left Trigger + **Y** and press Right, Right, Up, Down, Down, Left, Right, Left.

FORZA MOTORSPORT

START CAREER WITH 900,000,000 CREDITS
Start a new profile with the name **tEAm4za**.

FROGGER: ANCIENT SHADOW

UNLOCK LEVELS

To unlock various levels, select Cheat Codes and enter the following:

LEVEL	ENTER
Level 4-1	Lily, Lumpy, Frogger, Finnius
Level 4-2	Wani, Frogger, Lily, Berry
Level 5-1	Wani, Wani, Berry, Frogger
Level 5-2	Frogger, Finnius, Lily, Lily
Level 6-1	Wani, Lily, Lily, Frogger
Level 6-2	Lily, Lily, Wani, Lily
Level 6-3	Berry, Frogger, Lily, Lily
Level 7-1	Lumpy, Wani, Frogger, Frogger
Level 7-2	Lumpy, Frogger, Lily, Berry

UNLOCK LETTERS

To unlock various letters, select Cheat Codes and enter the following:

LEVEL	ENTER
Hyacinth Letter	Berry, Frogger, Lumpy, Berry
Cosmos Letter	Lumpy, Frogger, Frogger, Lumpy
Rose Letter	Frogger, Wani, Berry, Lumpy
Pansy Letter	Finnius, Lumpy, Lily, Wani

UNLOCK WIGS

To unlock various wigs, select Cheat Codes and enter the following:

LEVEL	ENTER
Lobster Wig	Finnius, Wani, Lumpy, Frogger
Bird Nest Wig	Lily, Lily, Lily, Lily
Sail Boat Wig	Lumpy, Lumpy, Lumpy, Lumpy
Skull Wig	Frogger, Lumpy, Lily, Frogger

UNLOCK ARTWORK

To unlock different kinds of artwork, select Cheat Codes and enter the following:

LEVEL	ENTER
Programmer Art 1	Wani, Wani, Wani, Wani
Programmer Art 2	Lumpy, Frogger, Berry, Lily
Programmer Art 3	Wani, Frogger, Lily, Finnius
Additional Art 1	Frogger, Frogger, Frogger, Frogger
Additional Art 2	Finnius, Finnius, Finnius, Finnius
Additional Art 3	Berry, Berry, Berry, Berry

DEVELOPER PICTURE 1

Select Cheat Codes and enter Wani, Frogger, Wani, Frogger.

DEVELOPER PICTURE 2

Select Cheat Codes and enter Berry, Berry, Berry, Wani.

FUTURE TACTICS: THE UPRISING

LEVEL SKIP

At the Game Select screen, press Left Trigger, **X**, Right Trigger, Right Trigger, Black, **X**, Left Trigger, Right Trigger, Black.

UNLIMITED TURNS AND MOVEMENT

During a game, press Up, Up, Down, Down, Left, Right, Left, Left, Right Trigger, Left Trigger.

BIG HEADS

During a game, press Up, Left, Down, Left, Down, Up, Up, Left.

DISCO MODE

During a game, press Left Trigger, Left, Left Trigger, Left, Right Trigger, Right, Right Trigger, Right.

LOW GRAVITY

During a game, press Up (x6), Down, Right, Up.

GOBLIN COMMANDER: UNLEASH THE HORDE

During a game, hold Right Trigger + Left Trigger + **Y** + Down until a message appears on the right side of the screen. Re-enter the code to disable it. Now you can enter the following codes. Note that a message appears when the code is entered correctly.

GOD MODE

Press Right Trigger (x3), Left Trigger (x3), Right Trigger, Left Trigger, **Y**, Right Trigger.

AUTOMATIC WIN

Press Right Trigger, Right Trigger, Left Trigger (x3), Right Trigger, Right Trigger, **Y** (x3).

ALL LEVEL ACCESS

Press **Y** (x3), Left Trigger, Right Trigger, Left Trigger, Left Trigger, Right Trigger, Left Trigger, Right Trigger, Right Trigger, Left Trigger, Right Trigger, Left Trigger, Left Trigger, Right Trigger, Left Trigger, Right Trigger, Left Trigger, Right Trigger, Left Trigger, Left Trigger, Right Trigger, Left Trigger, Right Trigger, Right Trigger, **Y** (x3). Start up a Campaign to select a level.

DISABLE FOG OF WAR

Press Right Trigger, Left Trigger, Right Trigger, Right Trigger, Left Trigger, Left Trigger, **Y**, **Y**, Left Trigger, Right Trigger.

GAME SPEED X1/2

Press Left Trigger (x5), **Y** (x4), Right Trigger.

GAME SPEED X2

Press Right Trigger (x5), Left Trigger, **Y**, Right Trigger (x3).

GOLD AND SOULS +1000

Press Right Trigger, Right Trigger, Left Trigger, Right Trigger, Right Trigger, **Y** (x3), Left Trigger, Left Trigger.

GOLD +100
Press Left Trigger, Right Trigger (x4), Left Trigger, **Y**, Left Trigger (x3).

SOULS +100
Press Right Trigger, Left Trigger (x4), Right Trigger, **Y**, Right Trigger (x3).

GODZILLA: SAVE THE EARTH

CHEAT MENU
At the Main menu, press and hold Left Trigger, **B**, Right Trigger in that order, then release **B**, Right Trigger, Left Trigger. Now you can enter the following cheats.

ALL CITIES
Enter **659996**.

ALL MONSTERS
Enter **525955**.

UNLOCK CHALLENGES
Enter **975013**.

HEALTH REGENERATES
Enter **536117**.

ENERGY DOESN'T REGENERATE
Enter **122574**.

INDESTRUCTIBLE BUILDINGS
Enter **812304**.

100,000 POINTS
Enter **532459**.

150,000 POINTS
Enter **667596**.

200,000 POINTS
Enter **750330**.

PLAYER 1: 4X DAMAGE
Enter **259565**.

PLAYER 1: INFINITE ENERGY
Enter **819342**.

PLAYER 1: INVISIBLE
Enter **531470**.

PLAYER 1: INVULNERABLE
Enter **338592**.

PLAYER 2: 4X DAMAGE
Enter **927281**.

PLAYER 2: INFINITE ENERGY
Enter **324511**.

PLAYER 2: INVISIBLE
Enter **118699**.

PLAYER 2: INVULNERABLE
Enter **259333**.

PLAYER 3: 4X DAMAGE
Enter **500494**.

PLAYER 3: INFINITE ENERGY
Enter **651417**.

PLAYER 3: INVISIBLE
Enter **507215**.

PLAYER 3: INVULNERABLE
Enter **953598**.

PLAYER 4: 4X DAMAGE
Enter **988551**.

PLAYER 4: INFINITE ENERGY
Enter **456719**.

PLAYER 4: INVISIBLE
Enter **198690**.

PLAYER 4: INVULNERABLE
Enter **485542**.

GALLERY
Enter **294206**.

GODZILLA FINAL WARS
Enter **409014**.

GREG HASTINGS' TOURNAMENT PAINTBALL

FLYING

During a game, hold Black + **X** + Right Trigger and press Up, Up, Down, Down, Right, Left, Down, Up.

GUN METAL

ALL MISSIONS

At the Mission Select screen, press Left Thumbstick, Black, Right Trigger, Right Thumbstick, White, Left Trigger.

MISSION SKIP

During a mission, press Left Thumbstick, White, White, Down, Right Thumbstick, White.

ALTERNATE MUSIC

At the Title screen, press Left Thumbstick, Left Thumbstick, Right Thumbstick, Right Thumbstick, Left Trigger, Right Trigger.

JOKE MISSION BREIFINGS

During Missions 1, 3, 6, 8, 9 or 14, press Left Trigger, Left Trigger, Right Trigger, Right Trigger, Left Thumbstick, Right Thumbstick.

HEROES OF THE PACIFIC

Note that the following cheats will disable game saving.

CHEAT MENU

At the Main menu, press **Y**, Left Trigger, Left on D pad, Right Trigger, Right on D-pad, White.

UPGRADE PLANES

At the Main menu, press Left Trigger, Left on the Right Thumbstick, Right Trigger, Right on the Right Thumbstick, White, **Y**.

ALL PLANES AND MISSIONS

At the Main menu, press Up on the Right Thumbstick, Down on the Right Thumbstick, White, Black, Left on the Right Thumbstick, Right on the Right Thumbstick.

JAPANESE PLANES

At the Main menu, press White, Black, Left Trigger, Right Trigger, Up on the Right Thumbstick, Left on the Right Thumbstick.

ICE AGE 2: THE MELTDOWN

INFINITE PEBBLES

Pause the game and press Down, Down, Left, Up, Up, Right, Up, Down.

INFINITE ENERGY

Pause the game and press Down, Left, Right, Down, Down, Right, Left, Down.

INFINITE HEALTH

Pause the game and press Up, Right, Down, Up, Left, Down, Right, Left.

THE INCREDIBLE HULK: ULTIMATE DESTRUCTION

You must first collect a specific comic in the game to activate each code. After collecting the appropriate comic, you can enter the following. If you don't have the comic and enter the code, you get the following message: "That code cannot be activated...yet". You can access the cheats on the Code Input screen.

UNLOCKED: CABS GALORE
Select Code Input from the Extras menu and enter **CABBIES**.

UNLOCKED: GORILLA INVASION
Select Code Input from the Extras menu and enter **KINGKNG**.

UNLOCKED: MASS TRANSIT
Select Code Input from the Extras menu and enter **TRANSIT**.

UNLOCKED: 5000 SMASH POINTS
Select Code Input from the Extras menu and enter **SMASH5**.

UNLOCKED: 10000 SMASH POINTS
Select Code Input from the Extras menu and enter **SMASH10**.

UNLOCKED: 15000 SMASH POINTS
Select Code Input from the Extras menu and enter **SMASH15**.

UNLOCKED: AMERICAN FLAG SHORTS
Select Code Input from the Extras menu and enter **AMERICA**.

UNLOCKED: CANADIAN FLAG SHORTS
Select Code Input from the Extras menu and enter **OCANADA**.

UNLOCKED: FRENCH FLAG SHORTS
Select Code Input from the Extras menu and enter **Drapeau**.

UNLOCKED: GERMAN FLAG SHORTS
Select Code Input from the Extras menu and enter **DEUTSCH**.

UNLOCKED: ITALIAN FLAG SHORTS
Select Code Input from the Extras menu and enter **MUTANDA**.

UNLOCKED: JAPANESE FLAG SHORTS
Select Code Input from the Extras menu and enter **FURAGGU**.

UNLOCKED: SPANISH FLAG SHORTS
Select Code Input from the Extras menu and enter **BANDERA**.

UNLOCKED: UK FLAG SHORTS
Select Code Input from the Extras menu and enter **FSHNCHP**.

UNLOCKED: COW MISSILES
Select Code Input from the Extras menu and enter **CHZGUN**.

UNLOCKED: DOUBLE HULK'S DAMAGE
Select Code Input from the Extras menu and enter **DESTROY**.

UNLOCKED: DOUBLE POWER COLLECTABLES
Select Code Input from the Extras menu and enter **BRINGIT**.

UNLOCKED: BLACK AND WHITE
Select Code Input from the Extras menu and enter **RETRO**.

UNLOCKED: SEPIA
Select Code Input from the Extras menu and enter **HISTORY**.

UNLOCKED: ABOMINATION
Select Code Input from the Extras menu and enter **VILLAIN**.

UNLOCKED: GRAY HULK
Select Code Input from the Extras menu and enter **CLASSIC**.

UNLOCKED: JOE FIXIT SKIN
Select Code Input from the Extras menu and enter **SUITFIT**.

UNLOCKED: WILD TRAFFIC
Select Code Input from the Extras menu and enter **FROGGIE**.

UNLOCKED: LOW GRAVITY
Select Code Input from the Extras menu and enter **PILLOWS**.

THE INCREDIBLES

To access the following codes, pause the game and select Secrets, then enter the following:

RESTORE SOME HEALTH
Enter **UUDDLRLRBAS**.

BIG HEADS
Enter **EINSTEINIUM**.

SMALL HEADS
Enter **DEEVOLVE**.

ONE-HIT KILLS
Enter **KRONOS**.

INFINITE INCREDI-POWER FOR ELASTIGIRL
Enter **FLEXIBLE**.

INFINITE INCREDI-POWER FOR MR. INCREDIBLE
Enter **SHOWTIME**.

EYE LASER
Enter **GAZERBEAM**.

SUPER SPEED INCREDI-POWER
Enter **DANIELTHEFLASH**.

DESTROYS EVERYTHING
Enter **SMARTBOMB**.

FIRE TRAIL
Enter **ATHLETESFOOT**.

FASTER GAMEPLAY
Enter **SASSMODE**.

SLOW MOTION
Enter **BWTHEMOVIE**.

BRIGHT COLORS
Enter **EMODE**.

INVERT HORIZONTAL CAMERA CONTROL
Enter **INVERTCAMERAX**.

INVERT VERTICAL CAMERA CONTROL
Enter **INVERTCAMERAY**.

TOGGLE HUD
Enter **BHUD**.

WATCH HEAVY IRON STUDIOS INTRO
Enter **HI**.

CREDITS
Enter **YOURNAMEINLIGHTS**.

THE INCREDIBLES: RISE OF THE UNDERMINER

BIG HEADS
Pause the game and press **B** to access the Options screen. Choose Secrets and enter **EGOPROBLEM**. Re-enter the code to disable it.

MR. INCREDIBLE GAINS 1000 EXPERIENCE POINTS
Pause the game and press **B** to access the Options screen. Choose Secrets and enter **MRIPROF**.

FROZONE GAINS 1000 EXPERIENCE POINTS
Pause the game and press **B** to access the Options screen. Choose Secrets and enter **FROZPROF**.

MR. INCREDIBLE GAINS A SUPER-MOVE
Pause the game and press **B** to access the Options screen. Choose Secrets and enter **MRIBOOM**.

FROZONE GAINS A SUPER-MOVE
Pause the game and press **B** to access the Options screen. Choose Secrets and enter **FROZBOOM**.

SHOWS THE GAME CREDITS
Pause the game and press **B** to access the Options screen. Choose Secrets and enter **ROLLCALL**.

TOUGHER GAME
Pause the game and press **B** to access the Options screen. Choose Secrets and enter **THISISTOOEASY**. This code cuts damage done to enemies in half, doubles damage caused to the Supers, there is no health recovery, and Experience Points are halved.

EASIER GAME
Pause the game and press **B** to access the Options screen. Choose Secrets and enter **THISISTOOHARD**. This code causes double damage to enemies, halves damage done to the Supers, and doubles the amount of health recovery and Experience Points!

ALL GALLERY ITEMS
Pause the game and press **B** to access the Options screen. Choose Secrets and enter **SHOWME**.

DOUBLE EXPERIENCE POINTS
Pause the game and press **B** to access the Options screen. Choose Secrets and enter **MAXIMILLION**.

L.A. RUSH

$5,000
During a game, press Up, Down, Left, Right, **B**, Left, **A**, Up.

UNLIMITED N2O
During a game, press Up, Down, Left, Right, **X**, Up, Down, **B**, Up.

ALL CARS IN GARAGE PIMPED
During a game, press Up, Down, Left, Right, **B**, **X**, **A**, **Y**, Up, Down, Left, Right.

DISABLE POLICE
During a game, press Up, Down, Left, Right, **A**, **X**, Right, **Y**, Left.

FAST TRAFFIC
During a game, press Up, Down, Left, Right, **X**, Right, **B**, Left.

NO CATCH UP
Use **C-VHARD** as a profile name.

SLOWER OPPONENTS
Use **C-EASY** as a profile name.

LEGO STAR WARS: THE VIDEO GAME

Extras
Pause the game and select Extras to toggle these cheats on and off.

INVINCIBILITY
At Dexter's Diner, select Enter Code and enter **4PR28U**.

BIG BLASTERS
At Dexter's Diner, select Enter Code and enter **IG72X4**.

CLASSIC BLASTERS
At Dexter's Diner, select Enter Code and enter **L449HD**.

SILLY BLASTERS
At Dexter's Diner, select Enter Code and enter **NR37W1**.

BRUSHES
At Dexter's Diner, select Enter Code and enter **SHRUB1**.

TEA CUPS
At Dexter's Diner, select Enter Code and enter **PUCEAT**.

MINIKIT DETECTOR
At Dexter's Diner, select Enter Code and enter **LD116B**.

MOUSTACHES
At Dexter's Diner, select Enter Code and enter **RP924W**.

PURPLE
At Depxter's Diner, select Enter Code and enter **YD77GC**.

SILHOUETTES

At Dexter's Diner, select Enter Code and enter **MS999Q**.

The following codes make each character available for purchase from Dexter's Diner.

BATTLE DROID

At Dexter's Diner, select Enter Code and enter **987UYR**.

BATTLE DROID (COMMANDER)

At Dexter's Diner, select Enter Code and enter **EN11K5**.

BATTLE DROID (GEONOSIS)

At Dexter's Diner, select Enter Code and enter **LK42U6**.

BATTLE DROID (SECURITY)

At Dexter's Diner, select Enter Code and enter **KF999A**.

BOBA FETT

At Dexter's Diner, select Enter Code and enter **LA811Y**.

CLONE

At Dexter's Diner, select Enter Code and enter **F8B4L6**.

CLONE (EPISODE III)

At Dexter's Diner, select Enter Code and enter **ER33JN**.

CLONE (EPISODE III, PILOT)

At Dexter's Diner, select Enter Code and enter **BHU72T**.

CLONE (EPISODE III, SWAMP)

At Dexter's Diner, select Enter Code and enter **N3T6P8**.

CLONE (EPISODE III, WALKER)

At Dexter's Diner, select Enter Code and enter **RS6E25**.

COUNT DOOKU

At Dexter's Diner, select Enter Code and enter **14PGMN**.

DARTH MAUL

At Dexter's Diner, select Enter Code and enter **H35TUX**.

DARTH SIDIOUS

At Dexter's Diner, select Enter Code and enter **A32CAM**.

DISGUISED CLONE

At Dexter's Diner, select Enter Code and enter **VR832U**.

DROIDEKA

At Dexter's Diner, select Enter Code and enter **DH382U**.

GENERAL GRIEVOUS

At Dexter's Diner, select Enter Code and enter **SF321Y**.

GEONOSIAN

At Dexter's Diner, select Enter Code and enter **19D7NB**.

GRIEVOUS' BODYGUARD

At Dexter's Diner, select Enter Code and enter **ZTY392**.

GONK DROID

At Dexter's Diner, select Enter Code and enter **U63B2A**.

JANGO FETT

At Dexter's Diner, select Enter Code and enter **PL47NH**.

KI-ADI MUNDI

At Dexter's Diner, select Enter Code and enter **DP55MV**.

LUMINARA

At Dexter's Diner, select Enter Code and enter **A725X4**.

MACE WINDU (EPISODE III)

At Dexter's Diner, select Enter Code and enter **MS952L**.

PADMÉ

At Dexter's Diner, select Enter Code and enter **92UJ7D**.

PK DROID

At Dexter's Diner, select Enter Code and enter **R840JU**.

PRINCESS LEIA
At Dexter's Diner, select Enter Code and enter **BEQ82H**.

REBEL TROOPER
At Dexter's Diner, select Enter Code and enter **L54YUK**.

ROYAL GUARD
At Dexter's Diner, select Enter Code and enter **PP43JX**.

SHAAK TI
At Dexter's Diner, select Enter Code and enter **EUW862**.

SUPER BATTLE DROID
At Dexter's Diner, select Enter Code and enter **XZNR21**.

LMA MANAGER 2005

QUICKER HEALING
Enter your name as **LMA2005A**.

£500,000,000
Enter your name as **LMA2005B**.

MOON BALL
Enter your name as **LMA2005MA**.

HELIUM SHOUTS
Enter your name as **LMA2005MB**.

BASS SHOUTS
Enter your name as **LMA2005MC**.

MADDEN NFL 2005

CHEAT CARDS

Select Madden Cards from the My Madden menu. Then select Madden Codes and enter the following:

CHEAT	ENTER
3rd Down, Opponent only get 3 downs to get a 1st down	Z28X8K
5th Down, Get 5 downs to get a 1st down	P66C4L
Aloha Stadium	G67F5X
Bingo!, Defensive interceptions increase by 75%	J33I8F
Da Bomb, Unlimited pass range	B61A8M
Da Boot, Unlimited field goal range	I76X3T
Extra Credit, Awards points for interceptions and sacks	M89S8G
First and Fifteen, Opponent must gain 15 yards to get a 1st down	V65J8P
First and Five, 1st down yards are set to 5	O72E9B
Fumbilitis, Opponent's fumble chance increases by 75% for game	R14B8Z
Human Plow, Break tackle increases by 75%	L96J7P
Lame Duck, Opponent throws lob passes	D57R5S
Mistake Free, Can't fumble or throw interceptions	X78P9Z
Mr. Mobility, Your QB can't get sacked	Y59R8R
Super Bowl XL	085P6I
Super Bowl XLI	P48Z4D
Super Bowl XLII	T67R10
Super Bowl XXXIX	D58F1B
Super Dive, Diving distance increases by 75%	D59K3Y
Tight Fit, Opponent's uprights become narrow	V34L6D
Unforced Errors, Opponent fumbles ball when he jukes	L48G1E

CLASSIC TEAM CARDS

Select Madden Cards from the My Madden menu. Then select Madden Codes and enter the following:

TEAM	ENTER	TEAM	ENTER
1958 Colts	P74X8J	1982 Redskins	F56D6V
1966 Packers	G49P7W	1983 Raiders	D23T8S
1968 Jets	C24W2A	1984 Dolphins	X23Z8H
1970 Browns	G12N1I	1985 Bears	F92M8M
1972 Dolphins	R79W6W	1986 Giants	K44F2Y
1974 Steelers	R12D9B	1988 49ers	F77R8H
1976 Raiders	P96Q8M	1990 Eagles	G95F2Q
1977 Broncos	O18T2A	1991 Lions	I89F4I
1978 Dolphins	G97U5X	1992 Cowboys	I44A1O
1980 Raiders	K71K4E	1993 Bills	Y66K3O
1981 Chargers	Y27N9A		

CHEERLEADER/PUMP UP THE CROWD CARDS

Select Madden Cards from the My Madden menu. Then select Madden Codes and enter the following:

TEAM	ENTER	TEAM	ENTER
Patriots	O59P9C	Jaguars	K32C2A
49ers	X61T6L	Jets	S45W1M
Bengals	Y22S6G	Lions	C18F4G
Bills	F26S6X	Packers	K26Y4V
Broncos	B85U5C	Panthers	M66N4D
Browns	B65Q1L	Raiders	G92L2E
Buccaneers	Z55Z7S	Rams	W73B8X
Cardinals	Q91W5L	Ravens	P98T6C
Chargers	Q68S3F	Redskins	N19D6Q
Chiefs	T46M6T	Saints	R99G2F
Colts	M22Z6H	Seahawks	A35T8R
Cowboys	J84E3F	Steelers	C98I2V
Dolphins	E88T2J	Texans	R74G3W
Eagles	Q88P3Q	Titans	Q81V4N
Falcons	W86F3F	Vikings	E26H4L
Giants	L13Z9J		

GOLD PLAYER CARDS

Select Madden Cards from the My Madden menu. Then select Madden Codes and enter the following:

PLAYER	ENTER	PLAYER	ENTER
Aaron Brooks	J95K1J	Amani Toomer	Z75G6M
Aaron Glenn	Q48E9G	Andre Carter	V76E2Q
Adewale Ogunleye	C12E9E	Andre Johnson	E34S1M
Ahman Green	T86L4C	Andy Reid	N44K1L
Al Wilson	G72G2R	Anquan Boldin	S32F7K
Alan Faneca	U32S9C	Antonio Winfield	A12V7Z

PLAYER	ENTER	PLAYER	ENTER
Bill Cowher	S54T6U	Dwight Freeney	G76U2L
Brad Hopkins	P44A8B	Edgerrin James	A75D7X
Brett Farve	L61D7B	Ed Reed	G18Q2B
Brian Billick	L27C4K	Eric Moulds	H34Z8K
Brian Dawkins	Y47B8Y	Flozell Adams	R54T1O
Brian Simmons	S22M6A	Fred Taylor	I87X9Y
Brian Urlacher	Z34J4U	Grant Wistrom	E46M4Y
Brian Westbrook	V46I2I	Herman Edwards	O19T2T
Bubba Franks	U77F2W	Hines Ward	M12B8F
Butch Davis	G77L6F	Jack Del Rio	J22P9I
Byron Leftwich	C55V5C	Jake Delhomme	M86N9F
Carson Palmer	O36V2H	Jake Plummer	N74P8X
Casey Hampton	Z11P9T	Jamie Sharper	W27I7G
Chad Johnson	R85S2A	Jason Taylor	O33S6I
Chad Pennington	B64L2F	Jason Webster	M74B3E
Champ Bailey	K89O9E	Jeff Fisher	N62B6J
Charles Woodson	F95N9J	Jeff Garcia	II32H7B
Chris Hovan	F14C6J	Jeremy Newberry	J77Y8C
Clinton Portis	Z28D2V	Jeremy Shockey	R34X5T
Corey Simon	R11D7K	Jerry Porter	F71Q9Z
Courtney Brown	R42R75	Jerry Rice	K34F8S
Curtis Martin	K47X3G	Jevon Kearse	A78B1C
Dallas Coach	O24U1Q	Jim Haslett	G78R3W
Damien Woody	E57K9Y	Jim Mora Jr.	N46C3M
Damien Woody	F78I1I	Jimmy Smith	I22J5W
Dante Hall	B23P8D	Joe Horn	P91A1Q
Dat Nguyen	Q86I2S	John Fox	Q98R7Y
Daunte Culpepper	O62O9K	Jon Gruden	H61I8A
Dave Wannstedt	W73D7D	Josh McCown	O33Y4X
David Boston	A25I9F	Julian Peterson	M89J8A
David Carr	C16E2Q	Julius Peppers	X54O4Z
Dennis Erickson	J83E3T	Junior Seau	W26K6Q
Dennis Green	C18J7T	Kabeer Gbaja-Biamala	U16I9Y
Derrick Brooks	P93I9Q	Keith Brooking	E12P4S
Derrick Mason	S98P3T	Keith Bulluck	M63N6V
Deuce Mcallister	D11H4J	Kendrell Bell	T96C7J
Dexter Coakley	L35K1A	Kevan Barlow	A23T5E
Dexter Jackson	G16B2I	Kevin Mawee	L76E6S
Dick Vermeil	F68V1W	Kris Jenkins	W6O3O3K
Dom Capers	B97I6R	Kyle Boller	A72F9X
Domanick Davis	L58S3J	Kyle Turley	Y46A8V
Donie Edwards	E18Y5Z	Ladainian Tomlinson	M64D4E
Donovin Darius	Q11T7T	Lavar Arrington	F19Q8W
Donovon Mcnabb	T98J1I	Laveranues Coles	R98I5S
Donte Stallworth	R75W3M	Lawyer Milloy	M37Y5B
Drew Bledsoe	W73M3E	La'roi Glover	K24L9K
Dre' Blv	Z68W8J	Lee Suggs	Z94X6Q

PLAYER	ENTER	PLAYER	ENTER
Leonard Davis	H14M2V	Rich Gannon	Q69I1Y
Lovie Smith	L38V3A	Richard Seymore	L69T4T
Marc Bulger	U66B4S	Ricky Williams	P19V1N
Marcel Shipp	R42X2L	Rod Smith	V22C4L
Marcus Stroud	E56I50	Rodney Harrison	O84I3J
Marcus Trufant	R46T5U	Rondel Barber	J72X8W
Mark Brunell	B66D9J	Roy Williams	J76C6F
Marshell Faulk	U76G1U	Rudi Johnson	W26J6H
Marty Booker	P51U4B	Sam Madison	Z87T5C
Marty Booker	H19Q2O	Samari Rolle	C69H4Z
Marty Shottenheimer	D96A7S	Santana Moss	H79E5B
Marvin Harrison	T11E80	Seattle Coach	V58U4Y
Marvin Lewis	P24S4H	Shaun Alexander	C95Z4P
Matt Hasselback	R68D5F	Shaun Ellis	Z54F2B
Michael Bennett	W81W2J	Shaun Rogers	J97X8M
Michael Strahan	O66T6K	Shawn Springs	J95K1J
Michael Vick	H67B1F	Simeon Rice	S62F9T
Mike Alstott	D89F6W	Stephen Davis	E39X9L
Mike Brown	F12J8N	Steve Mariucci	V74Q3N
Mike Martz	R64A8E	Steve Mcnair	S36T1I
Mike Mularkey	C56D6E	Steve Smith	W91O2O
Mike Rucker	K89O6S	T.J. Duckett	P67E1I
Mike Shanahan	H15L5Y	Takeo Spikes	B83A6C
Mike Sherman	F84X6K	Tedy Bruschi	K28Q3P
Mike Tice	Y31T6Y	Terence Newman	W57Y5P
New England Coach	N24L4Z	Terrell Suggs	V71A9Q
Nick Bernett	X95I7S	Tiki Barber	T43A2V
Norv Turner	F24K1M	Todd Heap	H19M1G
Olin Kreutz	R17R20	Tom Brady	X22V7E
Orlando Pace	U42U9U	Tom Coughlin	S71D6H
Patrick Surtain	H58T9X	Tony Dungy	Y96R8V
Peerless Price	X75V6K	Tony Gonzalez	N46E9N
Peter Warrick	D86P80	Torry Holt	W96U7E
Peyton Manning	L48H4U	Travis Henry	F36M2Q
Plaxico Burress	K18P6J	Trent Green	Y46M4S
Priest Holmes	X91N1L	Ty Law	F13W1Z
Quentin Jammer	V55S3Q	Walter Jones	G57P1P
Randy Moss	W79U7X	Washington Coach	W63V9L
Ray Lewis	B94X6V	Will Shields	B52S8A
Reggie Wayne	R29S8C	Zach Thomas	U63I3H
Rex Grossman	C46P2A		

MADDEN NFL 06

#55 DONOVAN MCNABB GOLD CARD

Select Madden Cards from My Madden. Then select Madden Codes and enter **8Q2J2X**.

#188 FIRST AND FIFTEEN BRONZE CARD

Select Madden Cards from My Madden. Then select Madden Codes and enter **2W4P9T**.

#189 FIRST AND FIVE BRONZE CARD

Select Madden Cards from My Madden. Then select Madden Codes and enter **2Y7L8B**.

#190 UNFORCED ERRORS BRONZE CARD

Select Madden Cards from My Madden. Then select Madden Codes and enter **2Z2F4H**.

#191 EXTRA CREDIT BRONZE CARD

Select Madden Cards from My Madden. Then select Madden Codes and enter **3D3Q3P**.

#192 TIGHT FIT BRONZE CARD

Select Madden Cards from My Madden. Then select Madden Codes and enter **3D8X6T**.

#193 5TH DOWN BRONZE CARD

Select Madden Cards from My Madden. Then select Madden Codes and enter **3E9R4V**.

#194 3RD DOWN BRONZE CARD

Select Madden Cards from My Madden. Then select Madden Codes and enter **3F9G4J**.

#195 HUMAN PLOW BRONZE CARD

Select Madden Cards from My Madden. Then select Madden Codes and enter **3H3U7F**.

#196 SUPER DIVE BRONZE CARD

Select Madden Cards from My Madden. Then select Madden Codes and enter **3H8M5U**.

#197 DA BOOT BRONZE CARD

Select Madden Cards from My Madden. Then select Madden Codes and enter **3J3S9Y**.

MAGIC: THE GATHERING—BATTLEGROUNDS

ALL QUESTS

At the Quest Select screen, press Left Trigger + Right Trigger, Down, Up, press the Left Thumbstick, White, Up, Right, Left, Down, Left Trigger + Right Trigger.

SECRET LEVEL

At the Arena Select screen, press Left Trigger + Right Trigger, Left, Up, **X**, Up, Right, **Y**, Left Trigger + Right Trigger.

ALL DUELISTS

At the Character Select screen, press Left Trigger + Right Trigger, Down, Up, **X**, White, Up, **X**, Black, Up, **X**, Left Trigger + Right Trigger.

MAJOR LEAGUE BASEBALL 2K5

ALL CHEATS
Create a new profile with the name **Ima Cheater**.

ALL CLASSIC TEAMS
Create a new profile with the name **Old Timers**.

ALL EXTRAS
Create a new profile with the name **Gimme Goods**.

MAJOR LEAGUE BASEBALL 2K5: WORLD SERIES EDITION

ALL CHEATS
Create a new profile with the name **Ima Cheater**.

ALL CLASSIC TEAMS
Create a new profile with the name **Old Timers**.

ALL EXTRAS
Create a new profile with the name **Gimme Goods**.

MAJOR LEAGUE BASEBALL 2K6

UNLOCK EVERYTHING
Select Enter Cheat Code from the My 2K6 menu and enter **Derek Jeter**.

TOPPS 2K STARS
Select Enter Cheat Code from the My 2K6 menu and enter **Dream Team**.

SUPER WALL CLIMB
Select Enter Cheat Code from the My 2K6 menu and enter **Last Chance**. Enable the cheats by selecting My Cheats or selecting Cheat Codes from the Options screen in-game.

SUPER PITCHES
Select Enter Cheat Code from the My 2K6 menu and enter **Unhittable**. Enable the cheats by selecting My Cheats or selecting Cheat Codes from the Options screen in-game.

ROCKET ARMS
Select Enter Cheat Code from the My 2K6 menu and enter **Gotcha**. Enable the cheats by selecting My Cheats or selecting Cheat Codes from the Options screen in-game.

BOUNCY BALL
Select Enter Cheat Code from the My 2K6 menu and enter **Crazy Hops**. Enable the cheats by selecting My Cheats or selecting Cheat Codes from the Options screen in-game.

MARVEL NEMESIS: RISE OF THE IMPERFECTS

UNLOCKS ALL FANTASTIC FOUR COMICS
Select Cheats from the Options screen and enter **SAVAGELAND**.

UNLOCKS ALL TOMORROW PEOPLE COMICS
Select Cheats from the Options screen and enter **NZONE**.

ELEKTRA BONUS CARD
Select Cheats from the Options screen and enter **THEHAND**.

SOLARA BONUS CARD
Select Cheats from the Options screen and enter **REIKO**.

STORM BONUS CARD
Select Cheats from the Options screen and enter **MONROE**.

MIDNIGHT CLUB II

Select Cheat Codes from the Options screen and enter the following:

ALL VEHICLES
Enter **hotwired**.

ALL CITIES IN ARCADE MODE
Enter **theworldismine**.

WEAPONS
Enter **lovenotwar**. Press the Left Thumbstick and White button to fire.

UNLIMITED NITROUS IN ARCADE MODE
Enter **zoomzoom4**.

ALL CAR ABILITIES
Enter **greasemonkey**.

EXTRA STAT
Enter **bigbrother**.

GAME SPEED
Enter one of the following (0 is the slowest, while 9 is the fastest):

    howfastcanitbe0
    howfastcanitbe1
    howfastcanitbe2
    howfastcanitbe3
    howfastcanitbe4
    howfastcanitbe5
    howfastcanitbe6
    howfastcanitbe7
    howfastcanitbe8
    howfastcanitbe9

CHANGE DIFFICULTY
Enter one of the following (0 is the easiest, while 9 is the most difficult):

    howhardcanitbe0
    howhardcanitbe1
    howhardcanitbe2
    howhardcanitbe3
    howhardcanitbe4
    howhardcanitbe5
    howhardcanitbe6
    howhardcanitbe7
    howhardcanitbe8
    howhardcanitbe9

MIDNIGHT CLUB 3: DUB EDITION

ALL CITIES AND RACES IN ARCADE MODE
Select Cheat Codes from the Options screen and enter **urbansprawl**, **roadtrip** or **crosscountry**.

NO DAMAGE
Select Cheat Codes from the Options screen and enter **ontheroad**.

ARGO SPECIAL MOVE
Select Cheat Codes from the Options screen and enter **dfens**.

ROAR SPECIAL MOVE
Select Cheat Codes from the Options screen and enter **Rjnr**.

ZONE SPECIAL MOVE
Select Cheat Codes from the Options screen and enter **allin**.

ADD $1 TO CAREER MONEY
Select Cheat Codes from the Options screen and enter **kubmir**.

SUBTRACT $1 OF CAREER MONEY
Select Cheat Codes from the Options screen and enter **rimbuk**.

BUNNY HEAD
Select Cheat Codes from the Options screen and enter **getheadl**.

CHROME HEAD
Select Cheat Codes from the Options screen and enter **haveyouseenthisboy**.

FLAMING HEAD
Select Cheat Codes from the Options screen and enter **trythisathome**.

SNOWMAN HEAD
Select Cheat Codes from the Options screen and enter **getheadm**.

PUMPKIN HEAD
Select Cheat Codes from the Options screen and enter **getheadk**.

YELLOW SMILE HEAD
Select Cheat Codes from the Options screen and enter **getheadj**.

MLB SLUGFEST: LOADED

CHEATS
At the Match-Up screen, press **X**, **Y**, and **B** to enter the following codes, then press the appropriate direction. For example, for 16" Softball press **X** (x2), **Y** (x4), **B** (x2), then press Down.

CODE	ENTER	CODE	ENTER
Bone Bat	0-0-1 Up	Little League Mode	1-0-1 Down
Blade Bat	0-0-2 Up	16" Softball	2-4-2 Down
Ice Bat	0-0-3 Up	Rubber Bball	2-4-2 Up
Log Bat	0-0-4 Up	Tiny Head	2-0-0 Left
Spike Bat	0-0-5 Up	Big Head	2-0-0 Right
Whiffle Bat	0-0-4 Right	Alien Team	2-3-1 Down
Max Batting	3-0-0 Left	Bobblehead Team	1-3-3 Down
Max Power	0-3-0 Left	Casey team	2-3-3 Down
Max Speed	0-0-3 Left	Dolphin Team	1-0-2 Down
Unlimited Turbo	4-4-4 Down	Dwarf Team	1-0-3 Down
Extra Time After Plays	1-2-3 Left	Eagle Team	2-1-2 Right

CODE	ENTER	CODE	ENTER
Evil Clown Team	2-1-1 Down	Scorpion Team	1 1-2 Down
Gladiator Team	1-1-3 Down	Terry Fitzgerald Team	3-3-3 Right
Horse Team	2-1-1 Right	Todd McFarlane Team	2-2-2 Right
Lion Team	2-2-0 Right	Atlantis Stadium	3-2-1 Left
Minotaur Team	1-1-0 Down	Coliseum Stadium	3-3-3 Up
Napalitano Team	2-3-2 Down	Empire Park Stadium	3-2-1 Right
Olshan Team	2-2-2 Down	Forbidden City Stadium	3-3-3 Left
Pinto Team	2-1-0 Right	Midway Park Stadium	3-2-1 Down
Rivera Team	2-2-2 Up	Monument Stadium	3-3-3 Down
Rodeo Clown Team	1-3-2 Down	Rocket Park Stadium	3-2-1 Up

MOTOCROSS MANIA 3

ALL TRACKS
At the Main menu, press Up, Left, Down, Right, Up, Left, Down, Left, Left, **X**.

ALL RIDERS AND BIKES
At the Main menu, press Up, Left, Down, Right, Up, Left, Down, Up, **X**.

ALL BIKE UPGRADES
At the Main menu, press Up, Left, Down, Right, Up, Down, Down, Left, Down, **X**.

ALL WEAPONS AND ARMOR
At the Main menu, press Up, Left, Down, Right, Up, Left, Down, Left, Down, **X**.

FREESTYLE
At the Main menu, press Up, Left, Down, Right, Up, Left, Down, Left, Left, **X**. Go to another menu and back out to access Freestyle.

MVP 06 NCAA BASEBALL

ALL CHALLENGE ITEMS
In Dynasty Mode, create a player with the name **Dee Jay Randall**.

LEVEL 1 CHALLENGE ITEMS
In Dynasty Mode, create a player with the name **Peter Termouth**.

ALL LEVEL 2 CHALLENGE ITEMS
In Dynasty Mode, create a player with the name **Trey Smith**.

MVP BASEBALL 2005

ALL STADIUMS, PLAYERS, UNIFORMS, & REWARDS
Create a player named **Katie Roy**.

GOOD HITTER WITH BIG BAT
Create a player named **Isaiah Paterson**, **Jacob Paterson** or **Keegan Paterson**.

BONE-SCALING CHEAT
Create a player named **Kenny Lee**.

MX vs. ATV UNLEASHED

UNLOCK EVERYTHING
Select Cheat Codes from the Options screen and enter **TOOLAZY**.

1,000,000 POINTS
Select Cheat Codes from the Options screen and enter **BROKEASAJOKE**. After entering the code, press Done multiple times for more points.

ALL PRO RIDERS
Select Cheat Codes from the Options screen and enter **WANNABE**.

ALL GEAR
Select Cheat Codes from the Options screen and enter **WARDROBE**.

50CC BIKE CLASS
Select Cheat Codes from the Options screen and enter **MINIMOTO**.

ALL MACHINES
Select Cheat Codes from the Options screen and enter **LEADFOOT**.

ALL FREESTYLE TRACKS
Select Cheat Codes from the Options screen and enter **HUCKIT**.

NASCAR 06: TOTAL TEAM CONTROL

UNLOCK EVERYTHING
In Fight to the Top mode, select Edit Driver. Enter **Gimme Gimme** as the first and last names.

$10,000,000
In Fight to the Top mode, select Edit Driver. Enter **Walmart Money** as the first and last names.

WALMART DRIVER AND TRACK
In Fight to the Top mode, select Edit Driver. Enter **Walmart Exclusive** as the first and last names.

MAX FAN LEVEL
In Fight to the Top mode, select Edit Driver. Enter **Super Star** as the first and last names.

MAX PRESTIGE
In Fight to the Top mode, select Edit Driver. **Enter MeMyself** AndI as the first and last names.

MAX TEAM PRESTIGE
In Fight to the Top mode, select Edit Driver. Enter **All ForOne** as the first and last names.

NASCAR 2005: CHASE FOR THE CUP

DALE EARNHARDT
At the Edit Driver screen, enter **The Intimidator** as your name.

$10,000,000
At the Edit Driver screen, enter **Walmart NASCAR** as your name.

2,000,000 PRESTIGE POINTS
At the Edit Driver screen, enter **You TheMan** as your name.

Exclusive Track
At the Edit Driver screen, enter Walmart Exclusive as your name.

All Thunder Plates
At the Edit Driver screen, enter Open Sesame as your name.

NBA 2K6

CELEBRITY STREET OPTION

Select Codes from the Features menu and enter **ballers**.

2KSPORTS TEAM

Select Codes from the Features menu and enter **2ksports**.

2K6 TEAM

Select Codes from the Features menu and enter **nba2k6**.

VC TEAM

Select Codes from the Features menu and enter **vcteam**.

NIKE SHOX MTX SHOES

Select Codes from the Features menu and enter **crazylift**.

NIKE ZOOM 20-5-5 SHOES

Select Codes from the Features menu and enter **lebronsummerkicks**.

NIKE ZOOM KOBE 1 SHOES

Select Codes from the Features menu and enter **kobe**.

NIKE ZOOM LEBRON III ALL-STAR COLORWAY SHOES

Select Codes from the Features menu and enter **lb allstar**.

NIKE ZOOM LEBRON III BLACK/CRIMSON SHOES

Select Codes from the Features menu and enter **lb crimsonblack**.

NIKE ZOOM LEBRON III SPECIAL BIRTHDAY EDITION SHOES

Select Codes from the Features menu and enter **lb bday**.

NIKE ZOOM LEBRON III WHITE/GOLD SHOES

Select Codes from the Features menu and enter **lb whitegold**.

NIKE UP TEMPO PRO SHOES

Select Codes from the Features menu and enter **anklebreakers**.

N

ALTERNATE UNIFORMS

To access various uniforms, select Codes from the Features menu and enter the following to unlock the different uniforms:

UNIFORM	ENTER
2006 All-Star	fanfavorites
St. Patrick's Day	gogreen
Bulls Retro	chi retro
Cavaliers Alternate	cle 2nd
Celtics Alternate	bos 2nd
Clippers Retro	lac retro
Grizzlies Retro	mem retro
Heat Retro	mia retro
Hornets Retro	no retro
Kings Alternate	sac 2nd
Knicks Retro	ny retro
Magic Retro	orl retro
Nets Retro	nj retro
Nuggets Alternate	den 2nd
2005-06 Pacers	31andonly

Pistons Alternate	det 2nd
Rockets Retro	hou retro
Sonics Retro	sea retro
Suns Retro	phx retro
Wizards Retro	was retro

+10 BONUS FOR DEFENSIVE AWARENESS

Find the PowerBar vending machine in The Crib. Choose Enter Code and enter **lockdown**.

+10 BONUS FOR OFFENSIVE AWARENESS

Find the PowerBar vending machine in The Crib. Choose Enter Code and enter **getaclue**.

MAX DURABILITY

Find the PowerBar vending machine in The Crib. Choose Enter Code and enter **noinjury**.

UNLIMITED STAMINA

Find the PowerBar vending machine in The Crib. Choose Enter Code and enter **nrgmax**.

POWERBAR TATTOO

Find the PowerBar vending machine in The Crib. Choose Enter Code and enter **pbink**. You can now use this feature in the game's Create Player feature.

ALL ITEMS IN THE CRIB

Find the PowerBar vending machine in The Crib. Choose Enter Code and enter **criball**.

NBA BALLERS

VERSUS SCREEN CHEATS

You can enter the following codes at the Vs screen. The **X** button corresponds to the first number in the code, the **Y** is the second number, and the **B** button corresponds to the last number. Press the D-pad in any direction to enter the code.

CODE	ENTER	CODE	ENTER
Tournament Mode	011	2x Juice Replenish	431
Big Head	134	Stunt Ability	374
Baby Ballers	423	Pass 2 Friend Ability	536
Kid Ballers	433	Alley-Oop Ability	725
Young Ballers1	443	Put Back Ability	313
Paper Ballers	354	Legal Goal Tending	756
Alternate Gear	123	Show Shot Percentage	012
Expanded Move Set	512	R2R Mode	008
Super Push	315	Play as Coach	567
Super Block Ability	124	Play as Agent	557
Great Handles	332	Play as Secretary	547
Unlimited Juice	763	Play as BiznezMan-A	537
Super Steals	215	Play as BiznezMan-B	527
Perfect Free Throws	327	Play as Afro Man	517
Speedy Players	213	Super Back-Ins	235
Better Free Throws	317	Half House	367
Fire Ability	722	Random Moves	300
Hotspot Ability	627	Pygmy	425
Back-In Ability	122		

PHRASE-OLOGY CODES/ALTERNATE GEAR

Select Phrase-ology from the Inside Stuff option and enter the following codes to unlock the Alternate Gear for the corresponding player.

PLAYER	PHRASE
Allan Houston	KNICKER BOCKER PLEASE
Allen Iverson	KILLER CROSSOVER
Alonzo Mourning	ZO
Amare Stoudemire	RISING SUN
Antoine Walker	BALL HAWK
Baron Davis	STYLIN' & PROFILIN'
Ben Wallace	RADIO CONTROLLED CARS
Bill Russell	CELTICS DYNASTY
Bill Walton	TOWERS OF POWER
Carmelo Anthony	NEW TO THE GAME
Chris Webber	24 SECONDS
Clyde Drexler	CLYDE THE GLIDE
Darko Milicic	NBA FASTBREAK
Darryl Dawkins	RIM WRECKER
Dejaun Wagner	NBA HANGTIME
Dikembe Mutumbo	IN THE PAINT
Dominique Wilkins	DUNK FEST
Eddie Jones	BALLER UPRISING
Elton Brand	REBOUND
Manu Ginobili	MANU
Gary Payton	GLOVE IS IN LA
George Gervin	THE ICE MAN COMETH
Grant Hill	GONE GOLD WITH IT
Isiah Thomas	TRUE BALLER
Jalen Rose	BRING IT
Jason Kidd	PASS THE ROCK
Jason Terry	BALL ABOVE ALL
Jason Williams	GIVE AND GO
Jerry Stackhouse	STOP DROP AND ROLL
John Stockton	COURT VISION
Julius Irving	ONE ON ONE
Karl Malone	SPECIAL DELIVERY
Kenyon Martin	TO THE HOLE
Kevin Garnett	BOSS HOSS
Kevin McHale	HOLLA BACK
Kobe Bryant	JAPANESE STEAK
Larry Bird	HOOSIER
Latrell Sprewell	SPREE
Lebron James	KING JAMES
Magic Johnson	LAKER LEGENDS
Michael Finley	STUDENT OF THE GAME
Mike Bibby	DREAMS & SCHEMES

PLAYER	PHRASE
Moses Malone	LOST FREESTYLE FILES
Nate "Tiny" Archibald	NATE THE SKATE
Nene Hilario	RAGS TO RICHES
Oscar Robertson	AINT NO THING
Pau Gasol	POW POW POW
Paul Pierce	CELTICS SUPREME
Pete Maravich	PISTOL PETE
Rashard Lewis	FAST FORWARD
Rasheed Wallace	BRING Down THE HOUSE
Ray Allen	ALL STAR
Reggie Miller	FROM DownTOWN
Richard Hamilton	RIP
Robert Parish	THE CHIEF
Scottie Pippen	PLAYMAKER
Shaquille O'Neal	DIESEL RULES THE PAINT
Shawn Marion	MAKE YOUR MARK
Stephon Marbury	PLATINUM PLAYA
Steve Francis	ANKLE BREAKER
Steve Francis	RISING STAR
Steve Nash	HAIR CANADA
Tim Duncan	MAKE IT TAKE IT
Tony Parker	RUN AND SHOOT
Tracy McGrady	LIVING LIKE A BALLER
Vince Carter	CHECK MY CRIB
Wally Szczerbiak	WORLD
Walt Frazier	PENETRATE AND PERPETRATE
Wes Unseld	OLD SCHOOL
Willis Reed	HALL OF FAME
Wilt Chamberlain	WILT THE STILT
Yao Ming	CENTER OF ATTENTION

CRIBS

Select Phrase-ology from the Inside Stuff option and enter the following to unlock player cribs.

CRIB	PHRASE
Allen Iverson's Recording Studio	THE ANSWER
Karl Malone's Devonshire Estate	ICE HOUSE
Kobe Bryant's Italian Estate	EURO CRIB
Scottie Pippen's Yacht	NICE YACHT
Yao Ming's Childhood Grade School	PREP SCHOOL

OTHER PHRASE-OLOGY CODES

Select Phrase-ology from the Inside Stuff option and enter the following to unlock that bonus.

BONUS	PHRASE
All Players, Alternate Gear, and Cinemas	NBA BALLERS TRUE PLAYA
Special Movie #1	JUICE HOUSE
Special Movie #2	NBA SHOWTIME
Special Movie #3	NBA BALLERS RULES
Special Movie #4	HATCHET MAN
Special Movie #5	SLAM IT
Special Shoe #2	COLD STREAK
Special Shoe #3	LOST YA SHOES

NBA BALLERS: PHENOM

VERSUS SCREEN CHEATS

Enter the following codes at the Vs screen. The **X** button corresponds to the first number in the code, the **Y** is the second number, and the **B** button corresponds to the last number. Press the D-pad in any direction to enter the code.

EFFECT	CODE
Tournament Mode	0 1 1
Big Head	1 3 4
Kid Ballers	4 3 3
Speedy Players	2 1 3
Alternate Gear	1 2 3

NBA LIVE 2004

Create a player with the following last name:

ALEKSANDER PAVLOVIC
Enter **WHSUCPOI**.

ANDREAS GLYNIADAKIS
Enter **POCKDLEK**.

CARLOS DELFINO
Enter **SDFGURKL**.

JAMES LANG
Enter **NBVKSMCN**.

JERMAINE DUPRI
Enter **SOSODEF**.

KYLE KORVER
Enter **OEISNDLA**.

MALICK BADIANE
Enter **SKENXIDO**.

MARIO AUSTIN
Enter **POSNEGHX**.

MATT BONNER
Enter **BBVDKCVM**.

NEDZAD SINANOVIC
Enter **ZXDSDRKE**.

PACCELIS MORLENDE
Enter **QWPOASZX**.

REMON VAN DE HARE
Enter **ITNVCJSD**.

RICK RICKERT
Enter **POILKJMN**.

SZYMON SZEWCZYK
Enter **POIOIJIS**.

SANI BECIROVIC
Enter **ZXCCVDRI**.

TOMMY SMITH
Enter **XCFWQASE**.

SOFOKLIS SCHORTSANITIS
Enter **IOUBFDCJ**.

XUE YUYANG
Enter **WMZKCOI**.

Select NBA Codes from the My NBA LIVE option and enter the following:

15,000 NBA STORE POINTS
Enter **87843H5F9P**.

ALL TEAM GEAR
Enter **YREY5625WQ**.

ALL HARDWOOD CLASSIC JERSEYS
Enter **725JKUpLMM**.

ALL SHOES
Enter **POUY985GY5**.

ALL NBA GEAR
Enter **ERT9976KJ3**.

UNLOCK SHOES
Select My NBA Live and enter the following NBA Codes to unlock the different shoes:

SHOES	ENTER
Air Bounds (black/white/blue)	7YSS0292KE
Air Bounds (white/black)	JA807YAM20
Air Bounds (white/green)	84HHST61QI
Air Flight 89 (black/white)	FG874JND84
Air Flight 89 (white/black)	63RBVC7423
Air Flight 89 (white/red)	GF9845JIIR4
Air Flightposite 2 (blue/gray)	2389JASE3E
Air Flightposite (white/black/gray)	74FDH7K94S
Air Flightposite (white/black)	6HJ874SFJ7
TtAir Flightposite (yellow/black/white)	MN54BV45C2
Air Flightposite 2 (blue/gray)	RB84UJHAS2
Air Flightposite 2 (blue/gray)	2389JASE3E
Air Foamposite 1 (blue)	OP5465UX12
Air Foamposite 1 (white/black/red)	D0D843HH7F
Air Foamposite Pro (blue/black)	DG56TRF446
Air Foamposite Pro (black/gray)	3245AFSD45
Air Foamposite Pro (red/black)	DSAKF38422
Air Force Max (black)	F84N845H92
Air Force Max (white/black/blue)	985KJF98KJ
Air Force Max (white/red)	8734HU8FFF
Air Hyperflight (white)	14TGU7DEWC
Air Hyperflight (black/white)	WW44YHU592

SHOES	ENTER
Air Hyperflight (blue/white)	A0K374HF8S
Air Hyperflight (yellow/black)	JCX93LSS88
Air Jordan 11 (black/red/white)	GF64H76ZX5
Air Jordan 11 (black/varsity royal/white)	HJ987RTGFA
Air Jordan 11 (cool grey)	GF75HG6332
Air Jordan 11 (white)	HG76HN765S
Air Jordan 11 (white/black)	A2S35TH7H6
Air Jordan 3 (white)	G9845HJ8F4
Air Jordan 3 (white/clay)	435SGF555Y
Air Jordan 3 (white/fire red)	RE6556TT90
Air Jordan 3 (white/true blue)	FDS9D74J4F
Air Jordan 3 (black/white/gray)	CVJ554TJ58
Air Max2 CB (black/white)	87HZXGFIU8
Air Max2 CB (white/red)	4545GFKJIU
Air Max2 Uptempo (black/white/blue)	NF8745J87F
Air Max Elite (black)	A4CD54T7TD
Air Max Elite (white/black)	966ERTFG65
Air Max Elite (white/blue)	FD9KN48FJF
Air Zoom Flight (gray/white)	367UEY6SN
Air Zoom Flight (white/blue)	92387HDO77
Zoom Generation (white/black/red)	23LBJNUMB1
Zoom Generation (black/red/white)	LBJ23CAVS1
Nike Blazer (khaki)	W3R57U9NB2
Nike Blazer (tan/white/blue)	DCT5YHMU90
Nike Blazer (white/orange/blue)	4G66JU99XS
Nike Blazer (black)	XCV6456NNL
Nike Shox BB4 (black)	WE424TY563
Nike Shox BB4 (white/black)	23ERT85LP9
Nike Shox BB4 (white/light purple)	668YYTRB12
Nike Shox BB4 (white/red)	424TREU777
Nike Shox VCIII (black)	SDFH764FJU
Nike Shox VCIII (white/black/red)	5JHD367JJT

NBA LIVE 06

EASTERN ALL-STARS 2005-06 AWAY JERSEYS
Select NBA Codes from My NBA Live and enter **XCVB5387EQ**.

EASTERN ALL-STARS 2005-06 HOME JERSEY
Select NBA Codes from My NBA Live and enter **234SDFGHMO**.

WESTERN ALL-STARS 2005-06 AWAY JERSEY
Select NBA Codes from My NBA Live and enter **39N56B679J**.

WESTERN ALL-STARS 2005-06 HOME JERSEY
Select NBA Codes from My NBA Live and enter **2J9UWABNP1**.

BOSTON CELTICS 2005-06 ALTERNATE JERSEY
Select NBA Codes from My NBA Live and enter **193KSHU88J**.

CLEVELAND CAVALIERS 2005-06 ALTERNATE JERSEY
Select NBA Codes from My NBA Live and enter **9922NVDKVT**.

DENVER NUGGETS 2005-06 ALTERNATE JERSEYS
Select NBA Codes from My NBA Live and enter **XWETJK72FC**.

DETROIT PISTONS 2005-06 ALTERNATE JERSEY
Select NBA Codes from My NBA Live and enter **JANTWIKBS6**.

INDIANA PACERS 2005-06 ALTERNATE AWAY JERSEY
Select NBA Codes from My NBA Live and enter **PSDF90PPJN**.

INDIANA PACERS 2005-06 ALTERNATE HOME JERSEY
Select NBA Codes from My NBA Live and enter **SDF786WSHW**.

SACRAMENTO KINGS 2005-06 ALTERNATE JERSEY
Select NBA Codes from My NBA Live and enter **654NNBFDWA**.

A3 GARNETT 3
Select NBA Codes from My NBA Live and enter **DRI239CZ49**.

JORDAN MELO V.5 WHITE & BLUE
Select NBA Codes from My NBA Live and enter **5223WERPII**.

JORDAN MELO V.5 WHITE & YELLOW
Select NBA Codes from My NBA Live and enter **ZXDR7362Q1**.

JORDAN XIV BLACK & RED
Select NBA Codes from My NBA Live and enter **144FVNHM35**.

JORDAN XIV WHITE & GREEN
Select NBA Codes from My NBA Live and enter **67YFH9839F**.

JORDAN XIV WHITE & RED
Select NBA Codes from My NBA Live and enter **743HFDRAU8**.

S. CARTER III LE
Select NBA Codes from My NBA Live and enter **JZ3SCARTVY**.

T-MAC 5 BLACK
Select NBA Codes from My NBA Live and enter **258SHQW95B**.

T-MAC 5 WHITE
Select NBA Codes from My NBA Live and enter **HGS83KP234P**.

ANSWER DMX 10
Select NBA Codes from My NBA Live and enter **RBKAIUSAB7**.

ANSWER IX AND THE RBK ANSWER IX VIDEO
Select NBA Codes from My NBA Live and enter **AI9BUBBA7T**.

THE QUESTION AND THE MESSAGE FROM ALLEN IVERSON VIDEO
Select NBA Codes from My NBA Live and enter **HOYAS3AI6L**.

NBA STREET VOL. 2

Select Pick Up Game, hold Left Trigger and enter the following codes when "Enter cheat codes now" appears at the bottom of the screen:

UNLIMITED TURBO
Press **X, X, Y, Y**.

ABA BALL
Press **B, X, B, X**.

WNBA BALL
Press **B, Y, Y, B**.

NO DISPLAY BARS
Press **X, B** (x3).

ALL JERSEYS
Press **B, Y, X, X**.

ALL COURTS
Press **X, Y, Y, X**.

ST. LUNATICS TEAM AND ALL STREET LEGENDS
Press **X, Y, B, Y**.

ALL NBA LEGENDS
Press **B, Y, Y, X**.

CLASSIC MICHAEL JORDAN
Press **B, Y, B, B**.

EXPLOSIVE RIMS
Press **B** (x3), **Y**.

SMALL PLAYERS
Press Y, Y, B, X.

ALL QUICKS
Press Y, B, Y, X.

BIG HEADS
Press B, X, X, B.

EASY SHOTS
Press Y, B, X, Y.

NO COUNTERS
Press Y, Y, B, B.

HARD SHOTS
Press Y, X, B, Y.

BALL TRAILS
Press Y, Y, Y, X.

NCAA FOOTBALL 2005

PENNANT CODES

At the Pennant Collection, press the Right Thumbstick and enter the following:

ENTER	CODE
EA Sports	Cuffed Cheat
Thanks	1st and 15
Sic Em	Baylor Power-up
For	Blink (ball spotted short)
Registering	Boing (dropped passes)
Tiburon	Crossed the Line
Oskee Wow	Illinois Team Boost
Hike	Jumbalaya
Home Field	Molasses Cheat
Elite 11	QB Dud
NCAA	Stiffed
Football	Take Your Time
Fight	Texas Tech Team Boost
2005	Thread The Needle
Tech Triumph	Virginia Tech Team Boost
Blitz	What a Hit
Fumble	2003 All-Americans
Roll Tide	Alabama All-time
Raising Cane	Miami All-time
Go Blue	Michigan All-time
Hail State	Mississippi State All-time
Go Big Red	Nebraska All-time
Rah Rah	North Carolina All-time
We Are	Penn State All-time
Death Valley	Clemson All-time
Glory	Colorado All-time
Victory	Kansas State All-time
Quack Attack	Oregon All-time
Fight On	USC All-time
Bow Down	Washington All-time
Bear Down	Arizona mascot team

ENTER	CODE
WooPigSooie	Arkansas All-time
War Eagle	Auburn All-time
U Rah Rah	Badgers All-time
Great To Be	Florida All-time
Great To Be	Florida All-time
Uprising	Florida State All-time
Hunker Down	Georgia All-time
On Iowa	Iowa All-time
Geaux Tigers	LSU All-time
Golden Domer	Notre Dame All-time
Boomer	Oklahoma All-time
Go Pokes	Oklahoma State All-time
Lets Go Pitt	Pittsburgh All-time
Boiler Up	Purdue All-time
Orange Crush	Syracuse All-time
Big Orange	Tennessee All-time
Gig Em	Texas A&M All-time
Hook Em	Texas All-time
Mighty	UCLA All-time
Killer Bucks	Ohio State All-time
Killer Nuts	Ohio State All-time
Wahoos	Virginia All-time
Ramblinwreck	Georgia Tech Mascot Team
Red And Gold	Iowa St. Mascot Team
Rock Chalk	Kansas Mascot Team
On On UK	Kentucky Mascot Team
Go Green	Michigan State Mascot Team
Rah Rah Rah	Minnesota Mascot Team
Mizzou Rah	Missouri Mascot Team
Go Pack	NC State Mascot Team
Go Cats	NU Mascot Team
Hotty Totty	Ole Miss Mascot Team
Hail WV	West Virginia Mascot Team
Go Deacs Go	Wake Forest Mascot Team
All Hail	WSU Mascot Team

NCAA FOOTBALL 06

PENNANT CODES

Select Pennant Collection from My NCAA. Press Select and enter the following codes:

CODE	ENTER	CODE	ENTER
Sic Em	#16 Baylor	Registering	#202 Boing
Oskee Wow	#63 Illinois	With EA	#204 Butter Fingers
Fight	#160 Texas Tech	Tiburon	#205 Crossed The Line
Thanks	#200 First and Fifteen	EA Sports	#206 Cuffed
For	#201 Blink	Touchdown	#207 Extra Credit

CODE	ENTER	CODE	ENTER
In The Zone	#208 Helium	Rah Rah	#290 All-North Carolina
Turnover	#209 Hurricane	Golden Domer	#291 All-Notre Dame
Impact	#210 Instant Freplay	Killer Nuts	#292 All-Ohio State
Heisman	#211 Jumbalaya	Boomer	#293 All-Oklahoma
Game Time	#212 Molasses	Go Pokes	#294 All-Oklahoma State
Break Free	#213 Nike Free	Quack Attack	#295 All-Oregeon
Hand Picked	#214 Nike Magnigrip	We Are	#296 All-Penn State
No Sweat	#215 Nike Pro	Lets Go Pitt	#297 All-Pittsburgh
Light Speed	#216 Nike Speed TD	Boiler Up	#298 All-Purdue
Elite 11	#219 QB Dud	Orange Crush	#299 All-Syracuse
NCAA	#222 Stiffed	Big Orange	#300 All-Tennessee
Football	#224 Take Your Time	Hook Em	#301 All-Texas
06	#225 Thread & Needle	Gig Em	#302 All-Texas A&M
Offense	#226 Tough As Nails	Mighty	#303 All-UCLA
Defense	#227 Trip	Fight On	#304 All-USC
Blitz	#228 What a Hit!	Wahoos	#305 All-Virginia
Sideline	#229 Kicker Hex	Tech Triumph	#306 All-Virginia Tech
Fumble	#273 2004 All-Americans	Bow Down	#307 All-Washington
Roll Tide	#274 All-Alabama	U Rah Rah	#308 All-Wisconsin
Woopigsooie	#276 All-Arkansas	Bear Down	#311 Ark Mascot
War Eagle	#277 All-Auburn	Red And Gold	#333 ISU Mascot
Death Valley	#278 All-Clemson	Rock Chalk	#335 KU Mascot
Glory	#279 All-Colorado	Go Green	#346 Michigan State Mascot
Great To Be	#280 All-Florida		
Uprising	#281 All-FSU	Rah Rah Rah	#341 Minn Mascot
Hunker Down	#282 All Georgia	Hotty Totty	#342 Miss Mascot
On Iowa	#283 All-Iowa	Mizzou Rah	#344 Mizzou Mascot
Victory	#284 All-Kansas State	Go Pack	#349 NCSU Mascot
Geaux Tigers	#285 All-LSU	Go Cats	#352 NU Mascot
Raising Cane	#286 All-Miami	On On UK	#371 UK Mascot
Go Blue	#287 All-Michigan	Go Deacs Go	#382 Wake Mascot
Hail State	#288 All-Mississippi State	All Hail	#385 WSU Mascot
Go Big Red	#289 All-Nebraska	Hail WV	#386 WVU Mascot

NCAA MARCH MADNESS 06

ALL TEAMS
Select My NCAA, then Cheat Codes from the lounge. Enter **PSDF9078VT**.

AIR JORDAN III SHOES
Select My NCAA, then Cheat Codes from the lounge. Enter **39N56BXC4S**.

FIRST AIR JORDANS
Select My NCAA, then Cheat Codes from the lounge. Enter **2J9UWAS44L**.

NEED FOR SPEED MOST WANTED

BURGER KING CHALLENGE
At the Title screen, press Up, Down, Up, Down, Left, Right, Left, Right.

CASTROL SYNTEC VERSION OF THE FORD GT
At the Title screen, press Left, Right, Left, Right, Up, Down, Up, Down.

MARKER FOR BACKROOM OF ONE-STOP SHOP
At the Title screen, press Up, Up, Down, Down, Left, Right, Up, Down.

PORSCHE CAYMAN
At the Title screen, press Left Trigger, Right Trigger, Right Trigger, Right Trigger, Right, Left, Right, Down.

NEED FOR SPEED UNDERGROUND 2

ALL CIRCUIT TRACKS
At the Main menu, press Down, Right Trigger, Right Trigger, Right Trigger, Black, Black, Black, **X**.

BEST BUY VINYL
At the Main menu, press Up, Down, Up, Down, Down, Up, Right, Left.

BURGER KING VINYL
At the Main menu, press Up, Up, Up, Up, Down, Up, Up, Left.

H2 CAPONE
At the Main menu, press Up, Left, Up, Up, Down, Left, Down, Left.

NISSIAN SKYLINE
At the Main menu, press Down, Down, Left Trigger, White, Left Trigger, White, Left Trigger, Down.

LEVEL 1 PERFORMANCE PARTS
At the Main menu, press Left Trigger, Right Trigger, Left Trigger, Right Trigger, Left, Left, Right, Up.

LEVEL 2 PERFORMANCE PARTS
At the Main menu, press Right Trigger, Right Trigger, Left Trigger, Right Trigger, Left, Right, Up, Down.

LEVEL 1 VISUAL PARTS
At the Main menu, press Right Trigger, Right Trigger, Up, Down, Left Trigger, Left Trigger, Up, Down.

LEVEL 2 VISUAL PARTS
At the Main menu, press Left Trigger, Right Trigger, Up, Down, Left Trigger, Up, Up, Down.

NFL STREET 2

FUMBLE MODE IN QUICK GAME
Enter **GreasedPig** as a code.

MAX CATCH IN QUICK GAME
Enter **MagnetHands** as a code.

NO CHAINS MODE IN QUICK GAME
Enter **NoChains** as a code.

NO FUMBLE MODE IN QUICK GAME
Enter **GlueHands** as a code.

UNLIMITED TURBO IN QUICK GAME
Enter **NozBoost** as a code.

EA FIELD
Enter **EAField** as a code.

AFC EAST ALL-STARS
Enter **EAASFSCT** as a code.

AFC NORTH ALL-STARS
Enter **NAOFRCTH** as a code.

AFC SOUTH ALL-STARS
Enter **SAOFUCTH** as a code.

AFC WEST ALL-STARS
Enter **WAEFSCT** as a code.

NFC EAST ALL-STARS
Enter **NNOFRCTH** as a code.

NFC NORTH ALL-STARS
Enter **NNAS66784** as a code.

NFC SOUTH ALL-STARS
Enter **SNOFUCTH** as a code.

NFC WEST ALL-STARS
Enter **ENASFSCT** as a code.

TEAM REEBOK
Enter **Reebok** as a code.

TEAM XZIBIT
Enter **TeamXzibit** as a code.

NHL 2K6

UNLOCK EVERYTHING
Select Manage Profiles from the Options screen. Create a New Profile with the name **Turco813**.

NIGHTCASTER

TEMPORARY INVINCIBILITY
Pause the game, hold Left Trigger + Right Trigger and press Left, Left, Up, Down.

ODDWORLD STRANGER'S WRATH

CHEAT MODE
During a game, insert a controller in port 2. Remove the controller and press **X, X, Y, Y, B, B, A, A** on controller 1.

INVINCIBILITY
After entering the Cheat Mode code, press **X, Y, A, B, X, Y.**

$1000
After entering the Cheat Mode code, press Left Thumbstick, Left Thumbstick, Right Thumbstick, Right Thumbstick, Left Thumbstick, Left Thumbstick, Right Thumbstick, Right Thumbstick. You can repeat this code multiple times.

OUTRUN 2

Select OutRun Challenge and go to the Gallery screen. Choose Enter Code and input the following:

ALL CARS
Enter **DREAMING**.

ALL MISSION STAGES
Enter **THEJOURNEY**.

BONUS TRACKS
Enter **TIMELESS**.

REVERSE TRACKS
Enter **DESREVER**.

ALL MUSIC
Enter **RADIOSEGA**.

ORIGINAL OUTRUN
Enter **NINETEEN86**.

ALL CARDS
Enter **BIRTHDAY**.

OUTRUN 2006: COAST 2 COAST

100% COMPLETE/UNLOCK EVERYTHING
Edit your license and change the name to **ENTIRETY**. Select Done, then back out of all menus.

1,000,000 OUTRUN MILES
Edit your license and change the name to **MILESANDMILES**. Select Done, then back out of all menus.

PANZER DRAGOON ORTA

ORIGINAL PANZER DRAGOON CODES
The following codes are for the original Panzer Dragoon. Unlock it first by defeating the game or playing for five hours. After doing so, enter the following codes at the Main menu of the original Panzer Dragoon.

INVINCIBLE
Press Left Trigger, Left Trigger, Right Trigger, Right Trigger, Up, Down, Left, Right.

STAGE SELECT
Press Up, Up, Down, Down, Left, Right, Left, Right, **X**, **Y**, White.

PLAY STAGE 0
Press Up, Up, Up, Down, Down, Down, Left, Right, Left, Right, Left, Right, Left Trigger, Right Trigger.

ROLLING MODE
Press Up, Right, Down, Left, Up, Right, Down, Left, Up, Right, Down, Left, Up, Right, Down, Left.

WIZARD MODE (FASTER GAMEPLAY)
Press Left Trigger, Right Trigger, Left Trigger, Right Trigger, Up, Down, Up, Down, Left, Right.

WATCH ENDING
Press Up, Up, Down, Up, Right, Right, Left, Right, Down, Down, Up, Down, Left, Left, Right, Left.

PETER JACKSON'S KING KONG: THE OFFICIAL GAME OF THE MOVIE

At the Main menu, hold Left Trigger + Right Trigger and press Down, **X**, Up, **Y**, Down, Down, Up, Up. Release Left Trigger + Right Trigger to get the Cheat option on the menu. The Cheat option is also available on the pause menu.

GOD MODE
Select Cheat and enter **8wonder**

ALL CHAPTERS
Select Cheat and enter **KKst0ry**.

AMMO 999
Select Cheat and enter **KK 999 mun**.

MACHINE GUN
Select Cheat and enter **KKcapone**.

REVOLVER
Select Cheat and enter **KKtigun**.

SNIPER RIFLE
Select Cheat and enter **KKsn1per**.

INFINITE SPEARS
Select Cheat and enter **lance 1nf**.

ONE-HIT KILLS
Select Cheat and enter **GrosBras**.

EXTRAS
Select Cheat and enter **KKmuseum**.

PINBALL HALL OF FAME: THE GOTTLIEB COLLECTION

LOVE METER MACHINE
Enter **LUV** at the Codes screen.

PAYOUT MODE
Enter **LAS** at the Codes screen.

XOLTEN MACHINE
Enter **XTN** at the Codes screen.

FACTORY TOUR
Enter **DGC** at the Codes screen

PRINCE OF PERSIA: THE SANDS OF TIME

CLASSIC PRINCE OF PERSIA ROOM
Start a new game. Then while on the balcony, press Left Thumbstick, **A, X, Y, B, Y, A, X, B**.

CLASSIC PASSWORDS

LEVEL	PASSWORD
Level 2	KIEJSC
Level 3	VNNNPC
Level 4	IYVPTC
Level 5	RWSWWC
Level 6	GONWUC
Level 7	DEFNUC
Level 8	SVZMSC
Level 9	DBJRPC
Level 10	MZFYSC
Level 11	BRAYQC
Level 12	UUGTPC
Battle with Jafar	LRARUC

PSYCHONAUTS

ALL POWERS
During a game, hold Left Trigger + Right Trigger and press **B**, **B**, **Y**, White, Left Thumbstick, **Y**.

9999 LIVES
During a game, hold Left Trigger + Right Trigger and press Left Thumbstick, White, White, **B**, **A**, Right Thumbstick.

9999 AMMO (BLAST, CONFUSION)
During a game, hold Left Trigger + Right Trigger and press Right Thumbstick, **A**, Left Thumbstick, Left Thumbstick, **Y**, **B**.

GLOBAL ITEMS (NO PSI-BALL COLORIZER, NO DREAM FLUFFS)
During a game, hold Left Trigger + Right Trigger and press Right Thumbstick, **B**, White, White, Left Thumbstick, **Y**.

ALL POWERS UPGRADED (MAX RANK)
During a game, hold Left Trigger + Right Trigger and press Left Thumbstick, Right Thumbstick, Left Thumbstick, White, **B**, White.

9999 ARROWHEADS
During a game, hold Left Trigger + Right Trigger and press **A**, Right Thumbstick, Right Thumbstick, White, **Y**, **X**.

INVINCIBILITY
During a game, hold Left Trigger + Right Trigger and press **B**, White, **B**, **B**, **Y**, Black.

WEIRD TEXT
During a game, hold Left Trigger + Right Trigger and press White, **A**, click Left Thumbstick, White, White, **B**.

RALLISPORT CHALLENGE 2

CARS AND TRACKS SET 1
Select Credits from the Options screen and press Down, Left, Down, Right, Up, Up.

CARS AND TRACKS SET 2
Select Credits from the Options screen and press Left, Left, Down, Down, Right, Right.

CARS AND TRACKS SET 3
Select Credits from the Options screen and press Down, Down, Left, Left, Up, Down.

CARS AND TRACKS SET 4
Select Credits from the Options and press Right, Down, Right, Down, Left, Up.

CARS AND TRACKS SET 5
Select Credits from the Options screen and press Left, Left, Right, Right, Down, Left.

CARS AND TRACKS SET 6
Select Credits from the Options screen and press Right, Up, Up, Up, Down, Left.

CARS AND TRACKS SET 7
Select Credits from the Options screen and press Left, Left, Left, Up, Up, Right.

CARS AND TRACKS SET 8
Select Credits from the Options screen and press Right, Up, Left, Up, Down, Right.

CARS AND TRACKS SET 9
Select Credits from the Options screen and press Down, Up, Down, Left, Left, Down.

CARS AND TRACKS SET 10
Select Credits from the Options screen and press Up, Up, Down, Down, Left, Right.

ROBOTECH: INVASION

Select Extras from the Options screen to enter the following codes:

INVINCIBILITY
Enter **supercyc**.

UNLIMMITED AMMO
Enter **trgrhpy**.

ONE-HIT KILLS
Enter **dustyayres**.

ALL LEVELS
Enter **reclamation**.

LANCER'S MULTIPLAYER SKIN
Enter **yllwfllw**.

SCOTT BERNARD'S MULTIPLAYER SKIN
Enter **ltntcmdr**.

RAND'S MULTIPLAYER SKIN
Enter **kidgloves**.

ROOK'S MULTIPLAYER SKIN
Enter **blueangls**.

ROBOTS

BIG HEAD FOR RODNEY
Pause the game and press Up, Down, Down, Up, Right, Right, Left, Right.

UNLIMITED HEALTH
Pause the game and press Up, Right, Down, Up, Left, Down, Right, Left.

UNLIMITED SCRAP
Pause the game and press Down, Down, Left, Up, Up, Right, Up, Down.

RUGBY LEAGUE 2

UNLOCK EVERYTHING
Create a player with the name **Darren Unlockyer**.

BIG HANDS
Create a player with the name **Jumbo Mittens**.

BIG HEADS
Create a player with the name **Planetoid**.

SMALL HEADS
Create a player with the name **micro noggin**.

BIG MUSCLES
Create a player with the name **Dale P Pugh**.

FAT PLAYERS
Create a player with the name **Cakemaster 3000**.

SKINNY PLAYERS
Create a player with the name **Crash Diet**.

TIRE IN BODY
Create a player with the name **Junkinthetrunk**.

TOGGLE MATRIX KICKING OFF
Create a player with the name **There is no spoon**.

SCALER

FULL HEALTH
Pause the game, select Audio from the Options screen and press Right Trigger, Left Trigger, Right Trigger, Left Trigger, Y, Y, X, X, Right Trigger, X.

200,000 KLOKKIES
Pause the game, select Audio from the Options screen and press Left Trigger, Left Trigger, Right Trigger, Right Trigger, Y, X, Y.

INFINITE ELECTRIC BOMBS
Pause the game, select Audio from the Options screen and press Right Trigger, Right Trigger, Left Trigger, Left Trigger, Y, Y, X.

SECRET WEAPONS OVER NORMANDY

ALL PLANES, ENVIRONMENTS, GALLERY, & MISSIONS
At the Main menu, press Y, Y, Y, X, X, X, Left Trigger, Right Trigger, Black, Black, White White.

ALL ENVIRONMENTS IN INSTANT ACTION
At the Main menu, press Up, Down, Left, Right, Left Trigger, Right Trigger, Left Trigger, Right Trigger.

INVINCIBILITY
At the Main menu, press Up, Down, Left, Right, Left, Left, Right, Right, Left Trigger, Left Trigger, Right Trigger, Right Trigger, White, Black.

UNLIMITED AMMUNITION
At the Main menu, press Up, Right, Down, Left, Up, Right, Down, Left, Left Trigger, Right Trigger.

BIG HEADS
At the Main menu, press Right, Up, Left, Down, Right, Up, Left, Down, Right, Left Trigger, Right Trigger, Left Trigger, Right Trigger.

SHATTERED UNION

SKIP CURRENT WEEK IN CAMPAIGN MODE
At the US Map, press Start for the Options. Then select Cheat Menu and press X, Y, X, B, A.

WIN CIVIL WAR IN CAMPAIGN MODE
At the US Map, press Start for the Options. Then select Cheat Menu and press X, B, A, B, Y.

$100,000
At the US Map, press Start for the Options. Then select Cheat Menu and press X, X, A, A, Y.

ARCADIA PLAINS
At the US Map, press Start for the Options. Then select Cheat Menu and press B, X, X, X, A.

ARIZONA TERRITORY
At the US Map, press Start for the Options. Then select Cheat Menu and press B, X, X, A, X.

CAROLINAS
At the US Map, press Start for the Options. Then select Cheat Menu and press **B, X, Y, X, A**.

CENTRAL CASCADES
At the US Map, press Start for the Options. Then select Cheat Menu and press **B, X, X, X, Y**.

CENTRAL HEARTLAND
At the US Map, press Start for the Options. Then select Cheat Menu and press **B, X, X, B, Y**.

CUMBERLANDS
At the US Map, press Start for the Options. Then select Cheat Menu and press **B, X, Y, X, Y**.

DAKOTAS
At the US Map, press Start for the Options. Then select Cheat Menu and press **B, X, X, B, X**.

EASTERN SHENANDOAH
At the US Map, press Start for the Options. Then select Cheat Menu and press **B, X, Y, Y, B**.

FLORIDA
At the US Map, press Start for the Options. Then select Cheat Menu and press **B, X, Y, X, B**.

GREAT BASIN
At the US Map, press Start for the Options. Then select Cheat Menu and press **B, X, X, Y, A**.

GREAT LAKES
At the US Map, press Start for the Options. Then select Cheat Menu and press **B, X, X, B, A**.

GREAT PLAINS
At the US Map, press Start for the Options. Then select Cheat Menu and press **B, X, X, B, B**.

MISSISSIPPI DELTA
At the US Map, press Start for the Options. Then select Cheat Menu and press **B, X, Y, X, X**.

NEW MEXICO
At the US Map, press Start for the Options. Then select Cheat Menu and press **B, X, X, Y, B**.

NEW YORK
At the US Map, press Start for the Options. Then select Cheat Menu and press **B, X, Y, Y, Y**.

NORTHERN CALIFORNIA
At the US Map, press Start for the Options. Then select Cheat Menu and press **B, X, X, Y, X**.

NORTHERN CASCADES
At the US Map, press Start for the Options. Then select Cheat Menu and press **B, X, X, X, B**.

NORTHERN NEW ENGLAND
At the US Map, press Start for the Options. Then select Cheat Menu and press **B, X, Y, Y, A**.

NORTHERN TEXAS
At the US Map, press Start for the Options. Then select Cheat Menu and press **B, X, X, A, A**.

OHIO VALLEY
At the US Map, press Start for the Options. Then select Cheat Menu and press **B, X, Y, Y, X**.

OKLAHOMA GRASSLANDS
At the US Map, press Start for the Options. Then select Cheat Menu and press **B, X, X, A, Y**.

SOUTHEASTERN CASCADES
At the US Map, press Start for the Options. Then select Cheat Menu and press **B, X, X, X, X**.

SOUTHERN CALIFORNIA
At the US Map, press Start for the Options. Then select Cheat Menu and press **B, X, X, Y, Y**.

SOUTHERN TEXAS
At the US Map, press Start for the Options. Then select Cheat Menu and press **B, X, X, A, B**.

SHREK 2

BONUS GAMES

Pause the game and select Scrapbook. Press Left, Up, **A**, **B**, Left, Up, **A**, **B**, Left, Up, **A**, **B**, **X**, **B**, **X**, **B**, **X**, **B**. Exit the level and select Bonus to access the games.

CHAPTER SELECT

Pause the game and select Scrapbook. Press Left, Up, **A**, **B**, Left, Up, **A**, **B**, Left, Up, **A**, **B**, Up (x5). Exit the level and choose Chapter Select to change chapters.

FULL HEALTH

Pause the game and select Scrapbook. Press Left, Up, **A**, **B**, Left, Up, **A**, **B**, Left, Up, **A**, **B**, Up, Right, Down, Left, Up.

1,000 COINS

Pause the game and select Scrapbook. Press Left, Up, **A**, **B**, Left, Up, **A**, **B**, Left, Up, **A**, **B** (x6).

SHREK SUPERSLAM

ALL CHALLENGES

At the Title screen, press **Y**, **Y**, **Y**, **B**, **B**, **B**, **Y**, **X**, **B**, **X**, **X**, **X**, Up, Down, Left, Right, Left Trigger, Right Trigger.

SUPER SPEED MODIFIER

At the Title screen, press Left Trigger, Left Trigger, Right Trigger, Right Trigger, Left Trigger, Right Trigger, Left Trigger, Right Trigger, **X**, **B**, **Y**, **Y**.

PIZZA ONE

At the Title screen, press Up, Up, **Y**, **Y**, Right, Right, **B**, **B**, Down, Down, Left Trigger, Right Trigger, Left, Left, **X**, **X**, Left Trigger, Right Trigger.

PIZZA TWO

At the Title screen, press **B**, **B**, **X**, **X**, Right Trigger, Right Trigger, Left, Left, Left Trigger, Left Trigger.

PIZZA THREE

At the Title screen, press Down, Down, Right, **B**, Up, **Y**, Left, **X**, Left Trigger, Left Trigger.

SLAMMAGEDDON

At the Title screen, press Up, Up, Down, Down, Left, Right, Left, Right, **Y**, **X**, **X**, Left Trigger, Right Trigger.

SID MEIER'S PIRATES!

FOOD NEVER DWINDLES

Name your character **Sweet Tooth**.

INVINCIBLE SHIP

Name your character **Bloody Bones Baz**.

JEFF BRIGGS AS ABBOTT

Name your character **Firaxis**.

SNAPPY DRESSER

Name your character **Bonus Frag**.

THE SIMS 2

During gameplay, press Left Trigger, Right Trigger, Up on D-pad, **A**, Black. Now you can enter the following cheats:

ALL LOCATIONS
Press **B**, White, Left, **B**, Up, **B**.

ALL CLOTHES
Press **X**, Black, Down, Right, **X**.

ALL OBJECTS
Press White, **B**, Down, Left, Up.

ALL RECIPES
Press Black, **X**, Up, Down, Right, **A**.

MAX ALL MOTIVES
Press Up, **B**, Up, Right, White.

§10,000
Press Right Trigger, Left Trigger, Black, Right, Left.

CHANGES SIM'S SKILL
Press **Y**, **B**, **X**, Black, D-pad Left.

JUMP AHEAD SIX HOURS
Press **B**, **X**, Left Trigger, Up, Down.

REMOVE MESSAGES
Press Right, Up, Right, Down, Right, Up, Down, Right.

THE SIMS BUSTIN' OUT

Pause the game to enter the following codes. Note that you must enter the Enable Cheats code first. After entering another code, select the gnome to access it.

ENABLE CHEATS
Press Right Trigger, Left Trigger, Down, Black, Left, **B**. A gnome appears in your yard when the code is entered correctly.

GIVE MONEY
Press Left Trigger, Black, Right, **X**, Left. Select the gnome to give money.

UNLOCK ALL LOCATIONS
Press Black, Down, Right Trigger, Left Trigger, Down, **Y**.

UNLOCK ALL OBJECTS
Press Black, Up, **Y**, Down, Right Trigger.

UNLOCK ALL SOCIAL OPTIONS
Press Left Trigger, Right Trigger, **A**, Down, Black.

SONIC HEROES

METAL CHARACTERS IN 2-PLAYER
After selecting a level in 2-Player mode, hold **A** + **Y**.

Comix Zone

INVINCIBILITY

Select the Jukebox from the Options screen and play the following tracks in order: 3, 12, 17, 2, 2, 10, 2, 7, 7, 11.

STAGE SELECT

Select the Jukebox from the Options screen and play the following tracks in order: 14, 15, 18, 5, 13, 1, 3, 18, 15, 6.

Dr. Robotnik's Mean Bean Machine

EASY PASSWORDS

Continue a game with the following passwords:

LEVEL	PASSWORD
2	Red Bean, Red Bean, Red Bean, Has Bean
3	Clear Bean, Purple Bean, Clear Bean, Green Bean
4	Red Bean, Clear Bean, Has Bean, Yellow Bean
5	Clear Bean, Blue Bean, Blue Bean, Purple Bean
6	Clear Bean, Red Bean, Clear Bean, Purple Bean
7	Purple Bean, Yellow Bean, Red Bean, Blue Bean
8	Yellow Bean, Green Bean, Purple Bean, Has Bean

LEVEL	PASSWORD
9	Yellow Bean, Purple Bean, Has Bean, Blue Bean
10	Red Bean, Yellow Bean, Clear Bean, Has Bean
11	Green Bean, Purple Bean, Blue Bean, Clear Bean
12	Red Bean, Has Bean, Has Bean, Yellow Bean
13	Yellow Bean, Has Bean, Blue Bean, Blue Bean

NORMAL PASSWORDS

LEVEL	PASSWORD
2	Has Bean, Clear Bean, Yellow Bean, Yellow Bean
3	Blue Bean, Clear Bean, Red Bean, Yellow Bean
4	Yellow Bean, Blue Bean, Clear Bean, Purple Bean
5	Has Bean, Green Bean, Blue Bean, Yellow Bean
6	Green Bean, Purple Bean, Purple Bean, Yellow Bean
7	Purple Bean, Blue Bean, Green Bean, Has Bean
8	Green Bean, Has Bean, Clear Bean, Yellow Bean
9	Blue Bean, Purple Bean, Has Bean, Has Bean
10	Has Bean, Red Bean, Yellow Bean, Clear Bean
11	Clear Bean, Red Bean, Red Bean, Blue Bean
12	Green Bean, Green Bean, Clear Bean, Yellow Bean
13	Purple Bean, Yellow Bean, Has Bean, Clear Bean

HARD PASSWORDS

LEVEL	PASSWORD
2	Green Bean, Clear Bean, Yellow Bean, Yellow Bean
3	Yellow Bean, Clear Bean, Purple Bean, Clear Bean
4	Blue Bean, Green Bean, Clear Bean, Blue Bean
5	Red Bean, Purple Bean, Green Bean, Green Bean
6	Yellow Bean, Yellow Bean, Clear Bean, Green Bean
7	Purple Bean, Clear Bean, Blue Bean, Blue Bean
8	Clear Bean, Yellow Bean, Has Bean, Yellow Bean
9	Purple Bean, Blue Bean, Blue Bean, Green Bean
10	Clear Bean, Green Bean, Red Bean, Yellow Bean
11	Blue Bean, Yellow Bean, Yellow Bean, Has Bean
12	Green Bean, Clear Bean, Clear Bean, Blue bean
13	Has Bean, Clear Bean, Purple Bean, Has Bean

HARDEST PASSWORDS

LEVEL	PASSWORD
2	Blue Bean, Blue Bean, Green Bean, Yellow Bean
3	Green Bean, Yellow Bean, Green Bean, Clear Bean
4	Purple Bean, Purple Bean, Red Bean, Has Bean
5	Green Bean, Red Bean, Purple Bean, Blue Bean
6	Blue Bean, Purple Bean, Green Bean, Yellow Bean
7	Blue Bean, Purple Bean, Green Bean, Has Bean
8	Clear Bean, Purple Bean, Has Bean, Yellow Bean
9	Purple Bean, Green Bean, Has Bean, Clear Bean
10	Green Bean, Blue Bean, Yellow Bean, Has Bean
11	Green Bean, Purple Bean, Has Bean, Red Bean
12	Red Bean, Green Bean, Has Bean, Blue Bean
13	Red Bean, Red Bean, Clear Bean, Yellow Bean

RISTAR

LEVEL SELECT
Enter **ILOVEU** as a password.

FIGHT ONLY BOSSES
Enter **MUSEUM** as a password.

TIME ATTACK
Enter **DOFEEL** as a password.

TONE DEAF SOUNDS
Enter **MAGURO** as a password.

TRUE SIGHT
Enter **MIEMIE** as a password.

SUPER HARD
Enter **SUPER** as a password.

VERY HARD
Enter **SUPERB** as a password.

CANCEL CODES
Enter **XXXXXX** as a password.

SPIDER-MAN 2

TREYARCH PASSWORD
Start a New Game and enter **HCRAYERT** as your name. This starts the
game at 44% complete, 201,000 Hero Points, some upgrades and more.

SPIKEOUT: BATTLE STREET

EASY MODE

Die twice and continue the game to unlock a new Easy Mode option.

SPONGEBOB SQUAREPANTS: BATTLE FOR BIKINI BOTTOM

The following codes must be entered quickly.

RESTORE HEALTH

Pause the game, hold Left Trigger + Right Trigger and press X, X, X, X, Y, X, Y, X, Y, Y, Y, Y.

EXPERT MODE

Pause the game, hold Left Trigger + Right Trigger and press X, X, X, Y, Y, X, X, X, Y, X, Y, Y, Y, X, Y, Y.

EARN 1,000 SHINY OBJECTS

Pause the game, hold Left Trigger + Right Trigger and press Y, X, X, Y, Y, X, X, Y.

EARN 10 GOLD SPATULAS

Pause the game, hold Left Trigger + Right Trigger and press X, Y, Y, X, X, Y, Y, X.

BUBBLE BOWL POWER-UP

Pause the game, hold Left Trigger + Right Trigger and press X, Y, X, Y, X, X, Y, Y. Press X to use.

CRUISE BUBBLE POWER-UP

Pause the game, hold Left Trigger + Right Trigger and press Y, X, Y, X, Y, Y, X, X.

INCREASE VALUE OF SHINY OBJECTS

Pause the game, hold Left Trigger + Right Trigger and press Y, X, Y, X, X, Y, X, X, X, Y, Y, Y, Y, X, X, Y.

MODIFIED CRUISE BUBBLE CONTROLS

Pause the game, hold Left Trigger + Right Trigger and press X, X, X, X, Y, Y, X, X, Y, Y, X, Y, Y.

VILLAGERS GIVE SHINY OBJECTS WHEN HIT

Pause the game, hold Left Trigger + Right Trigger and press Y, Y, Y, Y, Y, X, Y, X, X, Y, X, Y.

VILLAGERS RESTORE HEALTH WHEN NEAR

Pause the game, hold Left Trigger + Right Trigger and press Y, Y, Y, Y, Y, X, Y, X, X, X, Y, Y.

NO PANTS

Pause the game, hold Left Trigger + Right Trigger and press X, X, X, X, Y, X, X, Y, X, Y, Y, X.

BIG PLANKTON

Pause the game, hold Left Trigger + Right Trigger and press Y, Y, Y, Y, X, Y, X, Y, X, X, X, X.

SMALL CHARACTERS

Pause the game, hold Left Trigger + Right Trigger and press Y, Y, Y, Y, X, Y, X, Y, Y, Y, Y, Y.

SMALL VILLAGERS

Pause the game, hold Left Trigger + Right Trigger and press Y, Y, Y, Y, Y, X, Y, X, Y, X, Y, X.

SPONGEBOB BREAKS APART WHEN DEFEATED

Pause the game, hold Left Trigger + Right Trigger and press X, X, X, X, Y, Y, X, Y, X, X, X, Y.

INVERT LEFT/RIGHT CAMERA CONTROLS
Pause the game, hold Left Trigger + Right Trigger and press **Y**, **Y**, **X**, **X**, **X**, **X**, **Y**, **Y**.

INVERT UP/DOWN CAMERA CONTROLS
Pause the game, hold Left Trigger + Right Trigger and press **Y**, **X**, **X**, **X**, **X**, **X**, **X**, **Y**.

SPONGEBOB SQUAREPANTS: LIGHTS, CAMERA, PANTS!

SILVER STORY MODE
Select Rewards from the Bonuses menu, then select Codes and enter **486739**.

ALL ACTION FIGURES
Select Rewards from the Bonuses menu, then select Codes and enter **977548**.

HOOK, LINE & CHEDDAR GAME
Select Rewards from the Bonuses menu, then select Codes and enter **893634**.

SPONGEBOB SQUAREPANTS: THE MOVIE

ALL HEALTH
Pause the game, hold Left Trigger + Right Trigger and press **Y**, **Y**, **Y**, **Y**, **X**, **Y**, **X**, **Y**.

ALL TASKS
Pause the game, hold Left Trigger + Right Trigger and press **Y**, **X**, **Y**, **Y**, **X**, **Y**, **X**, **X**.

ALL MOVES
Pause the game, hold Left Trigger + Right Trigger and press **X**, **X**, **Y**, **X**, **Y**, **Y**, **X**, **X**.

ALL MOVES TO MACHO
Pause the game, hold Left Trigger + Right Trigger and press **X**, **X**, **Y**, **X**, **Y**, **Y**, **X**, **Y**.

SPONGEBOB CAVEMAN COSTUME
Pause the game, hold Left Trigger + Right Trigger and press **X**, **X**, **X**, **X**, **Y**, **X**, **X**, **X**.

SPONGEBOB RIPPED SHORTS COSTUME
Pause the game, hold Left Trigger + Right Trigger and press **X**, **X**, **X**, **X**, **Y**, **X**, **X**, **Y**.

PATRICK CAVEMAN COSTUME
Pause the game, hold Left Trigger + Right Trigger and press **X**, **X**, **X**, **X**, **Y**, **X**, **Y**, **Y**.

PATRICK GOOFY GOOBER COSTUME
Pause the game, hold Left Trigger + Right Trigger and press **X**, **X**, **X**, **X**, **Y**, **X**, **Y**, **X**.

SPY VS. SPY

ALL STORY MODE LEVELS
Select Cheats from the Extras menu, then enter **ANTONIO**.

ALL SINGLE-PLAYER MODERN MODE LEVELS
Select Cheats from the Extras menu, then enter **Prohias**.

MULTIPLAYER LEVELS
Select Cheats from the Extras menu, then enter **MADMAG**.

INVULNERABILITY
Select Cheats from the Extras menu, then enter **ARMOR**.

ALL SPY ATTACHMENTS
Select Cheats from the Extras menu, then enter **DISGUISE**.

PERMANENT FAIRY
Select Cheats from the Extras menu, then enter **FAIRY**.

SSX 3

CHEAT CHARACTERS

Select Options from the Main Menu. Next, choose Enter Cheat from the Options screen and enter the following codes to unlock each character. In the game, go to the Lodge and select Rider Details and choose Cheat Characters to find the new characters.

CHARACTER	ENTER	CHARACTER	ENTER
Brodi	zenmaster	Jurgen	brokenleg
Bunny San	wheresyourtail	Luther	bronco
Canhuck	greatwhitenorth	Marty	back2future
Churchill	tankengine	NW Legend	callhimgeorge
Cudmore	milkemdaisy	Snowballs	betyouveneverseen
Eddie	worm	Stretch	windmilldunk
Gutless	boneyardreject	Svelte Luther	notsosvelte
Hiro	slicksuit	Unknown Rider	finallymadeitin

OPEN ALL PEAKS
Enter **biggerthank7**.

PEAK 1 CLOTHES
Enter **shoppingspree**.

ALL PLAYLIST SONGS
Enter **djsuperstar**.

ALL POSTERS
Enter **postnobills**.

ALL ARTWORK
Enter **naturalconcept**.

ALL BOARDS
Enter **graphicdelight**.

ALL TOYS
Enter **nogluerequired**.

ALL TRADING CARDS
Enter **gotitgotitneedit**.

ALL VIDEOS
Enter **myeyesaredim**.

NEW THREADS
Select Cheats from the Extras menu and enter **FLYTHREADS**.

THE WORLD IS YOURS
Select Cheats from the Extras menu and enter **BACKSTAGEPASS**.

SHOW TIME (ALL MOVIES)
Select Cheats from the Extras menu and enter **THEBIGPICTURE**.

BLING BLING (INFINITE CASH)
Select Cheats from the Extras menu and enter **LOOTSNOOT**.

FULL BOOST, FULL TIME
Select Cheats from the Extras menu and enter **ZOOMJUICE**.

MONSTERS ARE LOOSE (MONSTER TRICKS)
Select Cheats from the Extras menu and enter **JACKALOPESTYLE**.

SNOWBALL FIGHT
Select Cheats from the Extras menu and enter **LETSPARTY**.

FEEL THE POWER (STAT BOOST)
Select Cheats from the Extras menu and enter **POWERPLAY**.

CHARACTERS ARE LOOSE
Select Cheats from the Extras menu and enter **ROADIEROUNDUp**.

UNLOCK CONRAD
Select Cheats from the Extras menu and enter **BIGPARTYTIME**.

UNLOCK NIGEL
Select Cheats from the Extras menu and enter **THREEISACROWD**.

UNLOCK MITCH KOOBSKI
Select Cheats from the Extras menu and enter **MOREFUNTHANONE**.

UNLOCK SKI PATROL
Select Cheats from the Extras menu and enter **FOURSOME**.

STARSKY AND HUTCH

UNLOCK EVERYTHING
Enter **VADKRAM** as a profile name.

STAR WARS: BATTLEFRONT

SMALL PEOPLE
Create a profile named **Jub Jub**.

STAR WARS EPISODE III: REVENGE OF THE SITH

INFINITE FORCE
Select Codes from the Settings menu and enter **KAIBURR**.

INFINITE HEALTH
Select Codes from the Settings menu and enter **XUCPHRA**.

QUICK HEALTH & FORCE RESTORATION
Select Codes from the Settings menu and enter **BELSAVIS**.

ALL STORY, BONUS & CO-OP MISSIONS AND DUELISTS
Select Codes from the Settings menu and enter **021282**.

ALL STORY MISSIONS
Select Codes from the Settings menu and enter **KORRIBAN**.

ALL BONUS MISSIONS
Select Codes from the Settings menu and enter **NARSHADDAA**.

ALL DUEL ARENAS
Select Codes from the Settings menu and enter **TANTIVIEV**.

ALL DUELISTS
Select Codes from the Settings menu and enter **ZABRAK**.

ALL POWERS & MOVES
Select Codes from the Settings menu and enter **JAINA**.

SUPER LIGHTSABER MODE
Select Codes from the Settings menu and enter **SUPERSABERS**.

TINY DRIOD MODE
Select Codes from the Settings menu and enter **071779**.

ALL REPLAY MOVIES
Select Codes from the Settings menu and enter **COMLINK**.

ALL CONCEPT ART
Select Codes from the Settings menu and enter **AAYLASECURA**.

STAR WARS KNIGHTS OF THE OLD REPUBLIC II: THE SITH LORDS

CHANGE VOICES
Add a controller to the fourth port and press Black or White to raise and lower character voices.

STAR WARS: OBI-WAN

ALL LEVELS
Create a Jedi with the name **GREYTHERAT**.

ALL LEVELS UP TO DARTH MAUL
Create a Jedi with the name **M1A2U3L4!?**.

STAR WARS REPUBLIC COMMANDO

GOD MODE
Pause the game and press **Y**, **Y**, Left Trigger, Up, **X**, Black, **X**, **Y**.

AMMO
Pause the game and press **Y**, **Y**, **X**, Down, Right Trigger, Left Trigger, Right Trigger, Up.

STOLEN

LEVEL SKIP
At the Title screen, press Right Trigger, Left Trigger, Start + Down.

99 OF ALL ITEMS
During gameplay, go to Equipment and press Right Trigger, Left Trigger, Right.

STRIKE FORCE BOWLING

ALL LEVELS
Name your bowler **!LEVELS!**.

ALL BOWLERS
Name your bowler **!BOWLER!**.

TAK: THE GREAT JUJU CHALLENGE

BONUS SOUND EFFECTS
In Juju's Potions, select Universal Card and enter the following numbers for Bugs, Crystals and Fruits: 20, 17, 5.

BONUS SOUND EFFECTS 2
In Juju's Potions, select Universal Card and enter the following numbers for Bugs, Crystals and Fruits: 50, 84, 92.

BONUS MUSIC TRACK 1
In Juju's Potions, select Universal Card and enter the following numbers for Bugs, Crystals and Fruits: 67, 8, 20.

BONUS MUSIC TRACK 2
In Juju's Potions, select Universal Card and enter the following numbers for Bugs, Crystals and Fruits: 6, 18, 3.

MAGIC PARTICLES
In Juju's Potions, select Universal Card and enter the following numbers for Bugs, Crystals and Fruits: 24, 40, 11.

MORE MAGIC PARTICLES
In Juju's Potions, select Universal Card and enter the following numbers for Bugs, Crystals and Fruits: 48, 57, 57.

VIEW JUJU CONCEPT ART
In Juju's Potions, select Universal Card and enter the following numbers for Bugs, Crystals and Fruits: Art 33, 22, 28.

VIEW VEHICLE ART
In Juju's Potions, select Universal Card and enter the following numbers for Bugs, Crystals and Fruits: 11, 55, 44.

VIEW WORLD ART
In Juju's Potions, select Universal Card and enter the following numbers for Bugs, Crystals and Fruits: 83, 49, 34.

TAK 2: THE STAFF OF DREAMS

BALLOON HEAD SHOWDOWN MINI-GAME
Select Universal Card from Juju Potions and enter the following numbers for Bugs, Crystals and Fruit: 48, 62, 19.

BARREL BLITZ MINI-GAME
Select Universal Card from Juju Potions and enter the following numbers for Bugs, Crystals and Fruit: 1, 105, 81.

CATAPULT CHAOS MINI-GAME
Select Universal Card from Juju Potions and enter the following numbers for Bugs, Crystals and Fruit: 103, 33, 20.

CHICKEN TENNIS MINI-GAME
Select Universal Card from Juju Potions and enter the following numbers for Bugs, Crystals and Fruit: 202, 17, 203.

CHUCKIN' CHICKENS MINI-GAME

Select Universal Card from Juju Potions and enter the following numbers for Bugs, Crystals and Fruit: 18, 71, 50.

DART TOOM DODGEM MINI-GAME

Select Universal Card from Juju Potions and enter the following numbers for Bugs, Crystals and Fruit: 83, 43, 142.

DINKY SNOWBOARD BIG AIR MINI-GAME

Select Universal Card from Juju Potions and enter the following numbers for Bugs, Crystals and Fruit: 233, 127, 204.

FLEA FLYER MINI-GAME

Select Universal Card from Juju Potions and enter the following numbers for Bugs, Crystals and Fruit: 22, 6, 17.

FROG DERBY MINI-GAME

Select Universal Card from Juju Potions and enter the following numbers for Bugs, Crystals and Fruit: 281, 62, 149.

GLIDE RIDE MINI-GAME

Select Universal Card from Juju Potions and enter the following numbers for Bugs, Crystals and Fruit: 131, 61, 179.

GLOOMLEAF ARENA MINI-GAME

Select Universal Card from Juju Potions and enter the following numbers for Bugs, Crystals and Fruit: 68, 13, 8.

KRASH KOURSE MINI-GAME

Select Universal Card from Juju Potions and enter the following numbers for Bugs, Crystals and Fruit: 5, 41, 41.

VINE CLIMB MINI-GAME

Select Universal Card from Juju Potions and enter the following numbers for Bugs, Crystals and Fruit: 8, 1, 3.

FAUNA IN MULTIPLAYER

Select Universal Card from Juju Potions and enter the following numbers for Bugs, Crystals and Fruit: 44, 13, 0.

JB IN MULTIPLAYER

Select Universal Card from Juju Potions and enter the following numbers for Bugs, Crystals and Fruit: 16, 19, 38.

LOK IN MULTIPLAYER

Select Universal Card from Juju Potions and enter the following numbers for Bugs, Crystals and Fruit: 2, 2, 5.

SKELETON JUJU SPIRIT IN MULTIPLAYER

Select Universal Card from Juju Potions and enter the following numbers for Bugs, Crystals and Fruit: 55, 171, 35.

TAK'S FEATHER COLOR

Select Universal Card from Juju Potions and enter the following numbers for Bugs, Crystals and Fruit: 4, 9, 23.

BETTER MANA MAGNET

Select Universal Card from Juju Potions and enter the following numbers for Bugs, Crystals and Fruit: 3, 27, 31.

TAK 1 GAME CINEMATIC SEQUENCE

Select Universal Card from Juju Potions and enter the following numbers for Bugs, Crystals and Fruit: 30, 21, 88.

CONCEPT ART
Select Universal Card from Juju Potions and enter the following numbers for Bugs, Crystals and Fruit: 30, 37, 51.

PICTURES OF THE TAK SUIT
Select Universal Card from Juju Potions and enter the following numbers for Bugs, Crystals and Fruit: 11, 4, 17.

SOUND EFFECTS SET ONE
Select Universal Card from Juju Potions and enter the following numbers for Bugs, Crystals and Fruit: 4, 55, 36.

VIEW COMMERICIALS
Select Universal Card from Juju Potions and enter the following numbers for Bugs, Crystals and Fruit: 6, 16, 6.

TAZ WANTED

ALL LEVELS
At the Start Game screen, select Marvin the Martian and enter **#OP**.

ALL BONUS GAMES
At the Start Game screen, select Daffy Duck and enter **?BN**.

2-PLAYER BOSS GAMES
At the Start Game screen, select Big red and enter ***JC**.

ART GALLERY
At the Start Game screen, select Tweety and enter **.RT**.

DISABLE WHACK IN THE BOXES
At the Start Game screen, select Taz and enter **!WB**.

TEENAGE MUTANT NINJA TURTLES 2: BATTLE NEXUS

Select Password from the Options screen and enter the following. Hold Left Trigger while selecting a turtle to get his New Nexus Turtle outfit.

CODE	PASSWORD
Challenge Code Abyss	SDSDRLD
Challenge Code Endurance	MRMDRMD
Challenge Code Fatal Blow	LRSRDRD
Challenge Code Lose Shuriken	RLMRDSL
Challenge Code Nightmare	SLSDRDL
Challenge Code Poison	DRSLLSR
Challenge Code Super-Tough	RDSRMRL
Cheat Code All-You-Can-Throw Shuriken	RSRLRSM
Cheat Code Health	DSRDMRM
Cheat Code Mighty Turtle	LSDRRDR
Cheat Code Pizza Paradise	MRLMRMR
Cheat Code Self Recovery	DRMSRLR
Cheat Code Squeaking	MLDSRDM
Cheat Code Super Defense Power	LDRMRLM
Cheat Code Super Offense Power	SDLSRLL
Cheat Code Toddling	SSSMRDD

CODE	PASSWORD
New Nexus Turtle outfit for Donatello	DSLRDRM
New Nexus Turtle outfit for Leonardo	LMRMDRD
New Nexus Turtle outfit for Michelangelo	MLMRDRM
New Nexus Turtle outfit for Raphael	RMSRMDR

TEENAGE MUTANT NINJA TURTLES 3: MUTANT NIGHTMARE

INVINCIBILITY
Select Passwords from the Options menu and enter **MDLDSSLR**.

HEALTH POWER-UPS TURN INTO SUSHI
Select Passwords from the Options menu and enter **SLLMRSLD**.

NO HEALTH POWER-UPS
Select Passwords from the Options menu and enter **DMLDMRLD**.

ONE-HIT DEFEATS TURTLE
Select Passwords from the Options menu and enter **LDMSLRDD**.

MAX OUGI
Select Passwords from the Options menu and enter **RRDMLSDL**.

UNLIMTED SHURIKEN
Select Passwords from the Options menu and enter **LMDRRMSR**.

NO SHURIKEN
Select Passwords from the Options menu and enter **LLMSRDMS**.

DOUBLE ENEMY ATTACK
Select Passwords from the Options menu and enter **MSRLSMML**.

DOUBLE ENEMY DEFENSE
Select Passwords from the Options menu and enter **SLRMLSSM**.

TOM & JERRY: WAR OF THE WHISKERS

REFILL HEALTH
Select Game Cheats from the Options screen and press **A, B, A, Y, Y, X, B, Y**.

ALL COSTUMES AND CHARACTERS
Select Game Cheats from the Options screen and press **B, B, A, X, B, Y, A, B**.

ALL MAPS IN VERSUS
Select Game Cheats from the Options screen and press **Y, B, Y, Y, A, X, B, X**.

TOMB RAIDER: LEGEND

The following codes must be unlocked in the game before using them.

BULLETPROOF

During gameplay, hold Left Trigger and press **A**, Right Trigger, **Y**, Right Trigger, **X**, Black.

DRAIN ENEMY HEALTH

During gameplay, hold Left Trigger and press **X**, **B**, **A**, Black, Right Trigger, **Y**.

INFINITE ASSAULT RIFLE AMMO

During gameplay, hold Black and press **A**, **B**, **A**, Left Trigger, **X**, **Y**.

INFINITE GRENADE LAUNCHER AMMO

During gameplay, hold Black and press Left Trigger, **Y**, Right Trigger, **B**, Left Trigger, **X**.

INFINITE SHOTGUN AMMO

During gameplay, hold Black and press Right Trigger, **B**, **X**, Left Trigger, **X**, **A**.

INFINITE SMG AMMO

During gameplay, hold Black and press **B**, **Y**, Left Trigger, Right Trigger, **A**, **B**.

EXCALIBUR

During gameplay, hold Black and press **Y**, **A**, **B**, Right Trigger, **Y**, Left Trigger.

SOUL REAVER

During gameplay, hold Black and press **A**, Right Trigger, **B**, Right Trigger, Left Trigger, **X**.

NO TEXTURE MODE

During gameplay, hold Left Trigger and press Black, **A**, **B**, **A**, **Y**, Right Trigger.

TIGER WOODS PGA TOUR 2005

Select Passwords from the Options screen and enter the following to unlock a variety of players, courses and other cool goodies:

CODE	ENTER
All Golfers and Courses	THEGIANTOYSTER
All Courses	THEWORLDISYOURS
All Accessories	TIGERMOBILE
The Roof in the Skillzone Game Mode	NIGHTGOLFER
Justin Timberlake	THETENNESSEEKID
Arnold Palmer	THEKING
Ben Hogan	PUREGOLF
Seve Ballesteros	THEMAGICIAN
Jack Nicklaus	GOLDENBEAR
Gary Player	BLACKKNIGHT
Tiffany "Tiff" Williamson	RICHGIRL
Jeb "Shooter" McGraw	SIXSHOOTER
Hunter "Steelhead" Elmore	GREENCOLLAR
Alastair" Captain" McFadden	NICESOCKS
Bev "Boomer" Buouchier	THEBEEHIVE

CODE	ENTER
Adriana "Sugar" Dulce	SOSWEET
Aphrodite Papadapolus	TEMPTING
Billy "Bear" Hightower	TOOTALL
Kendra "Spike" Lovette	ENGLISHPUNK
Dion "Double D" Douglas	DDDOUGLAS
Raquel "Rocky" Rogers	DOUBLER
Bunjiro "Bud" Tanaka	INTHEFAMILY
Ceasar "The Emperor" Rosado	LANDownER
Reginald "Reg" Weathers	REGGIE
The Hustler	ALTEREGO
Sunday Tiger Woods	NEWLEGEND
Adidas Items	91treSTR
Callaway Items	cgTR78qw
Cleveland Items	CL45etUB
Maxfli Items	FDGH597i
Nike Items	YJHk342B
Odyssey Items	kjnMR3qv
Ping Items	R453DrTe
Precept Items	BRi3498Z
TAG Items	cDsa2fgY
Tourstage Items	TS345329

T

TIGER WOODS PGA TOUR 06

ALL GOLFERS
Select Password from the Options screen and enter **WOOGLIN**.

ALL CLUBS
Select Password from the Options screen and enter **CLUB11**.

LEVEL 2 NIKE ITEMS
Select Password from the Options screen and enter **JUSTDOIT**.

ALL COURSES
Select Password from the Options screen and enter **ITSINTHEHOLE**.

TIGER WOODS IN HAT AND TIE
Select Password from the Options screen and enter **GOLDENAGE**.

TIGER WOODS IN STRIPED PANTS
Select Password from the Options screen and enter **TECHNICOLOR**.

TIGER WOODS IN OLD GOLF OUTFIT
Select Password from the Options screen and enter **OLDSKOOL**.

TIGER WOODS IN ALTERNATE OLD GOLF OUTFIT
Select Password from the Options screen and enter **THROWBACK**.

ARNOLD PALMER
Select Password from the Options screen and enter **ARNIESARMY**.

BEN HOGAN
Select Password from the Options screen and enter **THEHAWK**.

JACK NICKLAUS
Select Password from the Options screen and enter **GOLDENBEAR**.

OLD TOM MORRIS
Select Password from the Options screen and enter **FEATHERIE**.

TOMMY BLACK
Select Password from the Options screen and enter **IDONTHAVEAPROBLEM**.

WESLEY ROUNDER
Select Password from the Options screen and enter **POCKETPAIR**.

TIM BURTON'S THE NIGHTMARE BEFORE CHRISTMAS: OOGIE'S REVENGE

PUMPKIN KING AND SANTA JACK COSTUMES
During gameplay, press Down, Up, Right, Left, Left Thumbstick, Right Thumbstick.

TONY HAWK'S UNDERGROUND

Select Cheat Codes from the Options screen and enter the following codes. Pause the game and select Cheats from the Options screen to toggle the cheats on and off.

PERFECT RAIL
Enter **letitslide**.

PERFECT SKITCH
Enter **rearrider**.

PERFECT MANUAL
Enter **keepitsteady**.

MOON GRAVITY
Enter **getitup**.

TONY HAWK'S UNDERGROUND 2

Select Cheat Codes from the Game Options screen and enter the following. To access the cheats, pause the game and select Cheats to turn them on.

NATAS KAUPAS
Enter **bedizzy**.

NIGEL BEAVERHOPUSEN
Enter **skullet**.

PAULIE RYAN
Enter **4wheeler**.

PHIL MARGERA
Enter **notvito**.

ALL LEVELS
Enter **accesspass**.

ALWAYS SPECIAL CHEAT
Enter **likepaulie**.

PERFECT RAIL CHEAT
Enter **straightedge**.

ALL MOVIES
Enter **frontrowseat**.

TONY HAWK'S AMERICAN WASTELAND

ALWAYS SPECIAL

Select Cheat Codes from the Options screen and enter **uronfire**. Pause the game and select Cheats from the Game Options to enable the cheat.

PERFECT RAIL

Select Cheat Codes from the Options screen and enter **grindxpert**. Pause the game and select Cheats from the Game Options to enable the cheat.

PERFECT SKITCH

Select Cheat Codes from the Options screen and enter **h!tchar!de**. Pause the game and select Cheats from the Game Options to enable the cheat.

PERFECT MANUAL

Select Cheat Codes from the Options screen and enter **2wheels!**. Pause the game and select Cheats from the Game Options to enable the cheat.

MOON GRAVITY

Select Cheat Codes from the Options screen and enter **2them00n**. Pause the game and select Cheats from the Game Options to enable the cheat.

MAT HOFFMAN

Select Cheat Codes from the Options screen and enter **the_condor**.

JASON ELLIS

Select Cheat Codes from the Options screen and enter **sirius-dj**.

TY THE TASMANIAN TIGER 2: BUSH RESCUE

ALL BUNYIP KEYS

During a game, press Start, **Y**, Start, Start, **Y**, **X**, **B**, **X**, **A**.

ALL FIRST-LEVEL RANGS

During a game, press Start, **Y**, Start, Start, **Y**, **B**, **X**, **B**, **X**.

ALL SECOND-LEVEL RANGS

During a game, press Start, **Y**, Start, Start, **Y**, **X**, **B**, **X**, **Y**.

GET 100,000 OPALS

During a game, press Start, **Y**, Start, Start, **Y**, **B**, **A**, **B**, **A**.

CHEAT GNOME

During a game, press Left + **Y** + Down + **A** + **X**. Now you can enter the following cheats.

MAX ARTISTIC

Press **Y**, Down, Black, **A**, **B**.

MAX MENTAL

Press Left Trigger, **B**, **A**, Black, Down.

MAX PHYSTICAL

Press Left Trigger, Right Trigger, **A**, Down, Black.

ACQUIRE SKILL

Press Left Trigger, Black, Right, **X**, Left.

POWER SOCIAL

Press Down, Black, Right, **X**, Left.

TEAM PHOTO

At the Credits screen, press Up, Down, **X**, Up, Down.

TY THE TASMANIAN TIGER 3: NIGHT OF THE QUINKAN

100,000 OPALS
During a game, press Start, Start, Y, Start, Start, Y, B, A, B, A.

ALL RINGS
During a game, press Start, Start, Y, Start, Start, Y, B, X, B, X.

ULTIMATE SPIDER-MAN

ALL CHARACTERS
Pause the game and select Controller Setup from the Options screen. Press Right, Down, Right, Down, Left, Up, Left, Right.

ALL COVERS
Pause the game and select Controller Setup from the Options screen. Press Left, Left, Right, Left, Up, Left, Left, Down.

ALL CONCEPT ART
Pause the game and select Controller Setup from the Options screen. Press Down, Down, Down, Up, Down, Up, Left, Left.

ALL LANDMARKS
Pause the game and select Controller Setup from the Options screen. Press Up, Right, Down, Left, Down, Up, Right, Left.

WORLD CHAMPIONSHIP POOL 2004

PLACE CUE BALL ANYWHERE
At the Main menu, press Up, Down (x3), Left, Right, Down, Up.

WORLD RACING

ALL CARS
Enter **Full House** as a name.

ALL TRACKS
Enter **Free Ride** as a name.

ALL MISSIONS
Enter **Miss World** as a name.

ALL CHAMPIONSHIPS
Enter **JamSession** as a name.

ALMOST EVERY CAR
Enter **ALLUCANGET** as a name.

STATUS 1
Enter **Top 10** as a name.

STATUS 2
Enter **HUIBUH** as a name.

STATUS 3
Enter **N.I.C.E.** 2 as a name.

STATUS 4
Enter **TaxiDriver** as a name.

STATUS 5
Enter **Halbzeit** as a name.

STATUS 6
Enter **No Hat!** as a name.

STATUS 7
Enter **McRace** as a name.

STATUS 8
Enter **Jiu-Jitsu** as a name.

STATUS 9
Enter **Goodzpeed** as a name.

WRATH UNLEASHED

LARGE CHARACTERS
At the Title screen, press Left, **X**, Up, **Y**, Right, **B**, Down, **B**.

DOUBLE HEALTH AND SPEED
(VERSUS AND TEAM FIGHTER MODES)
At the Title screen, press Down, Down, Up, Down, Left, Right, Down, Up (x3), Right, Left, **X**.

ALTERNATE CHARACTERS (VERSUS MODE)
At the Character Select screen, press Left Trigger, Left Trigger, Down, Down, Black, White, Black, White, Right Trigger, Left Trigger, Black, Right Trigger, Right Trigger, White.

ALTERNATE CHARACTERS (TEAM FIGHTER MODE)
At the Title screen, press Left Trigger, Left Trigger, Down, Down, Black, White, Black, White, Right Trigger, Left Trigger, Black, Right Trigger (x3), White. Press the Black button for alternate characters.

WWE WRESTLEMANIA 21

ALL SHOPZONE UNLOCKED
At the Title screen, hold Left Trigger + Right Trigger, and press White + Black, press **X** + **Y** + **B** + **A**.

X-MEN LEGENDS II: RISE OF APOCALYPSE

ALL CHARACTERS
At the Team Management screen, press Right, Left, Left, Right, Up, Up, Up, Start.

ALL SKILLS
At the Team Management screen, press Left, Right, Left, Right, Down, Up, Start.

ALL SKINS
At the Team Management screen, press Down, Up, Left, Right, Up, Up, Start.

LEVEL 99
At the Team Management screen, press Up, Down, Up, Down, Left, Up, Left, Right, Start.

GOD MODE
Pause the game and press Down, Up, Down, Up, Right, Down, Right, Left, Start.

MOVE FASTER
Pause the game and press Up, Up, Up, Down, Up, Down, Start.

UNLIMITED XTREME TOKENS
Pause the game and press Left, Down, Right, Down, Up, Up, Down, Up, Start.

TOUCH OF DEATH
During a game, press Left, Left, Right, Left, Right, Up, Start.

100,000 TECH-BITS
At Forge or Beast's store, press Up, Up, Up, Down, Right, Right, Start.

ALL DANGER ROOM COURSES
At the Danger Room Course menu, press Right, Right, Left, Left, Up, Down, Up, Down, Start.

ALL COMICS
Select Review from the Main menu and press Right, Left, Left, Right, Up, Up, Right, Start.

ALL CINEMATICS
Select Review from the Main menu and press Left, Right, Right, Left, Down, Down, Left, Start.

ALL CONCEPTS
Select Review from the Main menu and press Left, Right, Left, Right, Up, Up, Down, Start.

ALL SCREENS
Select Review from the Main menu and press Right, Left, Right, Left, Up, Up, Down, Start.

X-MEN: THE OFFICIAL GAME

DANGER ROOM ICEMAN
At the Cerebro Files menu, press Right, Right, Left, Left, Down, Up, Down, Up, Start.

DANGER ROOM NIGHTCRAWLER
At the Cerebro Files menu, press Up, Up, Down, Down, Left, Right, Left, Right, Start.

DANGER ROOM WOLVERINE
At the Cerebro Files menu, press Down, Down, Up, Up, Right, Left, Right, Left, Start.

XGRA: EXTREME-G RACING ASSOCIATION

ALL LEVELS OF RACING
Enter **FREEPLAY** at the Cheat menu.

ALL TRACKS
Enter **WIBBLE** at the Cheat menu.

O2 LIVERIED
Enter **UCANDO** at the Cheat menu.

MESSAGE IN CREDITS
Enter **MUNCHKIN**, **EDDROOLZ** or **EDDIEPOO** at the Cheat menu.

YAGER

ALL LEVELS
Enter **lvl.activate 1** as a profile name.

9 CONTINUES
Enter set **MAXCNT 9** as a profile name.

COMPLETE DATABASE
Enter **data.setvis 1** as a profile name.

YU-GI-OH! THE DAWN OF DESTINY

COSMO QUEEN CARD IN DECK
Enter your name as **KONAMI**.

TRI-HORN DRAGON CARD IN DECK
Enter your name as **HEARTOFCARDS**.

ZERA THE MANT CARD IN DECK
Enter your name as **XBOX**.

ZAPPER

UNLIMITED LIVES
Pause the game, hold Left Trigger and press Up, Up, Up, Left, Left, Right, Left, Right.

UNLIMITED SHIELD
Pause the game, hold Left Trigger and press Up, Down, Up, Left, Right, Down, Up.

XBOX 360™

MAJOR LEAGUE BASEBALL 2K6

NBA 2K6

NBA LIVE 06

NHL 2K6

TIGER WOODS PGA TOUR 06

BASED ON A GAME RATED BY THE ESRB — T (TEEN)

AMPED 3

BATTLEFIELD 2: MODERN COMBAT

BLAZING ANGELS: SQUADRONS OF WWII

FIGHT NIGHT ROUND 3

FULL AUTO

NEED FOR SPEED MOST WANTED

PETER JACKSON'S KING KONG: THE OFFICIAL GAME OF THE MOVIE

TOMB RAIDER: LEGEND

TOM CLANCY'S GHOST RECON ADVANCED WARFIGHTER

TONY HAWK'S AMERICAN WASTELAND

Games Listing

AMPED 3

ALL SLEDS

Select Cheat Codes from the Options screen and press Right Trigger, X, Left Trigger, Down, Right, Left Bumper, Left Trigger, Right Trigger, Y, X.

ALL GEAR

Select Cheat Codes from the Options screen and press Y, Down, Up, Left, Right, Left Bumper, Right, Right Trigger, Right Trigger, Right Bumper.

A

ALL TRICKS

Select Cheat Codes from the Options screen and press Left Bumper, Right Trigger, Y, Up, Down, X, Left Trigger, Left, Right Bumper, Right Trigger.

ALL LEVELS

Select Cheat Codes from the Options screen and press X, Y, Up, Left, Left Bumper, Left Bumper, Right Trigger, X, Y, Left Trigger.

ALL CONFIGS

Select Cheat Codes from the Options screen and press Down, X, Right, Left Bumper, Right, Right Bumper, X, Right Trigger, Left Trigger, Y.

SUPER SPINS

Select Cheat Codes from the Options screen and press X (x4), Y (x3), X.

AWESOME METER ALWAYS FULL

Select Cheat Codes from the Options screen and press Up, Right Trigger, X, Y, Left Bumper, X, Down, Left Bumper, Right Trigger, Right Bumper.

ALL AWESOMENESS

Select Cheat Codes from the Options screen and press Right Bumper, Right Bumper, Down, Left, Up, Right Trigger, X, Right Bumper, X, X.

ALL BUILD LICENSES

Select Cheat Codes from the Options screen and press Left, Right Trigger, Left Bumper, Right Trigger, X, X, Y, Down, Up, X.

ALL BUILD OBJECTS

Select Cheat Codes from the Options screen and press Left Trigger, Right Trigger, Up, Up, Right Bumper, Left, Right, X, Y, Left Bumper.

ALL CHALLENGES

Select Cheat Codes from the Options screen and press Right, Left Bumper, Left Trigger, X, Left, Right Bumper, Right Trigger, Y, Left Trigger, X.

LOUD SPEAKERS

Select Cheat Codes from the Options screen and press Y, Right Trigger, Right Trigger, Left Bumper, Down, Down, Left, Left, Right, Left Bumper.

LOW GRAVITY BOARDERS

Select Cheat Codes from the Options screen and press Right Trigger, Down, Down, Up, X, Left Bumper, Y, Right Trigger, Y, Down.

NO AI

Select Cheat Codes from the Options screen and press X, X, Left Bumper, Down, Right, Right, Up, Y, Y, Left Trigger.

ALL MUSIC

Select Cheat Codes from the Options screen and press Up, Left, Right Trigger, Right Bumper, Right Trigger, Up, Down, Left, Y, Left Trigger.

BATTLEFIELD 2: MODERN COMBAT

ALL WEAPONS

During a game, hold Right Bumper + Left Bumper and quickly press Right, Right, Down, Up, Left, Left.

BLAZING ANGELS: SQUADRONS OF WWII

ALL MISSIONS, MEDALS, & PLANES

At the Main menu hold Left Trigger + Right Trigger and press X, Left Bumper, Right Bumper, Y, Y, Right Bumper, Left Bumper, X.

GOD MODE

Pause the game, hold Left Trigger and press X, Y, Y, X. Release Left Trigger, hold Right Trigger and press Y, X, X, Y. Re-enter the code to disable it.

INCREASED DAMAGE

Pause the game, hold Left Trigger and press Left Bumper, Left Bumper, Right Bumper. Release Left Trigger, hold Right Trigger and press Right Bumper, Right Bumper, Left Bumper. Re-enter the code to disable it.

FIGHT NIGHT ROUND 3

ALL VENUES

Create a champ with a first name of **NEWVIEW**.

FULL AUTO

ALL TRACKS, VEHICLES, & WEAPONS

Create a new profile with the name **magicman**.

MAJOR LEAGUE BASEBALL 2K6

UNLOCK EVERYTHING

Select Enter Cheat Code from the My 2K6 menu and enter **Derek Jeter**.

TOPPS 2K STARS

Select Enter Cheat Code from the My 2K6 menu and enter **Dream Team**.

SUPER WALL CLIMB
Select Enter Cheat Code from the My 2K6 menu and enter **Last Chance**. Enable the cheats by selecting My Cheats or selecting Cheat Codes from the in-game Options screen.

SUPER PITCHES
Select Enter Cheat Code from the My 2K6 menu and enter **Unhittable**. Enable the cheats by selecting My Cheats or selecting Cheat Codes from the in-game Options screen.

ROCKET ARMS
Select Enter Cheat Code from the My 2K6 menu and enter **Gotcha**. Enable the cheats by selecting My Cheats or selecting Cheat Codes from the in-game Options screen.

BOUNCY BALL
Select Enter Cheat Code from the My 2K6 menu and enter **Crazy Hops**. Enable the cheats by selecting My Cheats or selecting Cheat Codes from the in-game Options.

NBA 2K6

CELEBRITY STREET OPTION
Select Codes from the Features menu and enter **ballers**.

2KSPORTS TEAM
Select Codes from the Features menu and enter **2ksports**.

2K6 TEAM
Select Codes from the Features menu and enter **nba2k6**.

VC TEAM
Select Codes from the Features menu and enter **vcteam**.

NIKE SHOX MTX SHOES
Select Codes from the Features menu and enter **crazylift**.

NIKE ZOOM 20-5-5 SHOES
Select Codes from the Features menu and enter
lebronsummerkicks.

NIKE ZOOM KOBE 1 SHOES
Select Codes from the Features menu and enter **kobe**.

NIKE ZOOM LEBRON III ALL-STAR COLORWAY SHOES
Select Codes from the Features menu and enter **lb allstar**.

NIKE ZOOM LEBRON III BLACK/CRIMSON SHOES
Select Codes from the Features menu and enter **lb crimsonblack**.

NIKE ZOOM LEBRON III SPECIAL BIRTHDAY EDITION SHOES
Select Codes from the Features menu and enter **lb bday**.

NIKE ZOOM LEBRON III WHITE/GOLD SHOES
Select Codes from the Features menu and enter **lb whitegold**.

NIKE UP TEMPO PRO SHOES
Select Codes from the Features menu and enter **anklebreakers**.

2006 ALL-STAR UNIFORMS
Select Codes from the Features
menu and enter **fanfavorites**.

ST. PATRICK'S DAY UNIFORMS
Select Codes from the Features menu and enter **gogreen**.

BULLS RETRO UNIFORM
Select Codes from the Features
menu and enter **chi retro**.

CAVALIERS ALTERNATE UNIFORM
Select Codes from the Features menu and enter **cle 2nd**.

CELTICS ALTERNATE UNIFORM
Select Codes from the Features menu and enter **bos 2nd**.

CLIPPERS RETRO UNIFORM
Select Codes from the Features menu and enter **lac retro**.

GRIZZLIES RETRO UNIFORM
Select Codes from the Features menu and enter **mem retro**.

HEAT RETRO UNIFORM
Select Codes from the Features menu
and enter **mia retro**.

HORNETS RETRO UNIFORM
Select Codes from the Features
menu and enter **no retro**.

KINGS ALTERNATE UNIFORM
Select Codes from the Features menu and enter **sac 2nd**.

KNICKS RETRO UNIFORM
Select Codes from the Features menu and enter **ny retro**.

MAGIC RETRO UNIFORM
Select Codes from the Features menu and enter **orl retro**.

NETS RETRO UNIFORM
Select Codes from the Features
menu and enter **nj retro**.

NUGGETS ALTERNATE UNIFORM
Select Codes from the Features menu and enter **den 2nd**.

2005-06 PACERS UNIFORM
Select Codes from the Features menu and enter **31andonly**.

PISTONS ALTERNATE UNIFORM
Select Codes from the Features menu and enter **det 2nd**.

ROCKETS RETRO UNIFORM
Select Codes from the Features
menu and enter **hou retro**.

SONICS RETRO UNIFORM
Select Codes from the Features menu and enter **sea retro**.

SUNS RETRO UNIFORM
Select Codes from the Features menu and enter **phx retro**.

WIZARDS RETRO UNIFORM
Select Codes from the Features menu and enter **was retro**.

+10 BONUS FOR DEFENSIVE AWARENESS
Find the PowerBar vending machine in The Crib. Select Enter Code and enter **lockdown**.

+10 BONUS FOR OFFENSIVE AWARENESS
Find the PowerBar vending machine in The Crib. Select Enter Code and enter **getaclue**.

MAX DURABILITY
Find the PowerBar vending machine in The Crib. Select Enter Code and enter **noinjury**.

UNLIMITED STAMINA
Find the PowerBar vending machine in The Crib. Select Enter Code and enter **nrgmax**.

POWERBAR TATTOO
Find the PowerBar vending machine in The Crib. Select Enter Code and enter **pbink**. You can now use it in the game's Create Player feature.

NBA LIVE 06

EASTERN ALL-STARS 2005-06 AWAY JERSEYS
Select NBA Codes from My NBA Live and enter **XCVB5387EQ**.

EASTERN ALL-STARS 2005-06 HOME JERSEY
Select NBA Codes from My NBA Live and enter **234SDFGHMO**.

WESTERN ALL-STARS 2005-06 AWAY JERSEY
Select NBA Codes from My NBA Live and enter **39N56B679J**.

WESTERN ALL-STARS 2005-06 HOME JERSEY
Select NBA Codes from My NBA Live and enter **2J9UWABNP1**.

BOSTON CELTICS 2005-06 ALTERNATE JERSEY
Select NBA Codes from My NBA Live and enter **193KSHU88J**.

CLEVELAND CAVALIERS 2005-06 ALTERNATE JERSEY
Select NBA Codes from My NBA Live and enter **9922NVDKVT**.

DENVER NUGGETS 2005-06 ALTERNATE JERSEYS
Select NBA Codes from My NBA Live and enter **XWETJK72FC**.

DETROIT PISTONS 2005-06 ALTERNATE JERSEY
Select NBA Codes from My NBA Live and enter **JANTWIKBS6**.

INDIANA PACERS 2005-06 ALTERNATE AWAY JERSEY
Select NBA Codes from My NBA Live and enter **PSDF90PPJN**.

INDIANA PACERS 2005-06 ALTERNATE HOME JERSEY
Select NBA Codes from My NBA Live and enter **SDF786WSHW**.

SACRAMENTO KINGS 2005-06 ALTERNATE JERSEY
Select NBA Codes from My NBA Live and enter **654NNBFDWA**.

A3 GARNETT 3
Select NBA Codes from My NBA Live and enter **DRI239CZ49**.

JORDAN MELO V.5 WHITE & BLUE
Select NBA Codes from My NBA Live and enter **5223WERPII**.

JORDAN MELO V.5 WHITE & YELLOW
Select NBA Codes from My NBA Live and enter **ZXDR7362Q1**.

JORDAN XIV BLACK & RED
Select NBA Codes from My NBA Live and enter **144FVNHM35**.

JORDAN XIV WHITE & GREEN
Select NBA Codes from My NBA Live and enter **67YFH9839F**.

JORDAN XIV WHITE & RED
Select NBA Codes from My NBA Live and enter **743HFDRAU8**.

S. CARTER III LE
Select NBA Codes from My NBA Live and enter **JZ3SCARTVY**.

T-MAC 5 BLACK
Select NBA Codes from My NBA Live and enter **258SHQW95B**.

T-MAC 5 WHITE
Select NBA Codes from My NBA Live and enter **HGS83KP234P**.

ANSWER DMX 10
Select NBA Codes from My NBA Live and enter **RBKAIUSAB7**.

ANSWER IX AND THE RBK ANSWER IX VIDEO
Select NBA Codes from My NBA Live and enter **AI9BUBBA7T**.

THE QUESTION AND THE MESSAGE FROM ALLEN IVERSON VIDEO
Select NBA Codes from My NBA Live and enter **HOYAS3AI6L**.

NEED FOR SPEED MOST WANTED

BURGER KING CHALLENGE
At the Title screen, press Up, Down, Up, Down, Left, Right, Left, Right.

CASTROL SYNTEC VERSION OF THE FORD GT
At the Title screen, press Left, Right, Left, Right, Up, Down, Up, Down.

MARKER FOR BACKROOM OF THE ONE-STOP SHOP
At the Title screen, press Up, Up, Down, Down, Left, Right, Up, Down.

JUNKMAN ENGINE
At the Title screen, press Up, Up, Down, Down, Left, Right, Up, Down.

PORSCHE CAYMAN
At the Title screen, press L, R, R, R, Right, Left, Right, Down.

NHL 2K6

CHEAT MODE

Select Manage Profiles from the Options menu. Create a new profile with the name **Turco813**.

PETER JACKSON'S KING KONG: THE OFFICIAL GAME OF THE MOVIE

At the Main menu hold Left Bumper + Right Bumper + Left Trigger + Right Trigger and press Down, Up, Y, X, Down, Down, Y, Y. Release the buttons to access the Cheat option. The Cheat option will also be available on the pause menu. You cannot record your scores using cheat codes.

GOD MODE

Select Cheat and enter **8wonder**.

ALL CHAPTERS

Select Cheat and enter **KKst0ry**.

AMMO 999

Select Cheat and enter **KK 999 mun**.

MACHINE GUN

Select Cheat and enter **KKcapone**.

REVOLVER

Select Cheat and enter **KKtigun**.

SNIPER RIFLE
  Select Cheat and
  enter **KKsn1per**.

INFINITE SPEARS
  Select Cheat and enter **lance 1nf**.

ONE-HIT KILLS
  Select Cheat and enter **GrosBras**.

EXTRAS
  Select Cheat and
  enter **KKmuseum**.

TIGER WOODS PGA TOUR 06

ALL GOLFERS
Select Password from the Options screen and enter **itsinthegame**.

ALL CLUBS
  Select Password from the Options
  screen and enter **clubs11**.

GOLD COLLECTION EA
SPORTS BALL
  Select Password from the Options
  screen and enter **golfisfun**.

NICKLAUS ITEMS
Select Password from the Options
screen and enter **goldenbear**.

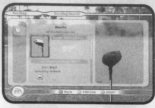

ALL COURSES
Select Password from the Options
screen and enter **eyecandy**.

VIJAY SINGH
Select Password from the Options screen and enter **victory**.

TOMB RAIDER: LEGEND

The following codes must be unlocked in the game before using them.

BULLETPROOF
During a game, hold Left Trigger
and press A, Right Trigger, Y, Right
Trigger, X, Left Bumper.

DRAIN ENEMY HEALTH
During a game, hold Left Trigger
and press X, B, A, Left Bumper, Right
Trigger, Y.

INFINITE ASSAULT RIFLE AMMO
During a game, hold Left Bumper
and press A, B, A, Left Trigger, X, Y.

INFINITE GRENADE LAUNCHER AMMO
During a game, hold Left Bumper
and press Left Trigger, Y, Right
Trigger, B, Left Trigger, X.

INFINITE SHOTGUN AMMO
During a game, hold Left Bumper
and press Right Trigger, B, X, Left
Trigger, X, A.

INFINITE SMG AMMO
During a game, hold Left Bumper
and press B, Y, Left Trigger, Right
Trigger, A, B.

EXCALIBUR
During a game, hold Left Bumper
and press Y, A, B, Right Trigger, Y,
Left Trigger.

SOUL REAVER
During a game, hold Left Bumper
and press A, Right Trigger, B, Right
Trigger, Left Trigger, X.

ONE-SHOT KILL
During a game, hold Left Trigger
and press Y, A, Y, X, Left Bumper, B.

TEXTURELESS MODE
During a game, hold Left Trigger
and press Left Bumper, A, B, A, Y,
Right Trigger.

TOM CLANCY'S GHOST RECON ADVANCED WARFIGHTER

ALL MISSIONS

At the Mission Select screen, hold Back + Left Trigger + Right Trigger and press Y, Right Bumper, Y, Right Bumper, X.

FULL HEALTH

Pause the game, hold Back + Left Trigger + Right Trigger and press Left Bumper, Left Bumper, Right Bumper, X, Right Bumper, Y.

INVINCIBLE

Pause the game, hold Back + Left Trigger + Right Trigger and press Y, Y, X, Right Bumper, X, Left Bumper.

TEAM INVINCIBLE

Pause the game, hold Back + Left Trigger + Right Trigger and press X, X, Y, Right Bumper, Y, Left Bumper.

UNLIMITED AMMO

Pause the game, hold Back + Left Trigger + Right Trigger and press Right Bumper, Right Bumper, Left Bumper, X, Left Bumper, Y.

TONY HAWK'S AMERICAN WASTELAND

ALWAYS SPECIAL

Select Cheat Codes from the Options screen and enter **uronfire**. Pause the game and select Cheats from the Game Options to enable the code.

PERFECT RAIL

Select Cheat Codes from the Options screen and enter **grindxpert**. Pause the game and select Cheats from the Game Options to enable the code.

PERFECT SKITCH

Select Cheat Codes from the Options screen and enter **h!tchar!de**. Pause the game and select Cheats from the Game Options to enable the code.

PERFECT MANUAL

Select Cheat Codes from the Options screen and enter **2wheels!**. Pause the game and select Cheats from the Game Options to enable the code.

MOON GRAVITY

Select Cheat Codes from the Options screen and enter **2them00n**. Pause the game and select Cheats from the Game Options to enable the code.

MAT HOFFMAN

Select Cheat Codes from the Options screen and enter **the_condor**.

GAMECUBE™

BASED ON A GAME RATED BY THE ESRB — **E** (EVERYONE)

1080° AVALANCHE

BEACH SPIKERS

BRATZ: ROCK ANGELZ

CHICKEN LITTLE

CRASH TAG TEAM RACING

DONKEY KONGA

FIFA STREET

FIFA STREET 2

FROGGER: ANCIENT SHADOW

ICE AGE 2: THE MELTDOWN

THE INCREDIBLES

THE INCREDIBLES: RISE OF THE UNDERMINER

JIMMY NEUTRON BOY GENIUS

JIMMY NEUTRON JET FUSION

MADDEN NFL 2005

MADDEN NFL 06

MARIO GOLF: TOADSTOOL TOUR

MARIO POWER TENNIS

MARIO SUPERSTAR BASEBALL

MEGA MAN X COLLECTION

MVP BASEBALL 2005

NAMCO MUSEUM: 50TH ANNIVERSARY

NASCAR 2005: CHASE FOR THE CUP

NBA LIVE 2004

NBA LIVE 2005

NBA LIVE 06

NBA STREET VOL.2

NCAA FOOTBALL 2005

NEED FOR SPEED UNDERGROUND 2

NFL STREET 2

PIKMIN 2

RAMPAGE: TOTAL DESTRUCTION

RAVE MASTER

ROBOTS

SHREK SUPERSLAM

SONIC GEMS COLLECTION

SONIC HEROES

SPONGEBOB SQUAREPANTS: BATTLE FOR BIKINI BOTTOM

SPONGEBOB SQUAREPANTS: LIGHTS, CAMERA, PANTS!

SSX 3

SSX ON TOUR

STRIKE FORCE BOWLING

TAK 2: THE STAFF OF DREAMS

TAK: THE GREAT JUJU CHALLENGE

TEENAGE MUTANT NINJA TURTLES 3: MUTANT NIGHTMARE

TIGER WOODS PGA TOUR 2004

TIGER WOODS PGA TOUR 2005

TIGER WOODS PGA TOUR 06

TY THE TASMANIAN TIGER 2: BUSH RESCUE

TY THE TASMANIAN TIGER 3: NIGHT OF THE QUINKAN

YU-GI-OH: FALSEBOUND KINGDOM

BASED ON A GAME RATED BY THE ESRB — **T** (TEEN)

ALIEN HOMINID

ARMY MEN: AIR COMBAT— THE ELITE MISSIONS

CABELA'S DANGEROUS HUNTS 2

THE CHRONICLES OF NARNIA: THE LION, THE WITCH AND THE WARDROBE

DRAGON BALL Z: SAGAS

FANTASTIC 4

FIRE EMBLEM: PATH OF RADIANCE

Games Listing

1080° AVALANCHE

Select Enter An Avalanche Code from the Options screen and enter the following codes:

NOVICE AVALANCHE CHALLENGE
Enter **JAS3IKRR**.

HARD AVALANCHE CHALLENGE
Enter **2AUNIKFS**.

EXPERT AVALANCHE CHALLENGE
Enter **EATFIKRM**.

EXTREME AVALANCHE CHALLENGE
Enter **9AVVIKNY**.

ALIEN HOMINID

ALL LEVELS, MINI-GAMES, AND HATS
Select Player 1 Setup or Player 2 Setup and change the name to **ROYGBIV**.

HATS FOR 2-PLAYER GAME
Go to the Options screen and rename your alien one of the following:

ABE	Top Hat	#11
APRIL	Blond Wig	#4
BEHEMOTH	Red Cap	#24
CLETUS	Hunting Hat	#3
DANDY	Flower Petal Hat	#13
GOODMAN	Black Curly Hair	#7
GRRL	Flowers	#10
PRINCESS	Tiara	#12
SUPERFLY	Afro	#6
TOMFULP	Brown Messy Hair	#2

ARMY MEN: AIR COMBAT—THE ELITE MISSIONS

UNLIMITED LIVES
During a game, press A, Y, X, Z, Down, Right, Up.

BEACH SPIKERS

UNIFORMS
In World Tour, name your player one of the following to unlock bonus outfits. The name disappears when entered correctly.

NAME	UNIFORMS
JUSTICE	105-106, Sunglasses 94
DAYTONA	107-108
FVIPERS	109-110, Face 51, Hair 75
ARAKATA	111-113, Face 52, Hair 76
PHANTA2	114-115, Face 53, Hair 77
OHTORII	116-117

BRATZ: ROCK ANGELZ

CHANGES CAMERRON
While in the Bratz Office, use the Cheat computer and enter **STYLIN**.

CHANGES DYLAN
While in the Bratz Office, use the Cheat computer and enter **MEYGEN**.

CHANGES LONDON BOY
While in the Bratz Office, use the Cheat computer and enter **BLINGZ**.

CHANGES PARIS BOY
While in the Bratz Office, use the Cheat computer and enter **ROCKIN**.

1000 BLINGZ
While in the Bratz Office, use the Cheat computer and enter **YASMIN**.

2000 BLINGZ
While in the Bratz Office, use the Cheat computer and enter **PHOEBE**.

2100 BLINGZ
While in the Bratz Office, use the Cheat computer and enter **DANCIN**.

3000 BLINGZ
While in the Bratz Office, use the Cheat computer and enter **WAYFAB**.

6000 BLINGZ
While in the Bratz Office, use the Cheat computer and enter **HOTTIE**.

RINGTONE 12
While in the Bratz Office, use the Cheat computer and enter **BLAZIN**.

RINGTONE 15
While in the Bratz Office, use the Cheat computer and enter **FIANNA**.

RINGTONE 16
While in the Bratz Office, use the Cheat computer and enter **ANGELZ**.

CABELA'S DANGEROUS HUNTS 2

DOUBLE HEALTH
Select the Codes option and enter Eye, Bolt, Skull, Hand, Boot.

HEALTH REGENERATES FASTER
Select the Codes option and enter Skull, Eye, Boot, Bolt, Hand.

DOUBLE DAMAGE
Select the Codes option and enter Hand, Boot, Skull, Eye, Bolt.

INFINITE AMMO
Select the Codes option and enter Bolt, Hand, Eye, Boot, Skull.

CHICKEN LITTLE

INVINCIBILITY
Select Cheat Codes from the Extras menu and enter Baseball, Baseball, Baseball, Shirt.

BIG FEET
Select Cheat Codes from the Extras menu and enter Hat, Glove, Glove, Hat.

BIG HAIR
Select Cheat Codes from the Extras menu and enter Baseball, Bat, Bat, Baseball.

BIG HEAD
Select Cheat Codes from the Extras menu and enter Hat, Helmet, Helmet, Hat.

PAPER PANTS
Select Cheat Codes from the Extras menu and enter Bat, Bat, Hat, Hat.

SUNGLASSES
Select Cheat Codes from the Extras menu and enter Glove, Glove, Helmet, Helmet.

UNDERWEAR
Select Cheat Codes from the Extras menu and enter Hat, Hat, Shirt, Shirt.

THE CHRONICLES OF NARNIA: THE LION, THE WITCH AND THE WARDROBE

ENABLE CHEATS
At the Title screen, press A then hold L + R and press Down, Down, Right, Up. The text should turn green when the code is entered correctly. Now you can enter the following:

LEVEL SELECT
At the wardrobe, hold L and press Up, Up, Right, Right, Up, Right, Down.

ALL BONUS LEVELS
At the Bonus Drawer, hold L and press Down, Down, Right, Right, Down, Right, Up.

LEVEL SKIP
During gameplay, hold L and press Down, Left, Down, Left, Down, Right, Down, Right, Up.

INVINCIBILITY
During gameplay, hold L and press Down, Up, Down, Right, Right.

RESTORE HEALTH
During gameplay, hold L and press Down, Left, Left, Right.

10,000 COINS
During gameplay, hold L and press Down, Left, Right, Down, Down.

ALL ABILITIES
During gameplay, hold L and press Down, Left, Right, Left, Up.

FILL COMBO METER
During gameplay, hold L and press Up, Up, Right, Up.

CRASH TAG TEAM RACING

FASTER VEHICLES
At the Main menu, hold L + R and press X, X, Y, Y.

ONE-HIT KO
At the Main menu, hold L + R and press A, X, X, A.

DISABLE HUD
At the Main menu, hold L + R and press A, B, Y, X.

CHICKEN HEADS
At the Main menu, hold L + R and press A, X, X, B.

JAPANESE CRASH
At the Main menu, hold L + R and press B, X, B, X.

DRIVE A BLOCK VEHICLE
At the Main menu, hold L + R and press X, X, Y, B.

DONKEY KONGA

100M VINE CLIMB (1 OR 2 PLAYERS)
Collect 4800 coins to unlock this mini-game for purchase at DK Town.

BANANA JUGGLE (1 OR 2 PLAYERS)
Collect 5800 coins to unlock this mini-game for purchase at DK Town.

BASH K. ROOL (1 PLAYER)
Collect 5800 coins to unlock this mini-game for purchase at DK Town.

DRAGON BALL Z: SAGAS

ALL UPGRADES
Pause the game, select Controller and press Up, Left, Down, Right, Start, Start, Y, A, X, B.

INVINCIBILITY
Pause the game, select Controller and press Down, A, Up, Y, Start, Start, Right, Left, X, B.

PENDULUM MODE
Complete the game.

FANTASTIC 4

BARGE ARENA AND STAN LEE INTERVIEW #1
At the Main menu, press B, X, B, Down, Down, X, Up.

INFINITE COSMIC POWER
At the Main menu, press Up, B, B, B, Left, Right, X.

BONUS LEVEL
At the Main menu, press Right, Right, B, X, Left, Up, Down.

FIFA STREET

ALL APPAREL
At the Main menu, hold L + Y and press Right, Right, Left, Up (x3), Down, Left.

MINI PLAYERS
Pause the game, hold L + Y and press Up, Left, Down, Down, Right, Down, Up, Left.

NORMAL SIZE PLAYERS
Pause the game, hold L + Y and press Right, Right, Up, Down, Down, Left, Right, Left.

FIFA STREET 2

ALL STAGES
At the Main menu, hold L + Y and press Left, Up, Up, Right, Down, Down, Right, Down.

FIRE EMBLEM: PATH OF RADIANCE

FIRE EMBLEM: PATH OF RADIANCE ART
Complete the game.

FIRE EMBLEM ART
Connect a GBA to the GameCube with the Fire Emblem game.

FE: THE SACRED STONES ART
Connect a GBA to the GameCube with the Fire Emblem: The Sacred Stones game.

FROGGER: ANCIENT SHADOW

UNLOCK LEVELS

Select the Secret Code option and enter the following to unlock various levels in the game.

LEVEL	ENTER
Dr. Wani's Mansion Level 1 with Berry	Berry, Lily, Lumpy, Lily

LEVEL	ENTER
Dr. Wani's Mansion Level 2 with Berry	Finnius, Frogger, Frogger, Wani
Elder Ruins Level 1 with Berry	Lily, Lily, Wani, Wani

LEVEL	ENTER
Elder Ruins Level 2 with Berry	Frogger, Berry, Finnius, Frogger
Doom's Temple Level 1 with Berry	Lily, Wani, Lily, Wani
Doom's Temple Level 2 with Berry	Frogger, Lily, Lily, Lily
Doom's Temple Level 3 with Berry	Frogger, Frogger, Frogger, Berry

LEVEL	ENTER
Sealed Heart Level 1 with Berry	Lily, Lily, Wani, Lumpy
Sealed Heart Level 2 with Berry	Lily, Frogger, Frogger, Lumpy

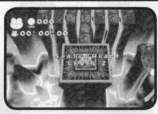

UNLOCK LETTERS

Select the Secret Code option and enter the following to unlock various letters in the game.

LETTER	ENTER
WHCinc Letter with Hyacinth Flower Seed	Lumpy, Frogger, Frogger, Berry

Opart's Letter with Cosmos Flower Seed	Berry, Lumpy, Frogger, Lumpy

Secret Admirer Letter with Rose Flower Seed	Wani, Lily, Wani, Frogger

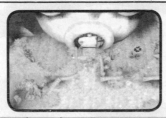

Dr. Wani's Letter with Pansy Flower Seed	Lumpy, Berry, Lumpy, Finnius

UNLOCK WIGS

Select the Secret Code option and enter the following to unlock various wigs in the game.

WIG	ENTER
Lobster Wig	Finnius, Wani, Lumpy, Frogger

F

WIG	ENTER
Bird Nest Wig	Lily, Lily, Lily, Lily
Masted Ship Wig	Lumpy, Lumpy, Lumpy, Lumpy

Skull Wig	Frogger, Lumpy, Lily, Frogger

UNLOCK ARTWORK

Select the Secret Code option and enter the following to unlock various artwork pieces from the game.

ARTWORK	ENTER
Developer Picture 1	Wani, Frogger, Wani, Frogger

Developer Picture 2	Berry, Berry, Berry, Wani
Programmer Art 1	Wani, Wani, Wani, Wani
Programmer Art 2	Lumpy, Frogger, Berry, Lily
Programmer Art 3	Wani, Frogger, Lily, Finnius

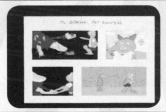

Additional Art 1	Frogger, Frogger, Frogger, Frogger

Additional Art 2	Finnius, Finnius, Finnius, Finnius
Additional Art 3	Berry, Berry, Berry, Berry

FUTURE TACTICS: THE UPRISING

UNLIMITED TURNS
During a game, press Up, Up, Down, Down, Left, Right, Left, Left, R, L.

BIG HEADS
During a game, press Up, Left, Down, Left, Down, Up, Up, Left.

DISCO MODE
During a game, press L, Left, L, Left, R, Right, R, Right.

LOW GRAVITY
During a game, press Up (x6), Down, Right, Up.

F-ZERO GX

SOUNDS OF BIG BLUE FOR PURCHASE
Select Customize and enter the shop. Press Z, Left, Right, Left, Z, Y, X, Z, Left, Right, Left, Right, Z, X, Z, X, Z. Select the Items option to find Sounds of Big Blue for sale.

SOUNDS OF MUTE CITY FOR PURCHASE
Select Customize and enter the shop. Press X (x3), Y, X (x3), Y, Z, Z, Left, Right, Left, Right, Left, Right. Select the Items option to find Sounds of Mute City for sale.

RUBY CUP CHAMPIONSHIP
Select Time Attack, then choose Records. Select Ruby Cup, hold L and press R, A, Z, A, C-Up, C-Left, A, C-Down, R, Z.

SAPPHIRE CUP CHAMPIONSHIP
Select Time Attack, then choose Records. Select Sapphire Cup, hold Z and press L, A, L, A, C-Up, L, C-Right, A, R, C-Up.

EMERALD CUP CHAMPIONSHIP
Select Time Attack, then choose Records. Select Emerald Cup, hold R and press Z, A, C-Down, L, C-Left, A, Z, C-Left, L, A.

GOBLIN COMMANDER: UNLEASH THE HORDE

During a game, hold R + L + Y + Down until a message appears in the upper-right corner of the screen. Re-enter the code to disable it. Now enter the following codes. A message appears when the code is entered correctly.

GOD MODE
Press R (x3), L (x3), R, L, Y, R.

AUTOMATIC WIN
Press R, R, L (x3), R, R, Y (x3).

ALL LEVEL ACCESS
Press Y (x3), L, R, L, L, R, L, R, R, L, R, L, L, R, L, R, L, L, R, L, L, R, L, R, R, Y (x3). Start a Campaign to select a level.

DISABLE FOG OF WAR
Press R, L, R, R, L, L, Y, Y, L, R.

GAME SPEED X1/2
Press L (x5), Y (x4), R.

GAME SPEED X2
Press R (x5), L, Y, R (x3).

GOLD AND SOULS +1000
Press R, R, L, R, R, Y (x3), L, L.

GOLD +100
Press L, R (x4), L, Y, L (x3).

SOULS +100
Press R, L (x4), R, Y, R (x3).

THE HAUNTED MANSION

SKELETON ZEKE
At the Legal screen, hold $A + B + X + Y$. Release the buttons at the Title screen.

LEVEL SELECT
During a game, hold Right and press X, X, B, Y, Y, B, X, A.

INVINCIBILITY
During a game, hold Right and press B, X (x3), B, X, Y, A.

WEAPON UPGRADE
During a game, hold Right and press B, B, Y, Y, X (x3), A.

ICE AGE 2: THE MELTDOWN

UNLIMITED PEBBLES
Pause the game and press Down, Down, Left, Up, Up, Right, Up, Down.

INFINITE ENERGY
Pause the game and press Down, Left, Right, Down, Down, Right, Left, Down.

INFINITE HEALTH
Pause the game and press Up, Right, Down, Up, Left, Down, Right, Left.

THE INCREDIBLE HULK: ULTIMATE DESTRUCTION

You must collect a specific comic in the game to activate each code. After collecting the appropriate comic, you can enter the following codes. If you don't have the comic and enter the code, you receive a message "That code cannot be activated... yet". Enter the cheats at the Code Input screen.

UNLOCKED: CABS GALORE
Select Code Input from the Extras menu and enter **CABBIES**.

UNLOCKED: GORILLA INVASION
Select Code Input from the Extras menu and enter **kingkng**.

UNLOCKED: MASS TRANSIT
Select Code Input from the Extras menu and enter **TRANSIT**.

UNLOCKED: 5000 SMASH POINTS
Select Code Input from the Extras menu and enter **SMASH5**.

UNLOCKED: 10000 SMASH POINTS
Select Code Input from the Extras menu and enter **SMASH10**.

UNLOCKED: 15000 SMASH POINTS
Select Code Input from the Extras menu and enter **SMASH15**.

UNLOCKED: AMERICAN FLAG SHORTS
Select Code Input from the Extras menu and enter **AMERICA**.

UNLOCKED: CANADIAN FLAG SHORTS
Select Code Input from the Extras menu and enter **OCANADA**.

UNLOCKED: FRENCH FLAG SHORTS
Select Code Input from the Extras menu and enter **Drapeau**.

UNLOCKED: GERMAN FLAG SHORTS
Select Code Input from the Extras menu and enter **DEUTSCH**.

UNLOCKED: ITALIAN FLAG SHORTS
Select Code Input from the Extras menu and enter **MUTANDA**.

UNLOCKED: JAPANESE FLAG SHORTS

Select Code Input from the Extras menu and enter **FURAGGU**.

UNLOCKED: SPANISH FLAG SHORTS

Select Code Input from the Extras menu and enter **BANDERA**.

UNLOCKED: UK FLAG SHORTS

Select Code Input from the Extras menu and enter **FSHNCHP**.

UNLOCKED: COW MISSILES

Select Code Input from the Extras menu and enter **CHZGUN**.

UNLOCKED: DOUBLE HULK'S DAMAGE

Select Code Input from the Extras menu and enter **DESTROY**.

UNLOCKED: DOUBLE POWER COLLECTABLES

Select Code Input from the Extras menu and enter **BRINGIT**.

UNLOCKED: BLACK AND WHITE

Select Code Input from the Extras menu and enter **RETRO**.

UNLOCKED: SEPIA

Select Code Input from the Extras menu and enter **HISTORY**.

UNLOCKED: ABOMINATION

Select Code Input from the Extras menu and enter **VILLAIN**.

UNLOCKED: GRAY HULK

Select Code Input from the Extras menu and enter **CLASSIC**.

UNLOCKED: JOE FIXIT SKIN

Select Code Input from the Extras menu and enter **SUITFIT**.

UNLOCKED: WILD TRAFFIC

Select Code Input from the Extras menu and enter **FROGGIE**.

UNLOCKED: LOW GRAVITY

Select Code Input from the Extras menu and enter **PILLOWS**.

THE INCREDIBLES

Pause the game and select the Secrets option to enter the following codes:

RESTORE SOME HEALTH
Enter **UUDDLRLRBAS**.

BIG HEADS
Enter **EINSTEINIUM**.

SMALL HEADS
Enter **DEEVOLVE**.

ONE-HIT KILLS
Enter **KRONOS**.

EYE LASER
Enter **GAZERBEAM**.

WEAKER BOMBS
Enter **LABOMBE**.

INFINITE INCREDI-POWER FOR ELASTIGIRL
Enter **FLEXIBLE**.

INFINITE INCREDI-POWER FOR MR. INCREDIBLE
Enter **SHOWTIME**.

INFINITE INCREDI-POWER FOR MR INCREDIBLE OR ELASTAGIRL
Enter **MCTRAVIS**.

DESTROYS EVERYTHING
Enter **SMARTBOMB**.

FIRE TRAIL
Enter **ATHLETESFOOT**.

BATTLE MODE
Enter **ROTAIDALG**.

FASTER GAMEPLAY
Enter **SASSMODE**.

SLOW MOTION
Enter **BWTHEMOVIE**.

DIFFERENT COLORS
Enter **DISCORULES**.

BRIGHT COLORS
Enter **EMODE**.

INVERT HORIZONTAL CAMERA CONTROL
Enter **INVERTCAMERAX**.

INVERT VERTICAL CAMERA CONTROL
Enter **INVERTCAMERAY**.

TOGGLE HUD
Enter **BHUD**.

WATCH HEAVY IRON STUDIOS INTRO
Enter **HI**.

CREDITS
Enter **YOURNAMEINLIGHTS**.

DEACTIVATE ALL CODES
Enter **THEDUDEABIDES**.

THE INCREDIBLES: RISE OF THE UNDERMINER

BIG HEADS
Pause the game and access the menu. Choose the Secrets option and enter **EGOPROBLEM**. Re-enter the code to disable it.

MR. INCREDIBLE GAINS 1000 EXPERIENCE POINTS
Pause the game and access the menu. Choose the Secrets option and enter **MRIPROF**.

FROZONE GAINS 1000 EXPERIENCE POINTS
Pause the game and access the menu. Choose the Secrets option and enter **FROZPROF**.

MR. INCREDIBLE GAINS A SUPER-MOVE
Pause the game and access the menu. Choose the Secrets option and enter **MRIBOOM**.

FROZONE GAINS A SUPER-MOVE
Pause the game and access the menu. Choose the Secrets option and enter **FROZBOOM**.

SHOWS THE GAME CREDITS
Pause the game and access the menu. Choose the Secrets option and enter **ROLLCALL**.

TOUGHER GAME
Pause the game and access the menu. Choose the Secrets option and enter **THISISTOOEASY**. This code cuts damage caused to enemies in half, doubles damage inflicted to the Supers, allows no health recovery, and Experience Points are halved!

EASIER GAME
Pause the game and access the menu. Choose the Secrets option and enter **THISISTOOHARD**. This code doubles damage caused to enemies, halves damage inflicted to the Supers, and doubles the amount of health recovery and Experience Points!

ALL GALLERY ITEMS
Pause the game and access the menu. Choose the Secrets option and enter **SHOWME**.

DOUBLE EXPERIENCE POINTS
Pause the game and access the menu. Choose the Secrets option and enter **MAXIMILLION**.

JIMMY NEUTRON BOY GENIUS

ALL KEY ITEMS
During a game, press R, R, L, A, B, B, A, R, L, R, Start, Down, A, Down.

JIMMY NEUTRON: JET FUSION

ALL MOVIES
During a game, press Z, L, R, R, B, X, X, B, R, R, L, L.

4-HIT COMBO
Pause the game, hold L + R and press A, B, A, Up.

MADDEN NFL 2005

CHEAT CARDS
Select Madden Cards from the My Madden menu. Then select Madden Codes and enter the following:

CHEAT	CODE
3rd Down, Opponent gets 3 downs to get a 1st down	Z28X8K
5th Down, Get 5 downs to get a 1st down	P66C4L
Aloha Stadium	G67F5X
Bingo!, Defensive interceptions increase by 75%	J33I8F
Da Bomb, Unlimited pass range	B61A8M
Da Boot, Unlimited field goal range	I76X3T
Extra Credit, Awards points for interceptions and sacks	M89S8G
1st and 15, Opponent must gain 15 yards for a 1st down	V65J8P
1st and 5, Opponent must gain 5 yards for a 1st down	O72E9B
Fumbilitis, Opponent's fumbles increase by 75%	R14B8Z
Human Plow, Break tackle increases by 75%	L96J7P
Lame Duck, Opponent will throw lob passes	D57R5S
Mistake Free, Can't fumble or throw interceptions	X78P9Z
Mr. Mobility, Your QB can't get sacked	Y59R8R
Super Bowl XL	O85P6I
Super Bowl XLI	P48Z4D
Super Bowl XLII	T67R1O
Super Bowl XXXIX	D58F1B
Super Dive, Diving distance increases by 75%	D59K3Y
Tight Fit, Opponent's uprights become narrow	V34L6D
Unforced Errors, Opponent fumbles ball when he jukes	L48G1E

CLASSIC TEAM CARDS
Select Madden Cards from the My Madden menu. Then select Madden Codes and enter the following:

TEAM	ENTER	TEAM	ENTER
1958 Colts	P74X8J	1978 Dolphins	G97U5X
1966 Packers	G49P7W	1980 Raiders	K71K4E
1968 Jets	C24W2A	1981 Chargers	Y27N9A
1970 Browns	G12N1I	1982 Redskins	F56D6V
1972 Dolphins	R79W6W	1983 Raiders	D23T8S
1974 Steelers	R12D9B	1984 Dolphins	X23Z8H
1976 Raiders	P96Q8M	1985 Bears	F92M8M
1977 Broncos	O18T2A	1986 Giants	K44F2Y

M

TEAM	ENTER
1988 49ers	F77R8H
1990 Eagles	G95F2Q
1991 Lions	I89F4I
1992 Cowboys	I44A1O
1993 Bills	Y66K3O

CHEERLEADER/PUMP UP THE CROWD CARDS

Select Madden Cards from the My Madden menu. Then select Madden Codes and enter the following:

TEAM	ENTER	TEAM	ENTER
Patriots	O59P9C	Jaguars	K32C2A
49ers	X61T6L	Jets	S45W1M
Bengals	Y22S6G	Lions	C18F4G
Bills	F26S6X	Packers	K26Y4V
Broncos	B85U5C	Panthers	M66N4D
Browns	B65Q1L	Raiders	G92L2E
Buccaneers	Z55Z7S	Rams	W73B8X
Cardinals	Q91W5L	Ravens	P98T6C
Chargers	Q68S3F	Redskins	N19D6Q
Chiefs	T46M6T	Saints	R99G2F
Colts	M22Z6H	Seahawks	A35T8R
Cowboys	J84E3F	Steelers	C98I2V
Dolphins	E88T2J	Texans	R74G3W
Eagles	Q88P3Q	Titans	Q81V4N
Falcons	W86F3F	Vikings	E26H4L
Giants	L13Z9J		

GOLD PLAYER CARDS

Select Madden Cards from the My Madden menu. Then select Madden Codes and enter the following:

PLAYER	ENTER	PLAYER	ENTER
Aaron Brooks	J95K1J	Brian Dawkins	Y47B8Y
Aaron Glenn	Q48E9G	Brian Simmons	S22M6A
Adewale Ogunleye	C12E9E	Brian Urlacher	Z34J4U
Ahman Green	T86L4C	Brian Westbrook	V46I2I
Al Wilson	G72G2R	Bubba Franks	U77F2W
Alan Faneca	U32S9C	Butch Davis	G77L6F
Amani Toomer	Z75G6M	Byron Leftwich	C55V5C
Andre Carter	V76E2Q	Carson Palmer	O36V2H
Andre Johnson	E34S1M	Casey Hampton	Z11P9T
Andy Reid	N44K1L	Chad Johnson	R85S2A
Anquan Boldin	S32F7K	Chad Pennington	B64L2F
Antonio Winfield	A12V7Z	Champ Bailey	K89O9E
Bill Cowher	S54T6U	Charles Woodson	F95N9J
Brad Hopkins	P44A8B	Chris Hovan	F14C6J
Bret Farve	L61D7B	Clinton Portis	Z28D2V
Brian Billick	L27C4K	Corey Simon	R11D7K

GAMECUBE™

186

PLAYER	ENTER	PLAYER	ENTER
Courtney Brown	R42R75	Jerry Rice	K34F8S
Curtis Martin	K47X3G	Jevon Kearse	A78B1C
Dallas Coach	O24U1Q	Jim Haslett	G70R3W
Damien Woody	E57K9Y	Jim Mora Jr.	N46C3M
Damien Woody	F78I11	Jimmy Smith	I22J5W
Dante Hall	B23P8D	Joe Horn	P91A1Q
Dat Nguyen	Q86I2S	John Fox	Q98R7Y
Daunte Culpepper	O6209K	Jon Gruden	H61I8A
Dave Wannstedt	W73D7D	Josh Mccown	O33Y4X
David Boston	A25I9F	Julian Peterson	M89J8A
David Carr	C16E2Q	Julius Peppers	X5404Z
Dennis Erickson	J83E3T	Junior Seau	W26K6Q
Dennis Green	C18J7T	Kabeer Gbaja-Biamala	U16I9Y
Derrick Brooks	P93I9Q	Keith Brooking	E12P4S
Derrick Mason	S98P3T	Keith Bulluck	M63N6V
Deuce Mcallister	D11H4J	Kendrell Bell	T96C7J
Dexter Coakley	L35K1A	Kevan Barlow	A23T5E
Dexter Jackson	G16B2I	Kevin Mawee	L76E6S
Dick Vermeil	F68V1W	Kris Jenkins	W6303K
Dom Capers	B97I6R	Kyle Boller	A72F9X
Domanick Davis	L58S3J	Kyle Turley	Y46A8V
Donie Edwards	E18Y5Z	Ladainian Tomlinson	M64D4E
Donovin Darius	Q11T7T	Lavar Arrington	F19Q8W
Donovon Mcnabb	T98J11	Laveranues Coles	R98I5S
Donte Stallworth	R75W3M	Lawyer Milloy	M37Y5B
Drew Bledsoe	W73M3E	La'roi Glover	K24L9K
Dre' Bly	Z68W8J	Lee Suggs	Z94X6Q
Dwight Freeney	G76U2L	Leonard Davis	H14M2V
Edgerrin James	A75D7X	Lovie Smith	L38V3A
Ed Reed	G18Q2B	Marc Bulger	U66B4S
Eric Moulds	H34Z8K	Marcel Shipp	R42X2L
Flozell Adams	R54T10	Marcus Stroud	E56I50
Fred Taylor	I87X9Y	Marcus Trufant	R46T5U
Grant Wistrom	E46M4Y	Mark Brunell	B66D9J
Herman Edwards	O19T2T	Marshell Faulk	U76G1U
Hines Ward	M12B8F	Marty Booker	P51U4B
Jack Del Rio	J22P9I	Marty Booker	H19Q20
Jake Delhomme	M86N9F	Marty Shottenheimer	D96A7S
Jake Plummer	N74P8X	Marvin Harrison	T11E80
Jamie Sharper	W27I7G	Marvin Lewis	P24S4H
Jason Taylor	O33S6I	Matt Hasselback	R68D5F
Jason Webster	M74B3E	Michael Bennett	W81W2J
Jeff Fisher	N62B6J	Michael Strahan	O66T6K
Jeff Garcia	H32H7B	Michael Vick	H67B1F
Jeremy Newberry	J77Y8C	Mike Alstott	D89F6W
Jeremy Shockey	R34X5T	Mike Brown	F12J8N
Jerry Porter	F71Q9Z	Mike Martz	R64A8E

PLAYER	ENTER	PLAYER	ENTER
Mike Mularkey	C56D6E	Santana Moss	H79E5B
Mike Rucker	K8906S	Seattle Coach	V58U4Y
Mike Shanahan	H15L5Y	Shaun Alexander	C95Z4P
Mike Sherman	F84X6K	Shaun Ellis	Z54F2B
Mike Tice	Y31T6Y	Shaun Rogers	J97X8M
New England Coach	N24L4Z	Shawn Springs	J95K1J
Nick Bernett	X95I7S	Simeon Rice	S62F9T
Norv Turner	F24K1M	Stephen Davis	E39X9L
Olin Kreutz	R17R20	Steve Mariucci	V74Q3N
Orlando Pace	U42U9U	Steve Mcnair	S36T1I
Patrick Surtain	H58T9X	Steve Smith	W91O2O
Peerless Price	X75V6K	T.J. Duckett	P67E1I
Peter Warrick	D86P8O	Takeo Spikes	B83A6C
Peyton Manning	L48H4U	Tedy Bruschi	K28Q3P
Plaxico Burress	K18P6J	Terence Newman	W57Y5P
Priest Holmes	X91N1L	Terrell Suggs	V71A9Q
Quentin Jammer	V55S3Q	Tiki Barber	T43A2V
Randy Moss	W79U7X	Todd Heap	H19M1G
Ray Lewis	B94X6V	Tom Brady	X22V7E
Reggie Wayne	R29S8C	Tom Coughlin	S71D6H
Rex Grossman	C46P2A	Tony Dungy	Y96R8V
Rich Gannon	Q69I1Y	Tony Gonzalez	N46E9N
Richard Seymore	L69T4T	Torry Holt	W96U7E
Ricky Williams	P19V1N	Travis Henry	F36M2Q
Rod Smith	V22C4L	Trent Green	Y46M4S
Rodney Harrison	O84I3J	Ty Law	F13W1Z
Rondel Barber	J72X8W	Walter Jones	G57P1P
Roy Williams	J76C6F	Washington Coach	W63V9L
Rudi Johnson	W26J6H	Will Shields	B52S8A
Sam Madison	Z87T5C	Zach Thomas	U63I3H
Samari Rolle	C69H4Z		

MADDEN NFL 06

#55 DONOVAN MCNABB GOLD CARD

Select Madden Cards from My Madden. Then select Madden Codes and enter **8Q2J2X**.

#188 FIRST AND FIFTEEN BRONZE CARD

Select Madden Cards from My Madden. Then select Madden Codes and enter **2W4P9T**.

#189 FIRST AND FIVE BRONZE CARD

Select Madden Cards from My Madden. Then select Madden Codes and enter **2Y7L8B**.

#190 UNFORCED ERRORS BRONZE CARD

Select Madden Cards from My Madden. Then select Madden Codes and enter **2Z2F4H**.

#191 EXTRA CREDIT BRONZE CARD
Select Madden Cards from My Madden. Then select Madden Codes and enter **3D3Q3P**.

#192 TIGHT FIT BRONZE CARD
Select Madden Cards from My Madden. Then select Madden Codes and enter **3D8X6T**.

#193 5TH DOWN BRONZE CARD
Select Madden Cards from My Madden. Then select Madden Codes and enter **3E9R4V**.

#194 3RD DOWN BRONZE CARD
Select Madden Cards from My Madden. Then select Madden Codes and enter **3F9G4J**.

#195 HUMAN PLOW BRONZE CARD
Select Madden Cards from My Madden. Then select Madden Codes and enter **3H3U7F**.

#196 SUPER DIVE BRONZE CARD
Select Madden Cards from My Madden. Then select Madden Codes and enter **3H8M5U**.

#197 DA BOOT BRONZE CARD
Select Madden Cards from My Madden. Then select Madden Codes and enter **3J3S9Y**.

MARIO GOLF: TOADSTOOL TOUR

At the Title screen, press Start + Z to access the Password screen. Enter the following to open up bonus tournaments:

TARGET BULLSEYE TOURNAMENT
Enter **CEUFPXJ1**.

HOLLYWOOD VIDEO TOURNAMENT
Enter **BJGQBULZ**.

CAMP HYRULE TOURNAMENT
Enter **0EKW5G7U**.

BOWSER BADLANDS TOURNAMENT
Enter **9L3L9KHR**.

BOWSER JR.'S JUMBO TOURNAMENT
Enter **2GPL67PN**.

MARIO OPEN TOURNAMENT
Enter **GGAA241H**.

PEACH'S INVITATIONAL TOURNAMENT
Enter **ELBUT3PX**.

MARIO POWER TENNIS

EVENT MODE
At the Title screen, press Z + Start.

MARIO SUPERSTAR BASEBALL

STAR DASH MINI GAME
Complete Star difficulty on all mini-games.

BABY LUIGI
Complete Challenge Mode with Yoshi.

DIXIE KONG
Complete Challenge Mode with Donkey Kong.

HAMMER BRO
Complete Challenge Mode with Bowser.

MONTY MOLE
Complete Challenge Mode with Mario.

PETEY PIRANHA
Complete Challenge Mode with Wario.

TOADETTE
Complete Challenge Mode with Peach.

KOOPA CASTLE STADIUM
Complete Challenge Mode.

MARVEL NEMESIS: RISE OF THE IMPERFECTS

ALL FANTASTIC FOUR COMICS
Select Cheats from the Options screen and enter **SAVAGELAND**.

ALL TOMORROW PEOPLE COMICS
Select Cheats from the Options screen and enter **NZONE**.

ELEKTRA BONUS CARD
Select Cheats from the Options screen and enter **THEHAND**.

SOLARA BONUS CARD
Select Cheats from the Options screen and enter **REIKO**.

STORM BONUS CARD
Select Cheats from the Options screen and enter **MONROE**.

MEGA MAN X COLLECTION

Mega Man X4
BLACK ZERO
At the Character Select screen, highlight Zero and hold R and press Right (x6). Release R, hold X and press Start. Continue holding X until the game starts.

ULTIMATE ARMOR FOR MEGA MAN X
At the Character Select screen, highlight Mega Man X and press X, X, Left (x6). Then hold L + Z and press Start. Continue holding L + Z until the game starts. Complete the level, then find the Leg power-up in the Jungle.

Mega Man X5
BLACK ZERO
At the Character Select screen, highlight Zero and press Down, Down, Up (x9).

ULTIMATE ARMOR FOR MEGA MAN X
At the Character Select screen, highlight Mega Man X and press Up, Up, Down (x9).

Mega Man X6
BLACK ZERO
At the Main menu, highlight Game Start and press L, L, L, R.

ULTIMATE ARMOR FOR MEGA MAN X

At the Main menu, highlight Game Start and press Left, Left, Left, Right.

MVP BASEBALL 2005

ALL STADIUMS, PLAYERS, UNIFORMS, AND REWARDS
Create a player named **Katie Roy**.

RED SOX ST. PATRICK'S DAY UNIFORM
Create a player named **Neverlose Sight**.

BAD HITTER WITH THIN BAT
Create a player named **Erik Kiss**.

GOOD HITTER WITH BIG BAT
Create a player named **Isaiah Paterson**, **Jacob Paterson** or **Keegan Paterson**.

BIGGER BODY
Create a player named **Kenny Lee**.

NAMCO MUSEUM: 50TH ANNIVERSARY

GALAGA '88
Get 40,000 points in Galaga.

PAC-MANIA
Get 15,000 points in Pac-Man and 20,000 points in Ms. Pac-Man

NASCAR 2005: CHASE FOR THE CUP

ALL BONUSES
At the Edit Driver screen, enter **Open Sesame** as your name.

DALE EARNHARDT
At the Edit Driver screen, enter **The Intimidator** as your name.

$10,000,000
At the Edit Driver screen, enter **Walmart NASCAR** as your name.

LAKESHORE DRIVE TRACK
At the Edit Driver screen, enter **Walmart Exclusive** as your name.

DODGE EVENTS
At the Edit Driver screen, enter **Dodge Stadium** as your name.

MR CLEAN DRIVERS
At the Edit Driver screen, enter **Mr.Clean Racing** as your name.

MR. CLEAN PIT CREW
At the Edit Driver screen, enter **Clean Crew** as your name.

2,000,000 PRESTIGE POINTS/LEVEL 10 IN FIGHT TO THE TOP MODE
At the Edit Driver screen, enter **You TheMan** as your name.

NBA LIVE 2004

Create a player with the following last name. The player will be placed in the Free Agents option.

ALEKSANDER PAVLOVIC
Enter **WHSUCPOI**.

ANDREAS GLYNIADAKIS
Enter **POCKDLEK**.

CARLOS DELFINO
Enter **SDFGURKL**.

JAMES LANG
Enter **NBVKSMCN**.

JERMAINE DUPRI
Enter **SOSODEF**.

KYLE KORVER
Enter **OEISNDLA**.

MALICK BADIANE
Enter **SKENXIDO**.

MARIO AUSTIN
Enter **POSNEGHX**.

MATT BONNER
Enter **BBVDKCVM**.

NEDZAD SINANOVIC
Enter **ZXDSDRKE**.

PACCELIS MORLENDE
Enter **QWPOASZX**.

REMON VAN DE HARE
Enter **ITNVCJSD**.

RICK RICKERT
Enter **POILKJMN**.

SANI BECIROVIC
Enter **ZXCCVDRI**.

SOFOKLIS SCHORTSANITIS
Enter **IOUBFDCJ**.

SZYMON SZEWCZYK
Enter **POIOIJIS**.

TOMMY SMITH
Enter **XCFWQASE**.

XUE YUYANG
Enter **WMZKCOI**.

Select NBA Codes from the My NBA LIVE option to enter the following:

15,000 NBA STORE POINTS
Enter **87843H5F9P**.

ALL HARDWOOD CLASSIC JERSEYS
Enter **725JKUPLMM**.

ALL NBA GEAR
Enter **ERT9976KJ3**.

ALL TEAM GEAR
Enter **YREY5625WQ**.

ALL SHOES
Enter **POUY985GY5**.

UNLOCK SHOES

Select My NBA Live and enter the following NBA Codes to unlock the different shoes:

SHOES	ENTER
Air Bounds (black/white/blue)	7YSS0292KE
Air Bounds (white/black)	JA807YAM20
Air Bounds (white/green)	84HHST61QI
Air Flight 89 (black/white)	FG874JND84
Air Flight 89 (white/black)	63RBVC7423
Air Flight 89 (white/red)	GF9845JHR4
Air Flightposite 2 (blue/gray)	2389JASE3E
Air Flightposite (white/black/gray)	74FDH7K94S
Air Flightposite (white/black)	6HJ874SFJ7
Air Flightposite (yellow/black/white)	MN54BV45C2
Air Flightposite 2 (blue/gray)	RB84UJHAS2
Air Flightposite 2 (blue/gray)	2389JASE3E
Air Foamposite 1 (blue)	OP5465UX12
Air Foamposite 1 (white/black/red)	D0D843HH7F
Air Foamposite Pro (blue/black)	DG56TRF446
Air Foamposite Pro (black/gray)	3245AFSD45
Air Foamposite Pro (red/black)	DSAKF38422
Air Force Max (black)	F84N845H92
Air Force Max (white/black/blue)	985KJF98KJ
Air Force Max (white/red)	8734HU8FFF
Air Hyperflight (white)	14TGU7DEWC

SHOES	ENTER
Air Hyperflight (black/white)	WW44YHU592
Air Hyperflight (blue/white)	A0K574HF8S
Air Hyperflight (yellow/black)	JCX93LSS88
Air Jordan 11 (black/red/white)	GF64H76ZX5
Air Jordan 11 (black/varsity royal/white)	HJ987RTGFA
Air Jordan 11 (cool grey)	GF75HG6332
Air Jordan 11 (white)	HG76HN765S
Air Jordan 11 (white/black)	A2S35TH7H6
Air Jordan 3 (white)	G9845HJ8F4
Air Jordan 3 (white/clay)	435SGF555Y
Air Jordan 3 (white/fire red)	RE6556TT90
Air Jordan 3 (white/true blue)	FDS9D74J4F
Air Jordan 3 (black/white/gray)	CVJ554TJ58
Air Max2 CB (black/white)	87HZXGFIU8
Air Max2 CB (white/red)	4545GFKJIU
Air Max2 Uptempo (black/white/blue)	NF8745J87F
Air Max Elite (black)	A4CD54T7TD
Air Max Elite (white/black)	966ERTFG65
Air Max Elite (white/blue)	FD9KN48FJF
Air Zoom Flight (gray/white)	367UEY6SN
Air Zoom Flight (white/blue)	92387HDO77
Zoom Generation (white/black/red)	23LBJNUMB1
Zoom Generation (black/red/white)	LBJ23CAVS1
Nike Blazer (khaki)	W3R57U9NB2
Nike Blazer (tan/white/blue)	DCT5YHMU90
Nike Blazer (white/orange/blue)	4G66JU99XS
Nike Blazer (black)	XCV6456NNL
Nike Shox BB4 (black)	WE424TY563
Nike Shox BB4 (white/black)	23ERT85LP9
Nike Shox BB4 (white/light purple)	668YYTRB12
Nike Shox BB4 (white/red)	424TREU777
Nike Shox VCIII (black)	SDFH764FJU
Nike Shox VCIII (white/black/red)	5JHD367JJT

NBA LIVE 2005

50,000 DYNASTY POINTS
Enter **YISS55CZOE** as an NBA Live Code.

ALL CLASSICS HARDWOOD JERSEYS
Enter **PRYI234N0B** as an NBA Live Code.

ALL TEAM GEAR
Enter **1NVDR89ER2** as an NBA Live Code.

ALL SHOES
Enter **FHM389HU80** as an NBA Live Code.

AIR UNLIMITED SHOES
Enter **XVLJD9895V** as an NBA Live Code.

HUARACHE 2K4 SHOES
Enter **VNBA60230T** as an NBA Live Code.

NIKE BG ROLLOUT SHOES
Enter **0984ADF90P** as an NBA Live Code.

NIKE SHOX ELITE SHOES
Enter **2388HDFCBJ** as an NBA Live Code.

ZOOM GENERATION LOW SHOES
Enter **234SDJF9W4** as an NBA Live Code.

ZOOM LEBRON JAMES II SHOES
Enter **1KENZO23XZ** as an NBA Live Code.

ATLANTA HAWKS ALTERNATE UNIFORM
Enter **HDI834NN9N** as an NBA Live Code.

BOSTON CELTICS ALTERNATE UNIFORM
Enter **XCV43MGMDS** as an NBA Live Code.

DALLAS MAVERICKS ALTERNATE UNIFORM
Enter **AAPSEUD09U** as an NBA Live Code.

NEW ORLEANS HORNETS ALTERNATE UNIFORM
Enter **JRE7H4D90F** as a NBA Live Code.

NEW ORLEANS HORNETS ALTERNATE UNIFORM 2
Enter **JRE7H4D9WH** as a NBA Live Code.

SEATTLE SONICS ALTERNATE UNIFORM
Enter **BHD87YY27Q** as a NBA Live Code.

GOLDEN STATE WARRIORS ALTERNATE UNIFORM
Enter **NAVNY29548** as an NBA Live Code.

NBA LIVE 06

EASTERN ALL-STARS 2005-06 AWAY JERSEYS
Select NBA Codes from My NBA Live and enter **XCVB5387EQ**.

EASTERN ALL-STARS 2005-06 HOME JERSEY
Select NBA Codes from My NBA Live and enter **234SDFGHMO**.

WESTERN ALL-STARS 2005-06 AWAY JERSEY
Select NBA Codes from My NBA Live and enter **39N56B679J**.

WESTERN ALL-STARS 2005-06 HOME JERSEY
  Select NBA Codes from My NBA Live
  and enter **2J9UWABNP1**.

BOSTON CELTICS 2005-06 ALTERNATE JERSEY
Select NBA Codes from My NBA Live and enter **193KSHU88J**.

**CLEVELAND CAVALIERS
2005-06 ALTERNATE JERSEY**
  Select NBA Codes from My NBA Live
  and enter **9922NVDKVT**.

DENVER NUGGETS 2005-06 ALTERNATE JERSEYS
Select NBA Codes from My NBA Live and enter **XWETJK72FC**.

DETROIT PISTONS 2005-06 ALTERNATE JERSEY
Select NBA Codes from My NBA Live and enter **JANTWIKBS6**.

INDIANA PACERS 2005-06 ALTERNATE AWAY JERSEY
Select NBA Codes from My NBA Live and enter **PSDF90PPJN**.

**INDIANA PACERS 2005-06
ALTERNATE HOME JERSEY**
  Select NBA Codes from My NBA Live
  and enter **SDF786WSHW**.

SACRAMENTO KINGS 2005-06 ALTERNATE JERSEY
Select NBA Codes from My NBA Live and enter **654NNBFDWA**.

A3 GARNETT 3
Select NBA Codes from My NBA Live and enter **DRI239CZ49**.

JORDAN MELO V.5 WHITE & BLUE
  Select NBA Codes from My NBA Live and enter **5223WERPII**.

JORDAN MELO V.5 WHITE & YELLOW
Select NBA Codes from My NBA Live and enter **ZXDR7362Q1**.

JORDAN XIV BLACK & RED
Select NBA Codes from My NBA Live and enter **144FVNHM35**.

JORDAN XIV WHITE & GREEN
Select NBA Codes from My NBA Live
and enter **67YFH9839F**.

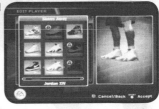

JORDAN XIV WHITE & RED
Select NBA Codes from My NBA Live and enter **743HFDRAU8**.

S. CARTER III LE
Select NBA Codes from My NBA Live
and enter **JZ3SCARTVY**.

T-MAC 5 BLACK
Select NBA Codes from My NBA Live
and enter **258SHQW95B**.

T-MAC 5 WHITE
Select NBA Codes from My NBA Live and enter **HGS83KP234P**.

ANSWER DMX 10
Select NBA Codes from My NBA Live
and enter **RBKAIUSAB7**.

ANSWER IX AND THE RBK ANSWER IX VIDEO
Select NBA Codes from My NBA Live and enter **AI9BUBBA7T**.

THE QUESTION AND THE MESSAGE FROM ALLEN IVERSON VIDEO

Select NBA Codes from My NBA Live and enter **HOYAS3AI6L**.

NBA STREET VOL. 2

Select the Pick Up Game option, hold L and enter the following when "Enter cheat codes now" appears at the bottom of the screen:

UNLIMITED TURBO
Press B, B, Y, Y.

ABA BALL
Press X, B, X, B.

WNBA BALL
Press X, Y, Y, X.

NO DISPLAY BARS
Press B, X (x3).

ALL JERSEYS
Press X, Y, B, B.

ALL COURTS
Press B, Y, Y, B.

ST. LUNATICS TEAM AND ALL STREET LEGENDS
Press X, Y, B, Y.

ALL NBA LEGENDS
Press X, Y, Y, B.

CLASSIC MICHAEL JORDAN
Press X, Y, X, X.

EXPLOSIVE RIMS
Press X (x3), Y.

SMALL PLAYERS
Press Y, Y, X, B.

BIG HEADS
Press X, B, B, X.

NO COUNTERS
Press Y, Y, X, X.

BALL TRAILS
Press Y, Y, Y, B.

ALL QUICKS
Press Y, X, Y, B.

EASY SHOTS
Press Y, X, B, Y.

HARD SHOTS
Press Y, B, X, Y.

NCAA FOOTBALL 2005

PENNANT CODES

Select My NCAA, then choose Pennant Collection. Now you can enter the following Pennant Codes:

ENTER	CODE
Cuffed Cheat	EA Sports
1st and 15	Thanks
Baylor power-up	Sic Em
Blink (ball spotted short)	For
Boing (dropped passes)	Registering
Crossed the Line	Tiburon
Illinois Team Boost	Oskee Wow
Jumbalaya	Hike

ENTER	CODE
Molasses Cheat	Home Field
QB Dud	Elite 11
Stiffed	NCAA
Take Your Time	Football
Texas Tech Team Boost	Fight
Thread the Needle	2005
Virginia Tech Team Boost	Tech Triumph
What a Hit	Blitz
2003 All-Americans	Fumble
Alabama All-time	Roll Tide
Miami All-time	Raising Cane
Michigan All-time	Go Blue
Mississippi State All-time	Hail State
Nebraska All-time	Go Big Red
North Carolina All-time	Rah Rah
Penn State All-time	We Are
Clemson All-time	Death Valley
Colorado All-time	Glory
Kansas State All-time	Victory
Oregon All-time	Quack Attack
USC All-time	Fight On
Washington All-time	Bow Down
Arizona Mascot team	Bear Down
Arkansas All-time	WooPigSooie
Auburn All-time	War Eagle
Badgers All-time	U Rah Rah
Florida All-time	Great To Be
Florida All-time	Great To Be
Florida State All-time	Uprising
Georgia All-time	Hunker Down
Iowa All-time	On Iowa
LSU All-time	Geaux Tigers
Notre Dame All-time	Golden Domer
Oklahoma All-time	Boomer
Oklahoma State All-time	Go Pokes
Pittsburgh All-time	Lets Go Pitt
Purdue All-time	Boiler Up
Syracuse All-time	Orange Crush
Tennessee All-time	Big Orange
Texas A&M All-time	Gig Em
Texas All-time	Hook Em
UCLA All-time	Mighty
Ohio State All-time	Killer Bucks
Ohio State All-time	Killer Nuts
Virginia All-time	Wahoos
Georgia Tech Mascot Team	Ramblinwreck
Iowa St. Mascot Team	Red And Gold

ENTER	CODE
Kansas Mascot Team	Rock Chalk
Kentucky Mascot Team	On On UK
Michigan State Mascot Team	Go Green
Minnesota Mascot Team	Rah Rah Rah
Missouri Mascot Team	Mizzou Rah
NC State Mascot Team	Go Pack
NU Mascot Team	Go Cats
Ole Miss Mascot Team	Hotty Totty
West Virginia Mascot Team	Hail WV
Wake Forest Mascot Team	Go Deacs Go
WSU Mascot Team	All Hail

NEED FOR SPEED MOST WANTED

BURGER KING CHALLENGE

At the Title screen, press Up, Down, Up, Down, Left, Right, Left, Right.

CASTROL SYNTEC VERSION OF FORD GT

At the Title screen, press Left, Right, Left, Right, Up, Down, Up, Down.

MARKER IN BACKROOM OF ONE-STOP SHOP

At the Title screen, press Up, Up, Down, Down, Left, Right, Up, Down.

NEED FOR SPEED UNDERGROUND 2

$200 IN CAREER MODE

At the Title screen, press Up, Up, Up, Left, R, R, R, Down.

$1000 IN CAREER MODE

At the Title screen, press Left, Left, Right, X, X, Right, L, R.

HUMMER H2 CAPONE

At the Title screen, press Up, Left, Up, Up, Down, Left, Down, Left.

BEST BUY VINYL

At the Title screen, press Up, Down, Up, Down, Down, Up, Right, Left.

BURGER KING VINYL

At the Title screen, press Up, Up, Up, Up, Down, Up, Up, Left.

PERFORMANCE LEVEL 1

At the Title screen, press L, R, L, R, Left, Left, Right, Up.

PERFORMANCE LEVEL 2

At the Title screen, press R, R, L, R, Left, Right, Up, Down.

VISUAL LEVEL 1

At the Title screen, press R, R, Up, Down, L, L, Up, Down.

VISUAL LEVEL 2

At the Title screen, press L, R, Up, Down, L, Up, Up, Down.

NFL STREET 2

Select Cheats from the Options screen and enter the following:

FUMBLE MODE

Enter **GreasedPig** as a code.

MAX CATCHING

Enter **MagnetHands** as a code.

NO FIRST DOWNS

Enter **NoChains** as a code.

NO FUMBLES MODE

Enter **GlueHands** as a code.

UNLIMITED TURBO

Enter **NozBoost** as a code.

EA FIELD

Enter **EAField** as a code.

GRIDIRON PARK
Enter **GRIDIRONPRK** as a code.

AFC EAST ALL-STARS
Enter **EAASFSCT** as a code.

AFC NORTH ALL-STARS
Enter **NAOFRCTH** as a code.

AFC SOUTH ALL-STARS
Enter **SAOFUCTH** as a code.

AFC WEST ALL-STARS
Enter **WAEFSCT** as a code.

NFC EAST ALL-STARS
Enter **NNOFRCTH** as a code.

NFC NORTH ALL-STARS
Enter **NNAS66784** as a code.

NFC SOUTH ALL-STARS
Enter **SNOFUCTH** as a code.

NFC WEST ALL STARS
Enter **ENASFSCT** as a code.

REEBOK TEAM
Enter **Reebo** as a code.

TEAM XZIBIT
Enter **TeamXzibit** as a code.

PETER JACKSON'S KING KONG: THE OFFICIAL GAME OF THE MOVIE

At the Main menu, hold L + R and press Down, X, Up, Y, Down, Down, Up, Up. Release L + R to access the Cheat option. The Cheat option is also available on the pause menu.

GOD MODE
Select Cheat and enter **8wonder**

ALL CHAPTERS
Select Cheat and enter **KKst0ry**.

AMMO 999
Select Cheat and enter **KK 999 mun**.

MACHINE GUN
Select Cheat and enter **KKcapone**.

REVOLVER
Select Cheat and enter **KKtigun**.

SNIPER RIFLE
Select Cheat and enter **KKsn1per**.

INFINITE SPEARS
Select Cheat and enter **lance 1nf**.

ONE-HIT KILLS
Select Cheat and enter **GrosBras**.

EXTRAS
Select Cheat and enter **KKmuseum**.

PIKMIN 2

TITLE SCREEN
At the Title screen, press the following for a variety of options:
Press R to make the Pikmin form NINTENDO.
Press L to go back to PIKMIN 2.
Press X to get a beetle.
Use the C-Stick to move it around.
Press L to dispose of the Beetle.
Press Y to get a Chappie.
Use the C-Stick to move it around.
Press Z to eat the Pikmin.
Press L to dispose of Chappie.

RAMPAGE: TOTAL DESTRUCTION

ALL MONSTERS AND CITIES
At the Main menu, press R + L to access the Cheat menu and enter **141421**.

ALL LEVELS
At the Main menu, press R + L to access the Cheat menu and enter **271828**.

INVULNERABLE TO ATTACKS
At the Main menu, press R + L to access the Cheat menu and enter **986960**.

ALL SPECIAL ABILITIES
At the Main menu, press R + L to access the Cheat menu and enter **011235**.

CPU VS CPU DEMO
At the Main menu, press R + L to access the Cheat menu and enter **082864**. This unlocks all of the monsters.

FAST CPU VS CPU DEMO
At the Main menu, press R + L to access the Cheat menu and enter **874098**. This unlocks all of the monsters.

ONE-HIT DESTROYS BUILDINGS
At the Main menu, press R + L to access the Cheat menu and enter **071767**.

OPENING MOVIE
At the Main menu, press R + L to access the Cheat menu and enter **667300**.

ENDING MOVIE
At the Main menu, press R + L to access the Cheat menu and enter **667301**.

CREDITS
At the Main menu, press R + L to access the Cheat menu and enter **667302**.

VERSION INFORMATION
At the Main menu, press R + L to access the Cheat menu and enter **314159**.

DISABLE CHEATS
At the Main menu, press R + L to access the Cheat menu and enter **000000**.

RAVE MASTER

REINA
At the Title screen, press Up, Up, Down, Down, Left, Right, Left, Right, B, A.

ROBOTS

BIG HEAD
Pause the game and press Up, Down, Down, Up, Right, Right, Left, Right.

INVINCIBLE
Pause the game and press Up, Right, Down, Up, Left, Down, Right, Left.

UNLIMITED SCRAP
Pause the game and press Down, Down, Left, Up, Up, Right, Up, Down.

SHREK SUPERSLAM

ALL CHARACTERS AND LEVELS
At the Title screen, press L, R, X, B.

ALL CHALLENGES
At the Title screen, press Y, Y, Y, X, X, X, Y, B, X, B, B, B, Up, Down, Left, Right, L, R.

ALL STORY MODE CHAPTERS
At the Title screen, press Y, B, R, X.

ALL MEDALS AND TROPHIES
At the Title screen, press R, L, Y, B.

SUPER SPEED MODIFIER
At the Title screen, press L, L, R, R, L, R, L, R, B, X, Y, Y.

PIZZA ONE
At the Title screen, press Up, Up, Y, Y, Right, Right, X, X, Down, Down, L, R, Left, Left, B, B, L, R.

PIZZA TWO
At the Title screen, press X, X, B, B, R, R, Left, Left, L, L.

PIZZA THREE
At the Title screen, press Down, Down, Right, X, Up, Y, Left, B, L, L.

SLAMMAGEDDON
At the Title screen, press Up, Up, Down, Down, Left, Right, Left, Right, Y, B, B, L, R.

THE SIMS: BUSTIN' OUT

Pause the game to enter the following codes. You must enter the Enable Cheats code first. After entering another code, select the gnome to access it.

ENABLE CHEATS
Press Down, L, Z, R, Left, X. When entered correctly, A gnome appears in front of your house.

FILL ALL MOTIVES
Press L, R, Y, Down, Down, X.

UNLOCK ALL LOCATIONS
Press Down, Z, R, L, Z.

UNLOCK ALL OBJECTS
Press Down, Z, Up, Y, R.

UNLOCK ALL SKINS
Press L, Y, A, R, Left.

UNLOCK ALL SOCIAL OPTIONS
Press L, R, Down, Down, Y.

SONIC GEMS COLLECTION

Sonic CD

STAGE SELECT
At the Title screen, press Up, Down, Down, Left, Right, A.

HIGH SCORES
At the Title screen, press Right, Right, Up, Up, Down, A.

SOUND TEST
At the Title screen, press Down, Down, Down, Left, Right, A.

Sonic R

SAME CHARACTER SELECT
When selecting your character in Multiplayer, hold L and press A or X. This will enable you to choose the same character as the other player.

Sonic Spinball

Enter the following codes by accessing the Options screen and entering them using the SFX option. The screen will shake to confirm that the code is entered correctly.

SKIP BOSS
Choose Sound Effects from the Options screen and play the following tracks in order: 00, 02, 01, 05, 06, 06. During a boss battle, pause the game, hold A + B + Start and press Down.

ANTI-GRAVITY SONIC
Choose Sound Effects from the Options screen and play the following tracks in order: 00, 09, 00, 01, 06, 08. Pause the game and press A + B + Start.

FAST MUSIC
Choose Sound Effects from the Options screen and play the following tracks in order: 00, 04, 02, 05, 05, 07.

Tails Skypatrol

SOUND AND STAGE TEST
At the Title screen, hold Up + A and press Start.

Vectorman 2

LEVEL SELECT AND SOUND TEST
Pause the game and press Up, Right, B, A, B, Down, Left, B, Down.

NEW WEAPONS
Pause the game and press X, B, Left, Left, Down, B, Down.

EXTRA LIFE
Pause the game and press Right, Up, A, B, Down, Up, A, Down, Up, A.

REFILL LIFE METER
Pause the game and press A, B, A, B, Left, Up, Up.

MAP COORDINATES
Pause the game and press A, B, Left, Left.

Vectorman

CHEAT MENU
At the Options screen, press B, A, A, B, Down, B, A, A, B.

REFILL LIFE METER
Pause the game and press B, A, Right, B, X, B, Down, B, A, Right, B.

SLOW MOTION
Pause the game and press Down, Right, B, X, Up, Left, B.

TAXI MODE
Pause the game and press X, B, Left, Left, B, X, B, A.

ALL ITEMS AND LEVEL SELECT
Enter the password ADE7 AA2A 51A6 6D12.

SONIC HEROES

METAL CHARACTERS IN 2-PLAYER
After selecting a level in 2-Player mode, hold A + Y.

SPIDER-MAN 2

TREYARCH PASSWORD
Start a New Game and enter **HCRAYERT** as your name. This code starts the game at 44% complete, 201,000 Hero Points, some upgrades and more.

SPONGEBOB SQUAREPANTS: BATTLE FOR BIKINI BOTTOM

The following codes must be entered quickly.

RESTORE HEALTH
Pause the game, hold L + R and press X, X, X, X, Y, X, Y, X, Y, Y, Y, Y.

EXPERT MODE
Pause the game, hold L + R and press X, X, X, Y, Y, X, X, X, Y, X, Y, Y, Y, Y, X, Y.

EARN 1,000 SHINY OBJECTS
Pause the game, hold L + R and press Y, X, X, Y, Y, X, X, Y.

EARN 10 GOLD SPATULAS
Pause the game, hold L + R and press X, Y, Y, X, X, Y, Y, X.

BUBBLE BOWL POWER-UP
Pause the game, hold L + R and press X, Y, X, Y, X, X, Y, Y. Press X to use the power-up.

CRUISE BUBBLE POWER-UP
Pause the game, hold L + R and press Y, X, Y, X, Y, Y, X, X. Press L to use the power-up.

INCREASE VALUE OF SHINY OBJECTS
Pause the game, hold L + R and press Y, X, Y, X, X, Y, X, X, X, Y, Y, Y, Y, X, X, Y.

MODIFIED CRUISE BUBBLE CONTROLS
Pause the game, hold L + R and press X, X, X, X, Y, Y, X, X, Y, X, Y, Y.

VILLAGERS GIVE SHINY OBJECTS WHEN HIT
Pause the game, hold L + R and press Y, Y, Y, Y, Y, X, Y, X, X, Y, X, Y.

VILLAGERS RESTORE HEALTH WHEN NEAR
Pause the game, hold L + R and press Y, Y, Y, Y, Y, X, Y, X, X, X, Y, Y.

BIG PLANKTON
Pause the game, hold L + R and press Y, Y, Y, Y, X, Y, X, Y, X, X, X, X.

SMALL CHARACTERS
Pause the game, hold L + R and press Y, Y, Y, Y, X, Y, X, Y, Y, Y, Y, Y.

SMALL VILLAGERS
Pause the game, hold L + R and press Y, Y, Y, Y, Y, X, Y, X, Y, X, Y, X.

SPONGEBOB BREAKS APART WHEN DEFEATED
Pause the game, hold L + R and press X, X, X, X, Y, Y, X, Y, X, X, X, Y.

INVERT LEFT/RIGHT CAMERA CONTROLS

Pause the game, hold L + R and press Y, Y, X, X, X, X, Y, Y.

INVERT UP/DOWN CAMERA CONTROLS

Pause the game, hold L + R and press Y, X, X, X, X, X, X, Y.

SPONGEBOB SQUAREPANTS: LIGHTS, CAMERA, PANTS!

SILVER STORY MODE

Select Rewards from the Bonuses menu, then choose Codes and enter **486739**.

ALL ACTION FIGURES

Select Rewards from the Bonuses menu, then choose Codes and enter **977548**.

HOOK, LINE & CHEDDAR GAME

Select Rewards from the Bonuses menu, then choose Codes and enter **893634**.

SSX 3

Select Options from the Main menu. Choose Cheat Codes from the Options screen and enter the following codes to unlock each character. To access the characters, go to the Lodge and select Rider Details, then select Cheat Characters to locate them.

BRODI

Enter **zenmaster**.

BUNNY SAN

Enter **wheresyourtail**.

CANHUCK

Enter **greatwhitenorth**.

CHURCHILL

Enter **tankengine**.

CUDMORE

Enter **milkemdaisy**.

EDDIE

Enter **worm**.

GUTLESS
Enter **boneyardreject**.

HIRO
Enter **slicksuit**.

JJ
Enter **potty**.

JURGEN
Enter **brokenleg**.

LUTHER
Enter **bronco**.

MARTY
Enter **back2future**.

NORTH WEST LEGEND
Enter **callhimgeorge**.

SNOWBALLS
Enter **betyouveneverseen**.

STRETCH
Enter **windmilldunk**.

SVELTE LUTHER
Enter **notsosvelte**.

UNKNOWN RIDER
Enter **finallymadeitin**.

PEAK 1 CLOTHES
Enter **shoppingspree**.

ALL PEAKS
Enter **biggerthank7**.

ALL ARTWORK
Enter **naturalconcept**.

ALL BOARDS
Enter **graphicdelight**.

ALL VIDEOS
Enter **myeyesaredim**.

ALL PLAYLIST SONGS
Enter **djsuperstar**.

ALL TOYS
Enter **nogluerequired**.

ALL TRADING CARDS
Enter **gotitgotitneedit**.

ALL POSTERS
Enter **postnobills**.

SSX ON TOUR

NEW THREADS
Select Cheats from the Extras menu and enter **FLYTHREADS**.

THE WORLD IS YOURS
Select Cheats from the Extras menu and enter **BACKSTAGEPASS**.

SHOW TIME (ALL MOVIES)
Select Cheats from the Extras menu and enter **THEBIGPICTURE**.

BLING BLING (INFINITE CASH)
Select Cheats from the Extras menu and enter **LOOTSNOOT**.

FULL BOOST, FULL TIME
Select Cheats from the Extras menu and enter **ZOOMJUICE**.

MONSTERS ARE LOOSE (MONSTER TRICKS)
Select Cheats from the Extras menu and enter **JACKALOPESTYLE**.

SNOWBALL FIGHT
Select Cheats from the Extras menu and enter **LETSPARTY**.

FEEL THE POWER (STAT BOOST)
Select Cheats from the Extras menu and enter **POWERPLAY**.

CHARACTERS ARE LOOSE
Select Cheats from the Extras menu and enter **ROADIEROUNDUP**.

UNLOCK CONRAD
Select Cheats from the Extras menu and enter **BIGPARTYTIME**.

UNLOCK MITCH KOOBSKI
Select Cheats from the Extras menu and enter **MOREFUNTHANONE**.

UNLOCK NIGEL
Select Cheats from the Extras menu and enter **THREEISACROWD**.

UNLOCK SKI PATROL
Select Cheats from the Extras menu and enter **FOURSOME**.

STAR WARS ROGUE SQUADRON III: REBEL STRIKE

Select Passcodes from the Options screen and enter the following. When there are two passcodes, enter the first one and Enter Code and then enter the second one and Enter Code.

UNLIMITED LIVES
Enter **IIOUAOYE**, then enter **WIMPIAM!**.

ACE MODE
Enter **YNMSFY?P**, then enter **YOUDAMAN**.

LEVEL SELECT (COOPERATIVE MODE)
Enter **SWGRCQPL**, then enter **UCHEATED**.

ALL SINGLE-PLAYER MISSIONS
Enter **HYWSCIWS**, then enter **NONGAMER**.

ALL SINGLE-PLAYER MISSIONS & BONUS MISSIONS
Enter **EEQQ?YPL**, then enter **CHEIATER**.

BEGGAR'S CANYON RACE (COOPERATIVE MODE)
Enter **FRLL!CSF**, then enter **FARMBOY?**.

ASTEROID FIELD MISSION (COOPERATIVE MODE)
Enter **RWALPIGC**, then enter **NOWAYOUT**.

DEATH STAR ESCAPE MISSION (COOPERATIVE MODE)
Enter **YFCEDFRH**, then enter **DSAGAIN?**.

ENDURANCE MISSION (COOPERATIVE MODE)
Enter **WPX?FGC!**, then enter **EXCERSIZ**.

ALL SHIPS (VERSUS MODE)
Enter **W!WSTPQB**, then enter **FREEPLAY**.

MILLENNIUM FALCON
Enter **QZCRPTG!**, then enter **HANSRIDE**.

NABOO STARFIGHTER
Enter **RTWCVBSH**, then enter **BFNAGAIN**.

SLAVE I
Enter **TGBCWLPN**, then enter **ZZBOUNTY**.

TIE BOMBER
Enter **JASDJWFA**, then enter **!DABOMB!**.

TIE HUNTER
Enter **FRRVBMJK**, then enter **LOOKOUT!**.

TIE FIGHTER (COOPERATIVE MODE)
Enter **MCKEMAKD**, then enter **ONESHOT!**.

TIE ADVANCE IN COOPERATIVE
Enter **VDX?WK!H**, then enter **ANOKSHIP**.

RUDY'S CAR
Enter **AXCBPRHK**, then enter **WHATTHE?**.

CREDITS
Enter **LOOKMOM!**. You can find this option in the Special Features menu.

STAR WARS ARCADE GAME
Enter **RTJPFC!G**, then enter **TIMEWARP**.

EMPIRE STRIKES BACK ARCADE GAME
Enter **!H!F?HXS**, then enter **KOOLSTUF**.

DOCUMENTARY
Enter **THEDUDES**.

ART GALLERY
Enter **!KOOLART**.

MUSIC HALL
Enter **HARKHARK**.

BLACK AND WHITE
Enter **NOCOLOR?**.

STRIKE FORCE BOWLING

ALL LEVELS
Name your bowler **!LEVELS!**.

ALL BOWLERS
Name your bowler **!BOWLER!**.

TAK 2: THE STAFF OF DREAMS

BALLOON HEAD SHOWDOWN MINI-GAME
Select Universal Card from Juju Potions and enter the following numbers for Bugs, Crystals and Fruit: 48, 62, 19.

BARREL BLITZ MINI-GAME
Select Universal Card from Juju Potions and enter the following numbers for Bugs, Crystals and Fruit: 1, 105, 81.

CATAPULT CHAOS MINI-GAME
Select Universal Card from Juju Potions and enter the following numbers for Bugs, Crystals and Fruit: 103, 33, 20.

CHICKEN TENNIS MINI-GAME
Select Universal Card from Juju Potions and enter the following numbers for Bugs, Crystals and Fruit: 202, 17, 203.

CHUCKIN' CHICKENS MINI-GAME
Select Universal Card from Juju Potions and enter the following numbers for Bugs, Crystals and Fruit: 18, 71, 50.

DART TOOM DODGEM MINI-GAME
Select Universal Card from Juju Potions and enter the following numbers for Bugs, Crystals and Fruit: 83, 43, 142.

DINKY SNOWBOARD BIG AIR MINI-GAME
Select Universal Card from Juju Potions and enter the following numbers for Bugs, Crystals and Fruit: 233, 127, 204.

FLEA FLYER MINI-GAME
Select Universal Card from Juju Potions and enter the following numbers for Bugs, Crystals and Fruit: 22, 6, 17.

FROG DERBY MINI-GAME
Select Universal Card from Juju Potions and enter the following numbers for Bugs, Crystals and Fruit: 281, 62, 149.

GLIDE RIDE MINI-GAME
Select Universal Card from Juju Potions and enter the following numbers for Bugs, Crystals and Fruit: 131, 61, 179.

GLOOMLEAF ARENA MINI-GAME
Select Universal Card from Juju Potions and enter the following numbers for Bugs, Crystals and Fruit: 68, 13, 8.

KRASH KOURSE MINI-GAME
Select Universal Card from Juju Potions and enter the following numbers for Bugs, Crystals and Fruit: 5, 41, 41.

VINE CLIMB MINI-GAME
Select Universal Card from Juju Potions and enter the following numbers for Bugs, Crystals and Fruit: 8, 1, 3.

FAUNA IN MULTIPLAYER
Select Universal Card from Juju Potions and enter the following numbers for Bugs, Crystals and Fruit: 44, 13, 0.

JB IN MULTIPLAYER
Select Universal Card from Juju Potions and enter the following numbers for Bugs, Crystals and Fruit: 16, 19, 38.

LOK IN MULTIPLAYER

Select Universal Card from Juju Potions and enter the following numbers for Bugs, Crystals and Fruit: 2, 2, 5.

SKELETON JUJU SPIRIT IN MULTIPLAYER

Select Universal Card from Juju Potions and enter the following numbers for Bugs, Crystals and Fruit: 55, 171, 35.

TAK'S FEATHER COLOR

Select Universal Card from Juju Potions and enter the following numbers for Bugs, Crystals and Fruit: 4, 9, 23.

BETTER MANA MAGNET

Select Universal Card from Juju Potions and enter the following numbers for Bugs, Crystals and Fruit: 3, 27, 31.

TAK 1 GAME CINEMATIC SEQUENCE

Select Universal Card from Juju Potions and enter the following numbers for Bugs, Crystals and Fruit: 30, 21, 88.

CONCEPT ART

Select Universal Card from Juju Potions and enter the following numbers for Bugs, Crystals and Fruit: 30, 37, 51.

PICTURES OF THE TAK SUIT

Select Universal Card from Juju Potions and enter the following numbers for Bugs, Crystals and Fruit: 11, 4, 17.

SOUND EFFECTS SET ONE

Select Universal Card from Juju Potions and enter the following numbers for Bugs, Crystals and Fruit: 4, 55, 36.

VIEW COMMERICIALS

Select Universal Card from Juju Potions and enter the following numbers for Bugs, Crystals and Fruit: 6, 16, 6.

TAK: THE GREAT JUJU CHALLENGE

BONUS SOUND EFFECTS

In Juju's Potions, select Universal Card and enter the following numbers for Bugs, Crystals and Fruit: 20, 17, 5.

BONUS SOUND EFFECTS 2

In Juju's Potions, select Universal Card and enter the following numbers for Bugs, Crystals and Fruit: 50, 84, 92.

BONUS MUSIC TRACK 1

In Juju's Potions, select Universal Card and enter the following numbers for Bugs, Crystals and Fruit: 67, 8, 20.

BONUS MUSIC TRACK 2

In Juju's Potions, select Universal Card and enter the following numbers for Bugs, Crystals and Fruit: 6, 18, 3.

MAGIC PARTICLES

In Juju's Potions, select Universal Card and enter the following numbers for Bugs, Crystals and Fruit: 24, 40, 11.

MORE MAGIC PARTICLES

In Juju's Potions, select Universal Card and enter the following numbers for Bugs, Crystals and Fruit: 48, 57, 57.

VIEW JUJU CONCEPT ART

In Juju's Potions, select Universal Card and enter the following numbers for Bugs, Crystals and Fruit: 33, 22, 28.

VIEW VEHICLE ART

In Juju's Potions, select Universal Card and enter the following numbers for Bugs, Crystals and Fruit: 11, 55, 44.

VIEW WORLD ART

In Juju's Potions, select Universal Card and enter the following numbers for Bugs, Crystals and Fruit: 83, 49, 34.

TEENAGE MUTANT NINJA TURTLES 2: BATTLE NEXUS

Select Password from the Options screen and enter the following. Hold L while selecting a turtle to get his New Nexus Turtle outfit.

EFFECT	PASSWORD
Challenge Code Abyss	SDSDRLD
Challenge Code Endurance	MRMDRMD
Challenge Code Fatal Blow	LRSRDRD
Challenge Code Lose Shuriken	RLMRDSL
Challenge Code Nightmare	SLSDRDL
Challenge Code Poison	DRSLLSR
Challenge Code Super-Tough	RDSRMRL
Cheat Code All-You-Can-Throw Shuriken	RSRLRSM
Cheat Code Health	DSRDMRM
Cheat Code Mighty Turtle	LSDRRDR
Cheat Code Pizza Paradise	MRLMRMR
Cheat Code Self Recovery	DRMSRLR
Cheat Code Squeaking	MLDSRDM
Cheat Code Super Defense Power	LDRMRLM
Cheat Code Super Offense Power	SDLSRLL
Cheat Code Toddling	SSSMRDD
New Nexus Turtle Outfit for Donatello	DSLRDRM
New Nexus Turtle Outfit for Leonardo	LMRMDRD

EFFECT	PASSWORD
New Nexus Turtle Outfit for Michelangelo	MLMRDRM
New Nexus Turtle Outfit for Raphael	RMSRMDR
Playmates Added to Bonus Materials	SRMLDDR

TEENAGE MUTANT NINJA TURTLES 3: MUTANT NIGHTMARE

INVINCIBILITY
Select Passwords from the Options screen and enter **MDLDSSLR**.

HEALTH POWER-UPS BECOME SUSHI
Select Passwords from the Options screen and enter **SLLMRSLD**.

NO HEALTH POWER-UPS
Select Passwords from the Options screen and enter **DMLDMRLD**.

ONE-HIT DEFEATS TURTLE
Select Passwords from the Options screen and enter **LDMSLRDD**.

MAX OUGI
Select Passwords from the Options screen and enter **RRDMLSDL**.

UNLIMITED SHURIKEN
Select Passwords from the Options screen and enter **LMDRRMSR**.

NO SHURIKEN
Select Passwords from the Options screen and enter **LLMSRDMS**.

DONATELLO'S LEVEL 2 DINO ARMOR SCROLL
Select Passwords from the Options screen and enter **MSSRDLMR**.

DONATELLO'S LEVEL 3 DINO ARMOR SCROLL
Select Passwords from the Options screen and enter **DLRLDMSR**.

LEO'S LEVEL 2 DINO ARMOR SCROLL
Select Passwords from the Options screen and enter **RLDMRMSD**.

LEO'S LEVEL 3 DINO ARMOR SCROLL
Select Passwords from the Options screen and enter **MLMSRRDS**.

MICHELANGELO'S LEVEL 2 DINO ARMOR SCROLL
Select Passwords from the Options screen and enter **SRDMMLRS**.

MICHELANGELO'S LEVEL 3 DINO ARMOR SCROLL
Select Passwords from the Options screen and enter **LSMRRDSL**.

RAPHAEL'S LEVEL 2 DINO ARMOR SCROLL
Select Passwords from the Options screen and enter **DRMDLLRS**.

RAPHAEL'S LEVEL 3 DINO ARMOR SCROLL
Select Passwords from the Options screen and enter **SMRDRSLD**.

DOUBLE ENEMY ATTACK
Select Passwords from the Options screen and enter **MSRLSMML**.

DOUBLE ENEMY DEFENSE
Select Passwords from the Options screen and enter **SLRMLSSM**.

TIGER WOODS PGA TOUR 2004

ALL GOLFERS AND COURSES
Enter **THEKITCHENSINK**.

ALL GOLFERS
Enter **CANYOUPICKONE**

ALL COURSES
Enter **ALLTHETRACKS**.

TARGET SHOOTOUT
Enter **sherwood target**.

ACE ANDREWS
Enter **ACEINTHEHOLE**.

CEDRIC THE ENTERTAINER
Enter **CEDDYBEAR**.

DOMINIC "THE DON" DONATELLO
Enter **DISCOKING**.

DOWNTOWN BROWN
Enter **DTBROWN**.

EDWIN "POPS" MASTERSON
Enter **EDDIE**.

ERICA ICE
Enter **ICYONE**.

HAMISH "MULLIGAN" MEGREGOR
Enter **DWILBY**.

MOA "BIG MO" TA'A VATU
Enter **ERUPTION**.

SOLITA LOPEZ
Enter **SHORTGAME**.

SUNDAY TIGER
Enter **4REDSHIRTS**.

TAKEHARU "TSUNAMI" MOTO
Enter **EMERALDCHAMP**.

VAL SUMMERS
Enter **BEVERLYHILLS**.

"YOSH" TANIGAWA
Enter **THENEWLEFTY**.

TIGER WOODS PGA TOUR 2005

Select Passwords and enter the following:

ALL GOLFERS AND COURSES
Enter **THEGIANTOYSTER**.

ALL COURSES
Enter **THEWORLDISYOURS**

THE CITY ROOFTOPS SKILL ZONE
Enter **NIGHTGOLFER**.

ADIDAS ITEMS
Enter **91treSTR**.

CALLAWAY ITEMS
Enter **cgTR78qw**.

CLEVELAND ITEMS
Enter **CL45etUB**.

MAXFLI ITEMS
Enter **FDGH597i**.

NIKE ITEMS
Enter **YJHk342B**.

ODYSSEY ITEMS
Enter **kjnMR3qv**.

PING ITEMS
Enter **R453DrTe**.

PRECEPT ITEMS
Enter **BRi3498Z**.

TAG ITEMS
Enter **cDsa2fgY**.

TOURSTAGE ITEMS
Enter **TS345329**.

TIFFANY WILLIAMSON
Enter **RICHGIRL**.

JEB "SHOOTER" MCGRAW
Enter **SIXSHOOTER**.

HUNTER "STEELHEAD" ELMORE
Enter **GREENCOLLAR**.

ALASTAIR "CAPTAIN" MCFADDEN
Enter **NICESOCKS**.

BEV "BOOMER" BUOUCHIER
Enter **THEBEEHIVE**.

ADRIANA "SUGAR" DULCE
Enter **SOSWEET**.

APHRODITE PAPADAPOLUS
Enter **TEMPTING**.

BILLY "BEAR" HIGHTOWER
Enter **TOOTALL**.

KENDRA "SPIKE" LOVETTE
Enter **ENGLISHPUNK**.

DION "DOUBLE D" DOUGLAS
Enter **DDDOUGLAS**.

RAQUEL "ROCKY" ROGERS
Enter **DOUBLER**.

BUNJIRO "BUD" TANAKA
Enter **INTHEFAMILY**.

CEASAR "THE EMPEROR" ROSADO
Enter **LANDOWNER**.

REGINALD WEATHERS
Enter **REGGIE**.

THE HUSTLER
Enter **ALTEREGO**.

SUNDAY TIGER WOODS
Enter **NEWLEGEND**.

SEVE BALLESTEROS
Enter **THEMAGICIAN**.

BEN HOGAN
Enter **PUREGOLF**.

JACK NICKLAUS
Enter **GOLDENBEAR**.

ARNOLD PALMER
Enter **THEKING**.

GARY PLAYER
Enter **BLACKKNIGHT**.

JUSTIN TIMBERLAKE
Enter **THETENNESSEEKID**.

TIGER WOODS PGA TOUR 06

ALL GOLFERS
Select Password from the Options screen and enter **WOOGLIN**.

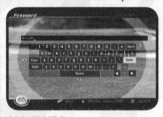

ALL CLUBS
Select Password from the Options screen and enter **CLUB11**.

LEVEL 2 NIKE ITEMS
Select Password from the Options screen and enter **JUSTDOIT**.

ALL COURSES
Select Password from the Options screen and enter **ITSINTHEHOLE**.

TIGER WOODS IN HAT AND TIE
Select Password from the Options screen and enter **GOLDENAGE**.

TIGER WOODS IN STRIPED PANTS
Select Password from the Options screen and enter **TECHNICOLOR**.

TIGER WOODS IN OLD GOLF OUTFIT
Select Password from the Options screen and enter **OLDSKOOL**.

TIGER WOODS IN A DIFFERENT OLD GOLF OUTFIT
Select Password from the Options screen and enter **THROWBACK**.

ARNOLD PALMER
Select Password from the Options screen and enter **ARNIESARMY**.

BEN HOGAN
Select Password from the Options screen and enter **THEHAWK**.

JACK NICKLAUS
Select Password from the Options screen and enter **GOLDENBEAR**.

OLD TOM MORRIS
Select Password from the Options screen and enter **FEATHERIE**.

TOMMY BLACK
Select Password from the Options screen and enter **IDONTHAVEAPROBLEM**.

WESLEY ROUNDER
Select Password from the Options screen and enter **POCKETPAIR**.

TONY HAWK'S AMERICAN WASTELAND

ALWAYS SPECIAL
Select Cheat Codes from the Options screen and enter **uronfire**. Pause the game and select Cheats from the Game Options to enable the cheat.

PERFECT RAIL
Select Cheat Codes from the Options screen and enter **grindxpert**. Pause the game and select Cheats from the Game Options to enable the cheat.

PERFECT SKITCH
Select Cheat Codes from the Options screen and enter **h!tchar!de**. Pause the game and select Cheats from the Game Options to enable the cheat.

PERFECT MANUAL
Select Cheat Codes from the Options and enter **2wheels!**. Pause the game and select Cheats from the Game Options to enable the cheat.

MOON GRAVITY
Select Cheat Codes from the Options screen and enter **2them00n**. Pause the game and select Cheats from the Game Options to enable the cheat.

MAT HOFFMAN
Select Cheat Codes from the Options screen and enter **the_condor**.

JASON ELLIS
Select Cheat Codes from the Options screen and enter **sirius-dj**.

TONY HAWK'S UNDERGROUND

Select Cheat Codes from the Options screen and enter the following. You must turn on some cheats by pausing the game and selecting Cheats from the Options menu.

PLAY AS T.H.U.D.
Enter **NOOO!!**.

PERFECT RAIL
Enter **letitslide**.

PERFECT SKITCH
Enter **rearrider**.

PERFECT MANUAL
Enter **keepitsteady**.

MOON GRAVITY
Enter **getitup**.

TONY HAWK'S UNDERGROUND 2

ALWAYS SPECIAL
Select Cheat Codes from the Game Options and enter likepaulie. Select Cheats from the Game Options to toggle the code on and off.

PERFECT RAIL
Select Cheat Codes from the Game Options and enter straightedge. Select Cheats from the Game Options to toggle the code on and off.

TY THE TASMANIAN TIGER 2: BUSH RESCUE

ALL BUNYIP KEYS
During a game, press Start, Y, Start, Start, Y, B, X, B, A.

ALL FIRST-LEVEL RANGS
During a game, press Start, Y, Start, Start, Y, X, B, X, B.

ALL SECOND-LEVEL RANGS
During a game, press Start, Y, Start, Start, Y, B, X, B, Y.

GET 100,000 OPALS
During a game, press Start, Y, Start, Start, Y, X, A, X, A.

HIGHLIGHT ALL COLLECTIBLES
During a game, press Start, Y, Start, Start, Y, Up, Down, Left, Right.

TY THE TASMANIAN TIGER 3: NIGHT OF THE QUINKAN

100,000 OPALS
During a game, press Start, Start, Y, Start, Start, Y, X, A, X, A.

ALL CHASSIS
During a game, press Start, Start, Y, Start, Start, Y, X, B, X, B.

THE URBZ: SIMS IN THE CITY

CHEAT GNOME
During a game, press Down, L, Z, R, X, Left. Now you can enter the following cheats.

ACQUIRE SKILL OBJECT
During a game, find the Gnome and press Down, Z, Up, Y, R.

ALL POWER SOCIALS
During a game, find the Gnome and press B, Left, X, R, L, A.

POWER SOCIALS
During a game, find the Gnome and press B, Left, X, R, L.

MAX ARTISTIC SKILL
During a game, find the Gnome and press R, Y, Up, Z, Down.

MAX MENTAL SKILL
During a game, find the Gnome and press Down, X, Left, R, Down.

MAX PHYSICAL SKILL
During a game, find the Gnome and press R, Z, Down, Y, Y.

WWE DAY OF RECKONING 2

SECRETS & UNLOCKABLES
Some items require that you complete certain Shows in Story Mode, while completing a specific number of matches in Exhibition Mode unlocks other extras. The specific requirements needed to earn each reward are listed in this section.

BONUS ATTRIBUTE POINTS

REWARD	REQUIREMENT
Increase Create a Superstar Experience to 800	Finish Show 16
Increase Create a Superstar Experience to 1100	Finish Show 21
Increase Create a Superstar Experience to 1400	Finish Show 32
Increase Create a Superstar Experience to 1700	Finish Show 43

BONUS ARENAS

REWARD	REQUIREMENT
Backlash Arena	Finish Show 08
Vengeance Arena	Finish Show 12
Summerslam Arena	Finish Show 16
Unforgiven Arena	Finish Show 20
No Mercy Arena	Finish Show 21
Survivor Series	Finish Show 26
Armageddon Arena	Finish Show 33
Royal Rumble	Finish Show 37
No Way Out Arena	Finish Show 40
Wrestlemania	Finish Show 43

LEGENDARY SUPERSTARS

REWARD	REQUIREMENT
The Rock	Finish Show 20
Steve Austin	Defeat the computer in Exhibition's Single Match Mode 5 times
Mankind	Defeat the computer in Exhibition's Single Match Mode 10 times
Hulk Hogan	Finish Show 43
Bret Hart	Defeat the computer in Exhibition's Single Match Mode 20 times

X2: WOLVERINE'S REVENGE

ALL MOVIES
At the Main menu, press B, X, B, Y, Y, Y, R, R, Z.

XGRA: EXTREME-G RACING ASSOCIATION

ALL LEVELS OF RACING
Enter **FREEPLAY** at the Cheat Menu.

ALL TRACKS
Enter **WIBBLE** at the Cheat Menu.

O2 LIVERIED
Enter **UCANDO** at the Cheat Menu.

MESSAGE IN CREDITS
Enter **MUNCHKIN**, **EDDROOLZ** or **EDDIEPOO** at the Cheat Menu.

X-MEN LEGENDS II: RISE OF APOCALYPSE

ALL CHARACTERS
At the Team Management screen, press Right, Left, Left, Right, Up, Up, Up, Start.

ALL SKINS
At the Team Management screen, press Down, Up, Left, Right, Up, Up, Start.

ALL SKILLS
At the Team Management screen, press Left, Right, Left, Right, Down, Up, Start.

LEVEL 99
At the Team Management screen, press Up, Down, Up, Down, Left, Up, Left, Right, Start.

GOD MODE
Pause the game and press Down, Up, Down, Up, Right, Down, Right, Left, Start.

MOVE FASTER
Pause the game and press Up, Up, Up, Down, Up, Down, Start.

UNLIMITED XTREME TOKENS
Pause the game and press Left, Down, Right, Down, Up, Up, Down, Up, Start.

TOUCH OF DEATH
During a game, press Left, Left, Right, Left, Right, Up, Start.

100,000 TECH-BITS
At Forge or Beast's store, press Up, Up, Up, Down, Right, Right, Start.

ALL DANGER ROOM COURSES
At the Danger Room Course menu, press Right, Right, Left, Left, Up, Down, Up, Down, Start.

ALL COMICS
Select Review from the Main menu and press Right, Left, Left, Right, Up, Up, Right, Start.

ALL CUTSCENES
Select Review from the Main menu and press Left, Right, Right, Left, Down, Down, Left, Start.

ALL CONCEPTS
Select Review from the Main menu and press Left, Right, Left, Right, Up, Up, Down, Start.

ALL SCREENS
Select Review from the Main menu and press Right, Left, Right, Left, Up, Up, Down, Start.

X-MEN: THE OFFICIAL GAME

DANGER ROOM ICEMAN
At the Cerebro Files menu, press Right, Right, Left, Left, Down, Up, Down, Up, Start.

DANGER ROOM NIGHTCRAWLER
At the Cerebro Files menu, press Up, Up, Down, Down, Left, Right, Left, Right, Start.

DANGER ROOM WOLVERINE
At the Cerebro Files menu, press Down, Down, Up, Up, Right, Left, Right, Left, Start.

YU-GI-OH: FALSEBOUND KINGDOM

GOLD COINS
On an empty piece of land and during a mission, press Up, Up, Down, Down, Left, Right, Left, Right, B, A.

ZOIDS: BATTLE LEGENDS

ENERGY LIGER
Select Config and play the following voices: 004, 044, 019, 066, 034.

LIGER ZERO PHOENIX
Select Config and play the following voices: 021, 001, 018, 006, 023.

MEGASAURER IN VS MODE
Select Config and play the following voices: 000, 007, 077, 041, 054.

SECRET CODES FOR CONSOLES 2006

BradyGames® Publishing
An Imprint of DK Publishing, Inc.
800 East 96th Street, Third Floor
Indianapolis, Indiana 46240

ISBN: 0-7440-0822-0

Printing Code: The rightmost double-digit number is the year of the book's printing; the rightmost single-digit number is the number of the book's printing. For example, 06-1 shows that the first printing of the book occurred in 2006.

09 08 07 06   4 3 2 1

Manufactured in the United States of America.

BradyGAMES Staff

Publisher
David Waybright

Editor-In-Chief
H. Leigh Davis

Director of Marketing
Steve Escalante

Creative Director
Robin Lasek

Licensing Manager
Mike Degler

Credits

Title Manager
Tim Cox

Screenshot Editor
Michael Owen

Book Designer
Colin King

Production Designers
Bob Klunder
Wil Cruz